The Last Courtly Lover
Yeats and the Idea of Woman

Studies in Modern Literature, No. 6

A. Walton Litz, General Series Editor

Professor of English
Princeton University

Richard J. Finneran

Consulting Editor for Titles on W.B. Yeats
Professor of English
Newcomb College, Tulane University

Other Titles in This Series

The Last Courtly Lover
Yeats and the Idea of Woman

by
Gloria C. Kline

UMI RESEARCH PRESS
Ann Arbor, Michigan

821
Y41zk

Produced and distributed by
UMI Research Press
an imprint of
University Microfilms International
Ann Arbor, Michigan 48106

Library of Congress Cataloging in Publication Data

Kline, Gloria C. (Gloria Cornelia)
  The last courtly lover.

  (Studies in modern literature ; no. 6)
  Revision of thesis (Ph.D.)—Florida State University,
1976.
  Bibliography: p.
  Includes index.
  1. Yeats, W. B. (William Butler), 1865-1939—Criticism
and interpretation. 2. Women in literature. 3. Sex role in
literature. 4. Courtly love.   I. Title. II. Series.
PR5908.W6K55 1983   821'.8   83-6941
ISBN 0-8357-1409-8

O do not love too long,
Or you will grow out of fashion
Like an old song. (CP81)

in memory of inspired teachers
Sallie Ratliff Taylor
William Hugh McEniry, Jr.

Contents

List of Illustrations and Figures

Illustrations

In text

Album

Figures

Acknowledgments

My thanks go first to George Mills Harper under whose guidance I wrote the dissertation that was the beginning of this book, then to Brendan P. O'Hehir and D. W. Robertson, Jr., for their information in matters of Celtic history and medieval intention and to Dr. Oliver Edwards for conversations about Yeats. I also thank all of my friends and colleagues who supported me with their encouragement and patience, especially Sallie G. Faloon, principal of Fort Lauderdale High School, and Howard D. Pearce, chairman of the Department of English at Florida Atlantic University. Finally, I am most grateful to the Reverend Hobart Jude Gary for his careful reading and theological criticism and to Ann Hitt for making the labor of indexing an almost enjoyable memory.

I make the following acknowledgments of permission to quote copyrighted material: to Michael B. Yeats, Anne Yeats, and Macmillan, London, Ltd., for quotations from *Letters on Poetry from W. B. Yeats to Dorothy Wellesley* (London: Oxford University Press, 1964) and for extracts from prose, poetry, and letters by W. B. Yeats; to Macmillan Publishing Co., Inc., for quotations from *Collected Plays of William Butler Yeats* (copyright 1934, 1952 by Macmillan Publishing Company) and from *The Variorum Edition of the Plays of W. B. Yeats*, ed. Russell K. Alspach (copyright © Russell K. Alspach and Bertha Georgie Yeats, 1966; copyright Macmillan & Co., Ltd., 1965); to Michael B. Yeats and Ann Yeats for quotations from W. B. Yeats, *Memoirs*, ed. Denis Donoghue (London: Macmillan, 1972); to the Estate of the late W. B. Yeats for quotations from Joseph Hone's *W. B. Yeats, 1865-1939* (Harmondsworth, Middlesex: Penguin Books, 1971).

Thanks are also due to Mme. Simone Bertin for permission to quote from letters of Margot Ruddock in *Ah! Sweet Dancer: A Correspondence*, ed. Roger McHugh (Macmillan, London, Ltd., 1970); to Sean MacBride, for permission to quote from Maud Gonne MacBride, *A Servant of the Queen* (London: Victor Gollancz, 1938); and to the Duke of Wellington for permission to quote letters of Dorothy Wellesley and the unpublished poem,

"The Squire, the Lady and the Serving Maid." Lines from "Leda" by Mona Van Duyn are reprinted by permission of Atheneum Publishers, from *To See, To Take*, copyright © 1970 by Mona Van Duyn.

Sources of additional shorter quotations are acknowledged in footnotes.

Abbreviations of Books by Yeats

A	*Autobiographies* (1955)
CP	*Collected Poems* (1956)
CPy	*Collected Plays* (1952)
EI	*Essays and Introductions* (1916)
FMM	*A Full Moon in March* (1935)
L	*Letters*, ed. Allan Wade (1955)
M	*Memoirs*, ed. Denis Donoghue (1972)
My	*Mythologies* (1959)
SR	*The Secret Rose* (1897)
V	*A Vision* (1938)
VPy	*Variorum Plays*, ed. Russell K. Alspach (1966)
WAR	*The Wind Among the Reeds* (1899)

Introduction

A romantic, when romanticism was in its final extravagance, I
thought one woman, whether wife, mistress, or incitement to Platonic
love, enough for a life-time: a Parsifal, a Tristram, Don Quixote,
without the intellectual prepossessions that gave them solidity. (A431)

—1—

"Yeats, the last romantic, was perhaps also the last courtly lover."[1] With this
statement Curtis Bradford opens his account of the relationship of W. B.
Yeats and Maud Gonne and the effects of that relationship upon the life and
work of the poet. The designation of Yeats as a courtly lover is, like his
designation as a believer in the occult or as an apologist for an elitist social
order, the sort of thing that causes his admirers, especially in this case
women, to say, "but he is a great poet in spite of that." To call him the last
courtly lover is to call him reactionary, to say that he failed to move along
with the maturing of sexual concepts that began with the work of many of
his contemporaries in psychology, sociology, medicine, and law.

But to call him the last courtly lover is also to call him a mythopoet in
the definition that Harry Slochower gives the term: a poet who, coming at
the close of an era, re-creates the ideals of its decaying social structures so
that "the hero's quest becomes *a critique* of the existing social norms and
points to a futuristic order which is envisaged as integrating the valuable
residues of the past and present."[2] Slochower cites Euripides and Dante,
both of whom wrote at times of crisis for their faiths, and Cervantes, whose
Don Quixote re-creates an idea of chivalry that was dead in Spain even as he
wrote. Coming at these particular times, the works of these poets present
"the supra-historical or symbolic reality"[3] of the passing faiths.

Because Yeats wrote steadily through half a century that not only saw a
great variety of experience in the poet's personal life but also spanned a
period of immense world change, his treatment of a single theme over that
half century invites study, more especially since that theme continues to bear
political and social as well as artistic significance.

Courtly love as applied to an understanding of Yeats's ideas about women and his use of female imagery and female personae must, of course, be courtly love as Yeats and his time understood it. Professor D. W. Robertson, Jr., who reads the medieval love poems as vehicles more of irony than of passion, says that the courtly love of Yeats's era is the only one that ever existed:

> I think it is time we stopped teaching medieval texts to the tune of "Hearts and Flowers." The sophistication of the tune with things like pseudo-Albigensian heresies, pseudo-Platonic philosophies, or pseudo-Arabic doctrines does not conceal its true nature, nor do these wailing ghosts on the sidelines make it any more respectable intellectually. The study of courtly love, if it belongs anywhere, should be conducted only as the subject is an aspect of nineteenth and twentieth century cultural history.[4]

The issues of this reading of Yeats are, therefore, to discover what he meant by "the old high way of love" (CP78–79), how his meaning functioned toward the cohesiveness of his entire work, and what he foresaw as the result of change or loss of this meaning.

For Yeats in the 1890s, the passing faith was what the twentieth century would call a life-style, the aristocratic life-style of ritualized or ceremonial order. He was fond of his friend Lionel Johnson's statement that "life is ritual," and he was certain that woman's role was its keystone: "How can life be ritual if woman had not her symbolical place?" (A302). The terms "ritual" and "ceremony" did not have for Yeats their twentieth-century superficiality. He came to see civilization itself as an interplay of roles, rituals, and ceremonies such as the "ceremony of innocence" whose drowning in the flood of anarchy signals the end of Western culture in "The Second Coming" (CP184).

The symbolical place of woman was, therefore, the center of order in the life of an individual man or of a culture, and Yeats maintained the idea for all phases of his life and work. In an early poem ("The Sorrow of Love" CP40), he celebrates the function of the feminine image in the artist's imposition of order on the chaos of nature. When he finally settled into marriage, he wrote of his wife that she had made his life "serene and full of order" (L634). When he received the Nobel Prize for Literature, he mused upon the service of women and of courts that had called forth high achievement from men in the past. In all instances—artistic, personal, and cultural—the woman at the center provides the image around which the unities that Yeats thought the greatest good could be achieved—Unity of Being and Unity of Culture.

The problem with this symbolical function is that it does not assure the Unities of Being and Culture to the woman. If she is herself an artist or a scholar, she must be so in terms of the masculine definition because no other exists. If she finds her identity in serving as the fixed center of things, then her intellectual activity, being "masculine" in nature, is somehow exterior to herself. If she is to be a self-directed individual, she must choose, on the one hand, to accept her dual role as symbol and as person and seek to fulfill herself as both, treading a narrow wire between frustration and fragmentation; or, on the other hand, to risk alienation through roles of her own devising in which she may, at crucial moments, find herself unrecognizable to herself or to her culture. She may, of course, remain unaware and undifferentiated, a passive reflection of whatever masculine attention is focused upon her from her father's generation to her husband's to her son's. If she does, she remains forever immature, and her intellect, untrained by its own experience, can express itself only in childish rebelliousness or in utter dependency.

Yeats never denied the presence of independent intellect in women, but he did for the greater part of his life see it as a threat to the woman, principally as a threat to her greatest good, her symbolical place as unifying image. His long struggle with Maud Gonne centered upon her intellect: "What would I not have given that she might think exactly right on all those great questions of the day?" (M42). To "think exactly right" meant, of course, to reflect what Yeats thought, to be symbol rather than activist. Yeats was not her only critic: even the *New York Times*' naming her "the Irish Joan of Arc," while apparently meant in compliment, still associated her with another woman who had donned masculine activism and so alienated herself from her culture that she died as a witch for it. The question of Maud's self-awareness and ultimate intellectual maturity is one for her biographers, but after their long struggle had lasted into middle age, Yeats could call her a child.[5]

Even as courtly love was being defined in the nineteenth century, women were rebelling—not at all childishly—at the symbolical place that it prepared for them. The slow assertion of woman's right to education and property begun in Yeats's youth was changing her from symbol to person except in that area closest to the intellect. As nineteenth-century psychologists associated her more and more with the unconscious mind, she became more and more the poets' Muse. But whereas Mallarmé, Baudelaire, and others were fascinated by the female in the abstract, Yeats attempted to find his symbolical woman in flesh and blood. He is, therefore, uniquely the last courtly lover in both art and practice.

Yeats's quests as lover can be divided into his personal quest for an image for Unity of Being and his cultural quest for an image for Unity of Culture. His personal quest is further divisible into his experience with a "woman lost"—Maud Gonne—and a "woman won"—his wife Georgie Hyde-Lees. His cultural quest was eminently satisfied by Lady Gregory from his first meeting with her in 1896 until her death in 1932. In his last years he recapitulated these two quests in his relationships with the actress Margot Ruddock and the poet Dorothy Wellesley. Such recapitulation, according to

Slochower, is one of the characteristics of the mythopoetic hero, who, like Sophocles's Oedipus and Goethe's Faust, repeats his initial act that brought calamity upon him in a symbolic reenactment that brings him "'heavenly gain.'"[6] Yeats's "heavenly gain" in the end can be demonstrated as a new understanding of and relationship to the intellect of women.

To trace Yeats's mythopoesis of courtly love, I will follow the course of his works in the courtly mode, that is, those poems and plays which present the woman as an elevated figure who has a spiritual influence on the man, can provide him a unifying image, and for that reason is reverently, sometimes fearfully, pursued or "courted" by him. The chapters will follow the elements of Slochower's definition of mythopoesis. Chapter 1 will introduce the myth of courtly love as it appeared in the nineteenth century. Chapter 2 will be concerned with Yeats's personal quests and Chapter 3 with his cultural quest. Chapter 4 will examine the recapitulations of the quests and the critique of the myth.

Before all that, however, the course of the great affair that "troubled" Yeats's life must be surveyed.

—2—

For a poet to be studied as a critic of sexual understanding, Yeats appears to be an inauspicious choice. Some of his statements read like the creed of the most extreme male chauvinist:

> Women do not keep their sanity in the presence of the abstract. (M24)

> A woman gets her thought through the influence of a man. (M232)

In his prayer for his infant daughter (CP185), he asks that she grow up to reject the analytical mind for that of a songbird:

> May she become a flourishing hidden tree
> That all her thoughts may like the linnet be,
> And have no business but dispensing round
> Their magnanimities of sound,
> Nor but in merriment begin a chase,
> Nor but in merriment a quarrel.

And in his famous love affair with Maud Gonne, he appears a man clinging to the patriarchal assumptions that a state of intellectual passivity is both natural and healthy for a woman, that a woman should hope for status through the good opinion of men, and that she should look to realize her own greatness through inspiring a man of genius. But the thoughts of the linnet were not Maud's thoughts. In fact, all the desired passive attributes of the daughter in the poem are marshalled to counter the errors Yeats believed Maud had made in her life: the "intellectual hatred," the "opinionated mind," the "crazy salad" of a marriage to a man who, in Yeats's eyes, was beneath her. Maud was as arrogant and independent as Aphrodite, "the great Queen, that rose out of the spray." She took no man's opinion as her measure, nor did she sit back enthralled by the male activity that her beauty inspired.

Maud Gonne was born December 21, 1866,[7] near Aldershot in Surrey, England. Her father, whom from infancy she called "Tommy," was a colonel in the British army, stationed for most of her life in Ireland. Her mother was English, of the propertied middle class. Her birth entitled her to presentation at the Viceregal Court in Dublin in her nineteenth year and assured her an independent income all her life. In her surroundings she learned an air of authority and assurance—Elizabeth Coxhead calls it "her Daughter of the Garrison manner,"[8]—that stayed with her all her life. Sean O'Casey describes its continued assertion in her very old age:

> There she sits stonily silent, once a sibyl of patriotism from whom no oracle ever came; now silent and aged; her deepset eyes now sad, agleam with disappointment; never quite at ease with the crowd, whose cheers she loved; the colonel's daughter still.[9]

Maud's earliest memory was a call to courage: she was four years old, and Tommy, holding her in his arms above her mother's coffin, said to her, "'You must never be afraid of anything, even of death.'" When she was older Tommy told her, "'Will is a strange incalculable force. It is so powerful that if, as a boy, I had willed to be the Pope of Rome, I would have been Pope.'" These two statements recur as motifs of her autobiography, *A Servant of the Queen* (1938).[10] Its title refers not to Victoria, against whom Maud railed and fomented rebellion, but to Cathleen ni Houlihan, the figure Yeats made famous as the feminine personification of Ireland.

The autobiography falls into three movements, each centered on a man in Maud's life: first on her father, then for the longest part on her French lover Lucien Millevoye, and then finally, on her husband, John MacBride. Yeats remains on the sidelines of Maud's adventures, depicted as ineffective and immature in comparison to a long list of the men she knew who became historical figures by their activities in the fight for Irish independence: Michael Davitt, J. F. Taylor, Arthur Griffith, James Connolly, Douglas Hyde, Tim Harrington, the Redmond brothers, the O'Briens, and the militant priest Father McFadden of 'Gweedore. Crusaders all, they were doing the things Maud wanted passionately to be doing herself. In regard to the two plays he wrote for her to act, *The Countess Cathleen* and *Cathleen ni Houlihan*, Yeats receives especially short shrift. His offer of the first play is treated as a temptation to the "detriment" of her revolutionary work:

> Willie Yeats was sad and tried hard to persuade me to act the part of Countess Kathleen. "I wrote it for you and if you don't act it we shall have to get an actress from London to take the part," which eventually he did with no marked success.[11]

And she makes certain that her readers understand that she acted in the second of the plays only in the interest of Ireland while implying at the same time that Yeats was not above using her patriotic fervor to his own ends:

> I did it because it was only on that condition that Willie Yeats would give us the right of producing his play, and I felt that play would have great importance for the National movement.

Nowhere can their characters be seen in stronger contrast than in their recollections in age of that play: hers full of business-like enthusiasm for the propaganda that will get the job done; his ruminating on the awesome power of the word:

> All that I have said and done,
> Now that I am old and ill,
> Turns into a question till
> I lie awake night after night
> And never get the answers right.
> Did that play of mine send out
> Certain men the English shot? (CP337)

Unlike Yeats, whose adolescent phases passed in dramatic imaginings, Maud grew up actively. Her mother, who had hated school, made Tommy promise on her deathbed that he would not send Maud and her younger sister Kathleen to board. He kept that promise until relatives and friends pointed out that the girls were growing up ignorant; the Irish peasant children they played with had had more schooling than they. Then Tommy sent them to Europe to study and travel with a French governess of independent, feminist ideals. For one moment, however, Maud's young life did parallel Willie's. Before they were sent to Europe, Maud and Kathleen lived with their nurse at Howth above Dublin, where they, like Yeats in his early teens, climbed the hills all day and slept at night in the tall heather. But while Yeats spent this time searching for a personality among the romantic figures Shelley had created, Maud was ready to assume the appearance of a woman:

> At fourteen I was five feet ten and, having a great desire to be grown up, I made Nurse lengthen my skirts and dress the masses of my gold-brown hair in great coils at the back of my head.[12]

The change brought thrilling results—not the attentions of young men but the misapprehension of strangers that she and her youthful-looking father were a honeymoon couple. When she was seventeen, Maud presided over her father's house and table and cultivated elderly generals at tea. Her romantic foolishness was already behind her. At sixteen she had accepted a young Italian's proposal in the moonlit Colosseum. Tommy had extracted her from that contract as he, a year or so later, removed her from Homburg, where the visiting Prince of Wales seemed about to invite her to supper. Maud makes it clear, however, that she could handle men on her own and tells with relish how she pulled a gun on three "guides" who tried to kidnap her in a lawless Mediterranean port.

Producing that revolver was no mere gesture. A few years later, when a French editor tried to blackmail her, she challenged him to a shooting match. After placing three of her six shots in the head of the cardboard target, Maud gave the editor her opinion on women and duelling:

> "Women have as good sight and as good nerve as men. It is unjust that they are debarred from the protection of duelling. But if any men insulted me in any way detrimental to my work, I should take the insult as a challenge, and that," pointing to the cardboard figure, "would be my answer."[13]

Calling herself "a horse that has to wear blinkers to prevent being sidetracked,"[14] Maud devoted body, mind, and spirit to her work for Ireland until her death at eighty-seven. Yeats tried to join her efforts, but the difference in their revolutionary aims and philosophies caused him to attempt awkward compromises while she would make none. Her real partner in this work, and according to Coxhead the only man she ever loved, was the Boulangist soldier and journalist Lucien Millevoye. She met him in 1887, the year after her father died, at the spa of Royat in Auvergne, where she was recovering her health after one of the pulmonary infections that plagued her all her life.

She recalled her first impression of "a tall man between thirty and forty . . . [who] looked ill."[15] He was unhappily married and separated from his wife but unable to get a divorce. The afternoon they met, a heavy thunderstorm began. While other ladies sought refuge behind drawn curtains, Maud stood on a balcony with her hands outstretched to the lashing rain, and Millevoye paid tribute to her fearlessness by kissing her dripping arms. With the reserve of a nineteenth-century lady, Maud says little of their personal relationship but much of their "alliance," in which Millevoye's ambition to win back Alsace-Lorraine from Germany figured as strongly as her devotion to Irish independence.

From Royat, Millevoye accompanied Maud to Marseilles, where she embarked alone for Constantinople. She bought a marmoset to be her chaperone; Millevoye gave her the revolver with which she was to become so proficient: "'It is to protect our alliance. . . . No woman should ever travel without a revolver.'"[16] Their alliance must have been already firm because on her return from Constantinople Maud went directly to Millevoye in Paris, where she agreed to carry a secret Boulangist dispatch into Russia.

On the train to St. Petersburg Maud noticed a distinguished man carrying an attaché case. He was clearly admiring her but, Maud later learned, hesitant to speak because he thought her long black traveling veil the habit of a religious order. When she was stopped at the Russian border for lack of visa, she saw him being officially welcomed and decided to speak first, saying that she regretted that she would not have the pleasure of traveling further with so courteous a gentleman. He promptly arranged that even without visa she should have that pleasure—in his private railway car. Maud had to act fast for more than personal qualms: she had sewn into her clothes Millevoye's dispatch, which competed with the message the Russian was carrying from Berlin:

> I took his hand and told him I too was happy to meet a Russian like him, who, I felt, would understand an Irish girl; that I had always believed that Russians were understanding people and not like others, English or Frenchmen, who looked on women in a vulgar way; that in my country women were very free because friendship between men and women could be beautiful and not commonplace.[17]

The appeal to national honor worked. The Russian—who has been identified as Count Pavel Andreevich, ambassador to Germany, 1885–1894—held Maud's hand to St. Petersburg and brought his wife the next day to meet her at her hotel. That was the winter of 1887; the marmoset died of the cold.

Through Millevoye's support and by his connections, Maud was able to work for Irish independence on the international level, hoping to make France bring pressure upon England for Ireland's sake. The editor of *Le Figaro* put his newspaper at her service; the British Embassy in Paris followed her movements. After Millevoye became editor of *La Patrie* in 1894, he helped her to found her own Irish news service, *L'Irelande libre*. W. T. Stead, an English journalist Maud met in Russia, later gave an unflattering assessment of what he called

> . . . the somewhat fantastic mission of Miss Maud Gonne to Paris for the purpose of founding an association of the "Friends of Irish Freedom" among the descendants of Hoche's expedition. Miss Gonne is one of the most beautiful women in the world. She is an Irish heroine, born a Protestant, who became a Buddhist, with theories of preexistence, but who, in all her pilgrimages from shrine to shrine, never ceased to cherish a passionate devotion to the cause of Irish independence. She is for the Irish republic and total separation, peaceably, if possible; but, if necessary, by the sword—by anybody's sword, that of France and Russia not excepted. She was in St. Petersburg in 1887, having travelled from Constantinople alone. Everywhere her beauty and her enthusiasm naturally make a great impression; and although she is hardly likely to be successful where

Wolfe Tone failed, her pilgrimage of passion is at least a picturesque incident that relieves the gloom of the political situation.[18]

According to Maud, however, her alliance with Millevoye grew so effective politically that Clemenceau himself intervened to destroy it. He did this by placing in Millevoye's way a beautiful cafe singer who was devoted to the reclamation of Alsace-Lorraine. Millevoye began to publish articles she wrote for that cause and pointed out to Maud that with the singer he did not have to share a rival interest. To Maud's regret Millevoye was influenced to support the Entente Cordiale, the alliance between France and England that she had fought hard to prevent. They saw each other only very rarely after 1897 and then in strained meetings.

Maud was in Holloway Prison on charges of suspected espionage in May 1918 when Millevoye died. Coxhead rather romantically suggests that the mourning Maud had worn, as she said, "for Ireland," since MacBride's execution for his part in the Easter Rising of 1916, was really thereafter worn for Millevoye.

Maud had borne him two children: a son "Georgette," who died in 1891, and a daughter Iseult, born in 1894 or 1895, to whom Yeats proposed marriage in 1917. Yeats learned of Iseult's birth when the child was about two years old (M133); Maud told him the details of her personal life in France at the time of her abandonment by Millevoye, but when these events were occurring Yeats knew nothing of them.

—3—

Yeats refers to January 30, 1889, when he met Maud, as the day that "the troubling of my life began" (M40). He was ready to welcome trouble. Under the influence of the romantics, he declared, "We begin to live when we have conceived of life as tragedy" (A189). In youth he dreamed less of having a woman than of having an experience in love that would shape him as a poet. He looked forward to such an experience, which no matter how painful would open to him the doors of a universal knowledge:

> I was about to learn that if a man is to write lyric poetry he must be shaped by nature and art to some one out of half a dozen traditional poses, and be lover or saint, sage or sensualist, or mere mocker of all life and that none but that stroke of luckless luck can open before him the accumulated expression of the world. And this thought before it could be knowledge was an instinct. (A87)

The "instinct" of which he speaks reveals an acceptance of what is now called "role-playing" for himself no less than for the woman to whom he assigned the role of center point of the social ritual. For Yeats, therefore, "role-playing" would not have held a superficial or pejorative connotation. A "traditional pose" was to him not an infertile stasis but a reliable footing for a point of view from which truth could be found out, an *understanding*, literal and practical. In this intuitive acceptance he was ahead of his time, more in line with the quantum physicists (L713–14), for whom point of view is essential to the reality perceived, than with the mechanistic physicists of his generation, for whom reality had an objectivity which point of view served only to distort. In his autobiographical recollection, therefore, Yeats reveals both his own role-playing and that which he proposed for Maud as intuitively existential rather than blindly chauvinistic.

All this, however, is in his retrospective analysis. While he was living through the experience, after "a hansom drove up to our door at Bedford Park with Miss Maud Gonne" and his "luckless luck" struck, Yeats's life and work became a classic study of infatuation. His condition, so common and so overwhelming for the inexperienced during those generations that preserved sexual innocence, has been anatomized in several psychoanalytical systems. Of these, the one most compatible with Yeats's own thought is that of Carl Gustav Jung, with whom Yeats has been compared by several scholars including Thomas Whitaker and Harold Bloom, who defend Yeats's general occultism, especially his "sacred book" *A Vision*, by stressing its psychological meaning in Jungian terms.[19]

By what Jung would later label the "projection" of an unconscious archetypal concept upon another person, Yeats seized upon Maud to be his mirror image. He read into her character those traits that were femininity as he dreamed of it. He fell in love, not with Maud, whom he scarcely knew, but with his own projected *anima*, the "woman within himself," a reference he would not actually use until near the end of his life in correspondence with Dorothy Wellesley (L868). Yeats, in fact, had his own version of *anima* projection, far more esoteric than Jung's:

> There is an astrological sense in which a man's wife or sweetheart is always an Eve made from a rib of his body. She is drawn to him because she represents a group of stellar influences on the radical horoscope. These influences also create an element in his character and his destiny, in things apart from love or marriage. Whether this element be good or evil she is therefore its external expression (M165).

It is ironic—and significant to the woman who has rejected the passive symbolical role in a masculine intellectual and cultural system—that Maud, a woman rare in her time, who refused to change her nature in accommodation or to assume a trait in response to a man's desire, should become the material of poetry. Maud always treated Yeats with blunt honesty and never led him to expect more of her than friendship and alliance in the Irish cause. And she was right. For the naive poet marriage, or even a liaison with her, would have been like hitching a ride on the tail of a comet. The projection of anima in Yeats's fascination with her appears in its interference between his consciousness and the realities of the situation. Her grasp of the reality and of its significance is clear in her famous rejection of his marriage proposal: "You would not be happy with me. You make beautiful poetry out of what you call your unhappiness and you are happy in that. . . . The world should thank me for not marrying you."[20]

By grace of his "traditional pose," the poet in love, Yeats was able—gradually and painfully—to gain control not of Maud but of his infatuation with her. This projecting and manipulating of images that we call the "creative imagination" in a poet seems akin to the process Jung later called "active imagination" and prescribed as the means of bringing an archetype to consciousness, where the intellect, or ego, can understand and assimilate it. Unconscious and unassimilated, a man's feminine characteristics impose between his ego and the outer world, tormenting him with self-doubt and illusion; made consciousness and positive, they form a bridge to his understanding of himself—his feelings and values—completing his personality and rendering him a "whole person," a "liberated" man.

As Yeats learned how Maud functioned in his creative imagination, he also met his identity as a poet and a man. The process occupied all his life. It did not lead to an idyllic old age but to an insight, a consciousness of choice:

> The intellect of man is forced to choose
> Perfection of the life or of the work,
> And if it take the second must refuse
> A heavenly mansion, raging in the dark. (CP242)

But the opposite choice, the seeking of reality without pose, is no guarantee of satisfaction either, for he provides no evidence of the existence of the "heavenly mansion." It, too, is an image, a role for reality to play. Reality without role, without pose is

> That old perplexity an empty purse,
> Or the day's vanity, the night's remorse.

—4—

Yeats's progress with his image of Maud falls into periods marked by change of consciousness. From their meeting in 1889 to the fall of 1891, Yeats was enthralled. The idea of the woman governed his consciousness. Although he saw little of her, he traced her activities through mutual friends more prominent than he in the Irish movement, and he mingled her image with his theosophic and hermetic studies, projecting her beauty into the eternal Idea, "The Rose of the World":

> Bow down, archangels, in your dim abode;
> Before you were, or any hearts to beat,
> Weary and kind, one lingered by His seat;
> He made the world to be a grassy road
> Before her wandering feet. (CP36)

In interpreting the feminine mood as "kind," Yeats employs the word used by the medieval poet to mean that the hard-hearted mistress is actually tolerating him for a moment. Commentary on the expression by Yeats's friend George Russell (the poet AE) serves to reveal the extent of imagination Yeats was using in his early courtly view of Maud. Russell, who did not especially like her, says that the poem was written at the end of a day when Yeats had walked Maud all over the cliffs of Howth (probably in the fall of 1891) and that she was only "in a gentler mood than usual" from fatigue.[21]

When rumors came to him of her connections in France or when the tart-tongued artist Sarah Purser teased him with descriptions of the "tall Frenchman" she had met lunching with Maud in Paris, he put these things from his mind (M63) and defended Maud in song:

> Half close your eyelids, loosen your hair,
> And dream about the great and their pride;
> They had spoken against you everywhere,
> But weigh this song with the great and their pride;
> I made it out of a mouthful of air,
> Their children's children shall say that they have lied.
> ("He Thinks of Those Who Have Spoken Evil of His Beloved," CP65)

He was playing the faithful courtly lover by one of the cardinal rules from the Middle Ages that the lover must nowise believe evil of his beloved. Yeats truly never seems to have realized or to have allowed himself to admit that when he first met Maud she must already have been pregnant with her first child by Millevoye. When, in the fall of 1891, she confided her grief to him at the death of Georgette, Maud said the child was adopted (M47–48), and despite the rumors, Yeats never questioned her statement. It remained for Maud to make a fuller confession of her life years later (M132).

The shared grief did, however, change the tack of his infatuated imagination. His worship of the ideal he had projected upon Maud became pity and protectiveness for her vulnerable soul. He associated her with the Countess Kathleen O'Shea, a woman of Irish legend who sacrificed her own soul to save others. He involved himself in the Irish Literary Society hoping that he might bring Maud also into the collecting of books and the founding of libraries that her soul might not be destroyed in pursuit of violent revolution.

This second period ended with a quarrel in summer 1893, and Yeats took a lover, Mrs. Olivia Shakespear, whose identity he masked as "Diana

Vernon." Their affair, although it led to a life-long friendship, was itself short-lived, for Yeats found that he had indeed made himself Maud's servant and prisoner of love in the manner of the courtly lovers that C. S. Lewis describes, "always weeping and always on their knees before ladies of inflexible cruelty."[22] Thinking of Maud, Yeats was unable to "bring the right mood round" with Mrs. Shakespear. "'There is someone else in your heart', she said" (M89), and she moved out of the rooms they were sharing in the Woburn Buildings, London. Yeats sang of the event to Maud:

> Pale brows, still hands and dim hair,
> I had a beautiful friend
> And dreamed that the old despair
> Would end in love in the end:
> She looked in my heart one day
> And saw your image was there;
> She was gone weeping away. (CP59)

As prisoner of love, Yeats assumed ritual and mythic identities through which he experienced real suffering both psychologically and physically. Of the period of this bondage that began with his separation from Olivia Shakespear, he wrote,

> It was a time of great personal strain and sorrow. Since my mistress had left me, no other woman had come into my life, and for nearly seven years none did. I was tortured by sexual desire and disappointed love. Often as I walked in the woods at Coole it would have been a relief to have screamed aloud. When desire became an unendurable torture, I would masturbate, and that, no matter how moderate I was, would make me ill. It never occurred to me to seek another love. I would repeat to myself again and again the last confession of Lancelot, and indeed it was my greatest pride, 'I have loved a queen beyond measure and exceeding long.' (M125)

In 1898, Maud's alliance with Millevoye having ended, Yeats began with her a "spiritual marriage," a relationship that, for all its intangibility, was based on their most solid mutual ground, their belief in what we now term "parapsychological phenomena." It had begun with Yeats's inducing Maud to "see visions" when she first began to confide her dreams to him in 1891, the period of his pity. He had also seen visions with Mrs. Shakespear. These were early instances of his mediumistic use of women that culminated around 1920 in his wife's automatic writing that provided the basis of *A Vision*.

In 1897, Yeats had caught Maud's interest in the planning of a "Castle of Heroes," to be a center for the revival of ancient Irish culture. It was a project in line with Yeats's concept of national identity asserted through indigenous culture rather than through the violent overthrow of the British government in Ireland. Yeats saw the Castle as the meeting place of a chivalric order with rites fashioned after the Eleusinian Mysteries. When he could make Maud find time, they would retreat into rural Ireland to "see visions" of those rites. Maud, ever in opposition to his mood, saw the Castle as a retreat housing the four ancient Irish symbols, the "jewels" of the Tuatha de Danaan—cauldron, stone, spear, and sword—to which fatigued revolutionists could retire for rest and inspiration.

It was in the intimacy that grew out of these adventures that Maud confessed the unhappy details of her life to him, and one day they shared a vision reminiscent of St. Theresa's. Yeats heard a voice announcing it as the "initiation of the spear," the third step in the rites they had planned for the Castle:

> We became silent; a double vision unfolded itself, neither speaking till all was finished. She thought herself a great stone statue through which passed flame, and I felt myself becoming flame and mounting up through and looking out of the eyes of a great stone Minerva. Were the beings which stand behind human life trying to unite us, or had we brought it by our own dreams? (M134)

During this period Yeats created for Maud the only role in which she acquiesced, that of the militant Cathleen ni Houlihan. Maud returned from a speaking tour of the United States to appear in his play in April 1902. In spite of her revelation to him that she had "a horror and terror of physical love" (M134), Yeats believed that she was close to accepting his repeated offers of marriage, but again he was not privy to her affairs. She had decided upon marriage to Major John MacBride, a dashing figure who had achieved celebrity by leading the Irish Brigade in support of the Boers against England in the South African War. MacBride was Maud's speaking partner in America, and after performing in Yeats's play, she rejoined him there. Yeats knew nothing of her intention until he was handed her telegram on the day of her marriage in Paris, February 21, 1903. He read it moments before making a speech about the Irish National Theatre, of which he was a founder. Later he said that although people complimented the speech, he could not remember a word he had said. Curtis Bradford believes that Yeats's poem, "Reconciliation," written after their reunion in September 1908, refers to the experience of the telegram:

> Some have blamed you that you took away
> The verses that could move them on the day
> When, the ears being deafened, the sight of the eyes blind
> With lightning, you went from me. (CP89)[23]

But a poem written on the occasion of Maud's return from America in 1902 indicates that love on the astral plain alone had paled for Yeats:

I had a thought for no one's but your ears;
That you were beautiful, and that I strove
To love you in the old high way of love;
That it had all seemed happy, and yet we'd grown
As weary-hearted as that hollow moon. (CP79)

Maud lived with MacBride for nearly two years and had one child by him. They were legally separated, and although Yeats contrived with John Quinn, a friend in New York, to have MacBride followed in the hope of turning up grounds for divorce, he did not see Maud again until 1908, when she offered a renewal of the spiritual marriage. He turned to astrology for guidance and kept a record of their attempted astral meetings in private papers known as the Maud Gonne Notebook. Two of the few surviving letters from Maud to him are preserved in it. They contain somewhat wifely advice on his worrisome involvement with the Abbey Theatre and reveal a higher evaluation of him and his work then does her autobiography. She says that she had not wanted to see him involved in politics in the 1890s because that would have taken him from his writing and "cheated Ireland of a greater gift."[24]

The resumption of the spiritual marriage seems to have been more successful for Maud than for Yeats, who had turned to more earthly relationships in the interim of Maud's marriage, including probably a reunion with Olivia Shakespear. In her letter dated 26 July [1908], Maud rapturously describes a spiritual union she had had with Yeats. She tells him, with underscoring, how united they became "one being, a being greater than ourselves." This epiphany, however, was followed by an ordinary dream in which they discussed their union. Maud was troubled in this dream when Yeats said that the spiritual meeting would increase physical desire. She argued in her letter that "material union" would be a pale shadow compared to the spiritual.[25]

But for Yeats the last period of his infatuation had begun. He had moved out of his Celtic Twilight of dim-haired goddesses and had published stringent criticism of those poets who had been his early guides in romantic love: Spenser, Morris, and Shelley.[26] He had read Nietzsche; he no longer conceived of life as tragedy. The Maud Gonne Notebook begins with daily entries of the efforts Yeats was making to send his spirit to Maud in dreams. On the night of her vision, July 25, 1909, he had "evoked" the signs of the sun and moon in union, the emblem of their spiritual marriage of "Sol and Luna," and had seen it "for the first time bright and shining." But he slept that night without dreaming. When her "extraordinary" letter came, he went "over and over the thing" in his mind, wondering whether her physical desire was being kindled toward him at last.[27]

Gradually his efforts became more objective, more a study of the possibility of spiritual union in itself. He blamed "her fears and my irritations" for driving him "from the threshold of wisdom." At the same time he could not, as he had twenty years earlier, return to the role of Lancelot and content himself with spirit alone. During the time of this second spiritual marriage to Maud he was involved physically with an unidentified woman who nearly trapped him into marriage by announcing that she was pregnant. As Maud continued to repel physical desire, she lost maturity in Yeats's sight: "Now she is my child more than my sweetheart," he said of this woman in her forties. The vicissitudes of this long struggle, which began in June 1909, are reflected over the years in the abortive drafts of *The Player Queen*. He began the play just after their reunion in 1908, in his old romantic style of verse drama; he found that he could finish it only as a prose comedy after his marriage to Georgie Hyde-Lees in October 1917.

Yeats remained Maud's loyal friend during the war years while she lived in France and nursed wounded soldiers. When MacBride was executed for his part in the Easter Rising of 1916, Yeats made a last proposal to her. Coxhead, for one, is certain that he was relieved when she refused him. Then he proposed to Iseult because she reminded him of her mother when young. Now past fifty, Yeats felt the loss of the years; he wanted a family. In the preface poem of *Responsibilities* (1914), he had written:

> Pardon, old fathers, if you still remain
> Somewhere in ear-shot for the story's end. . . .
> Pardon that for a barren passion's sake,
> Although I have come close on forty-nine,
> I have no child, I have nothing but a book
> Nothing but that to prove your blood and mine. (CP99)

Iseult seemed to offer a chance of turning back the calendar, but he had become too much of a father to her. She declined with genuine regret.

Yeats's last act for Maud before his marriage was to escort her and Iseult through the hostile British officials on their return from France in the summer of 1917. Under the Defense of the Realm Act, the British refused to allow Maud to return to Ireland. One year later she was imprisoned at Holloway but removed to a sanatorium where she fell ill. She escaped disguised as a nurse and appeared the next day in Dublin at the door of her own house in Stephens Square, where Yeats and his wife were living as her tenants. Placing the interest of his wife, who was pregnant and had been ill, above Maud's danger, Yeats turned her away. Their friendship cooled, and after further disagreement over the founding of an Irish republic in the twenties, they avoided each other.

After the poet's death in 1939, Maud contributed an essay to a memorial collection, in which, without slighting her memory of her own striking appearance when young, she sets out a candid statement of the differences that kept her and Yeats apart:

A tall, lanky boy, with deep-set eyes behind glasses, over which a lock of dark hair was constantly falling, to be pushed back impatiently by long sensitive fingers, often stained with paint—dressed in shabby clothes that none noticed (except himself, as he confessed long after)—a tall girl with masses of gold-brown hair and a beauty which made her Paris clothes equally unnoticeable. . . . I, having studied for the stage, in those days had better diction, and though very proud of the praise I felt it was unfair, for Willie's speeches were more sincere than mine; I was always concealing the foolishness of a thought which kept intruding on my mind—how few had ever read those dusty volumes on the shelves. . . . Being young and hasty, I secretly felt action not books was needed; I did not then realise how the written word may lead to action and I drifted off to speak at other meetings held on wild hillsides.[28]

In the same essay Maud gives her version of Yeats's last proposal and its aftermath. Having come to her in France immediately after MacBride's execution, Yeats wrote his commemorative poem "Easter 1916" there with its image of the stone symbolizing a life frozen to a single intent:

Hearts with one purpose alone
Through summer and winter seem
Enchanted to a stone
To trouble the living stream. . . .
Too long a sacrifice
Can make a stone of the heart. (CP 177–80)

Maud remembers,

Standing by the seashore in Normandy in September 1916 he read me that poem; he had worked on it all the night before, and he implored me to forget the stone and its inner fire for the flashing, changing joy of life; but when he found my mind dull with the stone of the fixed idea of getting back to Ireland, kind and helpful as ever, he helped me to overcome political and passport difficulties and we traveled as far as London together. In London we parted; my road led to jail . . . , but Willie's road was more difficult, a road of outer peace and inner confusion, discernible in his later work. He was too old to cut a way for himself and for Ireland out of the confusion which, after the Treaty of 1921, spread like a wizard's mist over the country, obscuring both the stone and the glory and joy of changing life.[29]

—5—

Maud remained poetic symbol to Yeats but, now that the infatuation was finished, a symbol under his artistic and emotional control. He last celebrated her in "Beautiful Lofty Things" as one of the "Olympians" he had known:

. . . Maud Gonne at Howth station waiting a train,
Pallas Athene in that straight back and arrogant head. (CP300)

But conversely in "A Bronze Head" he viewed her as the "withered and mummy-dead" image of the heroic culture he had dreamed when young (CP328). Bradford wrily comments that even what Yeats calls a "bronze" head of Maud by the sculptor Laurence Campbell "was but painted plaster."[30] Yeats surely would have rejected this comment as a slight not on his poetic license but on his understanding of Maud. That she was not Intellectual Beauty and Wisdom incarnate as in his early phase of enchantment he would have had her does not mean that she was only facade, only "painted plaster." One result of Yeats's mythopoesis of courtly love is his realization that while feminine beauty is in East and West a poetic symbol of intellectual abstractions by a symbolism far older than Christianity or the Eastern philosophies, these abstractions cannot be read into an individual woman, even into one so outwardly fitted for them as Maud Gonne. This realization may have begun for him in the brief affair with Olivia Shakespear.

What brought Yeats and Mrs. Shakespear together at first was his willingness to read and discuss the several novels that she wrote between 1894 and 1896. The gist of his criticism is that she drew better women than men characters: "You do not know mankind anything like as well as womankind" (L240). Mrs. Shakespear allowed womankind to speak for her in her story "Beauty's Hour":

> It's such an old story. You fall in love with a girl's beautiful face—it's not the first time you've done it; you endow her with all sorts of qualities; you make her into an idol; and the whole thing only means that your aesthetic sense is gratified. That's a poor way of loving.[31] . . . What happens if you find she does not possess the soul, which she never claimed to have, but which you insisted on crediting her with? You dethrone her with ignominy. The case of the other woman is hard: she has a face that does not attract you, so you deny her the soul that you forced on the other one.[32]

The passage presages lines Yeats published after his marriage when his prime intellectual interests had become the resolution of antinomies in the marriage bed and the search for the self of the loved one. He had also realized that the assumption of any role, while it may serve its purpose for art's sake, must be in practicality a sometime thing, else it would indeed lead to "raging in the dark":

> *The Girl.* I rage at my own image in the glass
> That's so unlike myself that when you praise it
> It is as though you praised another, or even
> Mocked me with praise of my mere opposite. . . .
> *The Hero.* I have raged at my own strength because
>   you have loved it.
> *The Girl.* If you are no more strength than I am beauty
> I had better find a convent and turn nun. (CP216–17)

Concurrent with the maturing of his concepts of personal sexual relationships, he sought a system of belief by which he could both organize the chaos of de-Christianized history and provide himself with coherent metaphors for poetry. In this search he retained the ancient symbolic role of the female, seeking it anew in the "fardel of stories, and of personages, and of emotions, inseparable from their first expression, passed on from generation to generation by poets and painters with some help from philosophers and theologians" from which he looked to found "a new religion, an almost infallible church of poetic tradition" (A116). He had even created dogma: "'Because those imaginary people are created out of the deepest instinct of man, to be his measure and his norm, whatever I can imagine those mouths speaking may be the nearest I can go to truth.'" This credo provided Yeats with the "intellectual prepossessions" to give to his role of courtly lover the solidity of the courtly lovers of legend: Parsifal, Tristram, and Don Quixote.

1

The Myth

And this brought forth a dream and soon enough
This dream itself had all my thought and love. (CP336)

—1—

The attitude toward love and sex that expressed the final extravagance of
romanticism served many creative men of the later nineteenth century—
Swinburne, Baudelaire, Mallarmé, Villiers de l'Isle Adam—as a metaphorical system to replace the Christian allegory that they could not transfer
from the Middle Ages to the new Age of Science. The phrase for this
extravagant attitude, "courtly love," was itself not medieval but coined in
1883, when Gaston Paris referred to the humble service that Lancelot
renders to Guenevere in Chrétien de Troyes' poem, *Le Conte de la Charrette*,
as *amour courtois*.[1] In that poem, Lancelot, *en route* to rescue his queen who
is imprisoned in the land of Gorre, loses his horse and is offered a ride by a
dwarf driving a tumbril, a cart of shame for transporting criminals. He
accepts the ride after a brief hesitation. When he meets the queen, he finds
her furious with him. That momentary hesitation on behalf of his dignity
has, in her opinion, overshadowed all the dangers and trials he has undergone for her. To make up to her for the slight, Guenevere demands that the
great knight deliberately play the coward in a tournament. On hearing her
demand, he sends her thanks and promises to fulfill it. His return to
unthinking obedience and humility redeems him in Guenevere's sight, and
she receives him again into her favor. The material for this tale and its
manner of treatment were allegedly dictated to Chrétien by his sponsor
Marie, wife of Henry the Liberal, count of Champagne, in the last quarter of
the twelfth century.

Literary historians of the late nineteenth and early twentieth centuries
applied Paris's term for Lancelot's behavior in this story to what they
believed to be a highly stylized code of sexual behavior between men and
women of position and property. They believed this code to have been
actually practiced in the Middle Ages and to have represented a basic change

from previous sexual attitudes that had treated the passion of love as either comic or insane. They devoted much time and effort to ascertaining the cause of the change and to justifying it in relation to other medieval religious and social attitudes. They were not clearly successful in either endeavor. Collectively, their studies prove that courtly love is not Platonic in origin and not Ovidian, not Arabic and not Germanic, and neither Christian nor Manichean. C. S. Lewis, one of the most respected scholars to write on the subject, credits the change in sexual attitude to a spontaneous change in human sentiment, of which, he says without specification, "there are perhaps three or four on record."[2] Yeats admits that he cannot explain it:

> When the tide changed and faith no longer sufficed, something must have happened in the courts and castles of which history has perhaps no record, for with the first vague dawn of the ultimate *antithetical* revelation man, under the eyes of the Virgin, or upon the breast of his mistress, became but a fragment. Instead of that old alternation, brute or ascetic, came something obscure or uncertain that could not find its full explanation for a thousand years. (V285)

A modern medical definition agrees with Yeats's assessment of the new attitude as a departure from two previous modes: "Sex is biological and animal, love is social and human. . . . When love and sex unite, we have 'romantic love,' which is different from either of its precursors though it encompasses both."[3]

The new attitude appeared rather suddenly in Spain, then in southern France, and later in Germany during the second feudal age, or Little Renaissance. For centuries there had been the sensual tradition in literature, as exemplified in Ovid's *Ars Amatoria*, *Remedia Amoris*, and *Amores*, but in 1022, the Andalusian Ibn Hazm wrote *The Dove's Neck-Ring*, presenting sexual love in a serious and spiritual manner. Duke William of Aquitaine, the "first troubadour," was believed to have brought the idea from Spain to his own province, where it became a family literary tradition handed down through William's granddaughter Eleanor of Aquitaine. By her first marriage to Louis II of France and her second to Henry II of England, Eleanor carried it to those countries. Marie of Champagne, whom Chrétien served, was Eleanor's daughter. Marie's chaplain Andreas (Capellanus) has been traditionally credited with codifying the new attitude toward love in a book called *De Amore* or *De arte honeste amandi* that follows the plan of the works of Ovid, but whether it also follows Ovid's satirical viewpoint has been the crux of the recent controversy. In Germany, the code of courtly love, called *Frauendienst*, or "the service of women," was the subject of the *minnesingers*, who praised *Frau Minne*, a feminine counterpart of the god Amor. Love was at first an alien theme among the Germans, who, as C. S. Lewis says, "preferred to hear how a holy man went to heaven or how a brave man went to battle,"[4] but in time it was accepted, and it in turn absorbed some of the primitive Germanic view of women as "uncanny and prophetic beings." The combination of Latin and Germanic attitudes invested the beloved Lady with an aura of magical-spiritual power.

From the time of Paris's work until after the Second World War, an understanding of the code of courtly love was considered basic to criticism of all medieval literature on the theme of love and much that is on other themes. As late as 1941, John Jay Parry, in his translation of *De Amore*, took the view that Andreas's work is " 'one of those capital works which reflect the thought of a great epoch, which explain the secret of a civilization'."[5] But in 1952, D. W. Robertson, Jr., began a reappraisal of the subject.[6] He takes the position that Andreas, far from promulgating the adulterous passion and the abasement of the lover that his Rules seem to demand, is really employing irony and deliberate self-contradiction to preach against yielding to the governance of fleshly appetites. Robertson explains that the judgments on love that Andreas puts into the mouth of Eleanor of Aquitaine as she presides over Courts of Love would be understood as self-incriminating by those who knew her private life and that they certainly do not prove, as earlier scholars thought they did, that Eleanor and her daughter actually presided over elaborately staged trials of lovers.[7] Robertson interprets Chrétien's tale of Lancelot and Guenevere as an allegory of a man's loss of the grace of God through climbing on the cart of sin to ride off into the land of vanity (a suggested etymological origin of "Gorre").

Now contemporary scholars are much less certain as to whether courtly love ever existed in practice and whether, if it existed as a literary convention, it was employed only to entertain or to convey profounder meanings, either heretical or orthodox. In short, courtly love has fallen on hard times both socially and academically. Professor Robertson insists that the very idea is a cultural artifact of the nineteenth and early twentieth centuries and, therefore, an impediment to the understanding of medieval life and literature. In 1967, John F. Benton moved that the term be banned from all future conferences of the Center for Medieval and Early Renaissance Studies.[8]

But in the nineteenth century, courtly love became a metaphor for the poets on the one hand and a romantic rationale for middle-class sexual attitudes on the other. Yeats—a poet and a middle-class man who admired the aristocracy—exemplifies the efforts of both groups to make the romantic extravagance viable. It may have been this dual identity of Yeats that made him so conscious of facing a choice between perfection of the work and perfection of the life and that has left his critics so much ground on which to argue whether he succeeded or failed in either or both of the choices. The dual identity certainly gave his love quest both personal and philosophical dimensions.

Perhaps it was the middle-class quality of the British Royal Family's life in the nineteenth century that made middle-class people of the English-speaking nations feel that courtly love provided a model of sexual attitude for them. The middle class did not know Andreas, but they did know Malory and Dante; from the former, by way of such interpreters as Tennyson, they drew the ideal of chivalric behavior, and from the latter, the idea of love as a spiritually transforming power.

To transform the spirit, love must be "pure," that is, "above" the flesh. Andreas says that pure love "consists in the contemplation of the mind and the affection of the heart; it goes as far as the kiss and the embrace and the modest contact with the nude lover, omitting the final solace, for that is not permitted to those who wish to love purely."[9] Benton finds this definition too broadly drawn to be believed:

> To do so requires the expectation that it is easy and in fact common for two naked lovers embracing together to avoid intercourse if one of them, presumably the woman, will only call a halt, thereby sublimating sexual desire into a spiritual relationship. The idea could be held in the Victorian period, when it was widely assumed that decent women did not enjoy sexual relations, and it still seems to linger on today. But it is a view which clashes with medieval views on physiology and the sexuality of women.[10]

It cannot be ignored in the consideration of "pure love" that Dante, who, as Yeats said, "found / The most exalted lady loved by man" (CP157), was inspired by the idealized memory of a woman who was dead. James Joyce referred to such idealization of love as "the spiritual-heroic refrigerating apparatus, invented and patented in all countries by Dante Alighieri."[11]

What the literati of the nineteenth century thought to have belonged originally to property and power came popularly to be a matter of morals and manners. A young woman of no worldly worth could smooth her dress, comb her hair, straighten her back, lower her voice, and call herself a "lady," and it was believed that if she acted like a lady, she could indeed command the respect and, if need be, the protection of any decent man. It was also believed that the love of a good woman could redeem a dissolute man. This transforming power was indicated even for the Royal Family by W. T. Stead in his comment on the engagement of the popular Princess May of Teck to the unpopular Duke of Clarence in December 1891: "The genial influence of a true-hearted girl is often the making of a man."[12]

In his personal quest to find the true-hearted girl who would both inspire him and respond to his chivalry, Yeats experienced dramatic disappointment with Maud Gonne and unusual success with Georgie Hyde-Lees, the woman he married in 1917. His double experience led him to ask:

> Does the imagination dwell the most
> Upon a woman won or a woman lost? (CP195)

The answer is, of course, upon a woman lost, but not because Yeats was unable to relinquish his personal dream of Maud as a wife, partner in magical evocations, and hostess to his literary friends. All these things he found in his marriage to "George," as he always called her, after he had clearly decided that Maud either never would or never could provide them.

The woman lost fascinates the imagination as symbol of all that is lost or elusive or unrealized as the woman won cannot. The very satisfying of the quest quells the imagination. Denis de Rougement, who saw the roots of courtly love in the Catharist heresy which denied sexual love to those who would attain perfection and translated the energy from that denial into passionate yearning for the spiritual realm, contends that passion, in order to exist, must be unsatisfied, must cause suffering, and cannot lead to fruitful contentment in marriage.[13] Similarly, Yeats wrote at the height of his marital contentment that

> There's not a thing but love can make
> The world a narrow pound (CP136)

even for such minds as Solomon and Sheba possessed. Yeats, who had early adopted the romantic attitude that "We begin to live when we have conceived life as tragedy" (A189), became over the years realistic enough to end his disappointed personal quest in the comedy of *The Player Queen*, in which he shares, at least for the moment, the attitude of the frustrated Cavalier depicted by Sir John Suckling:

> Nothing can make her:
> The Devil take her!

But Yeats the poet clung to the woman lost as metaphor. As he grew older, that metaphor image began to demonstrate a will of her own. She came to stand more and more in the way of the timeless beauty he wanted to create, but over the same years she provided him entry to wider understanding. After his experiments with female persona, Yeats wrote to Dorothy Wellesley:

> It seems that I can make a woman express herself as never before. I have looked out of her eyes. I have shared her desire. (L868)

It is here, on the metaphorical level, that the old high way of love leads into a dark maze. In the poetic metaphor of courtly love, the good and evil Powers of Christianity, expressed in the masculine figures of God the Father and of the Fallen Archangel, revert to feminine images, the Virgin and the Witch. They, unlike the Father and Satan of orthodox interpretation, may be one and the same Person. The Powers can be said to "revert" because, according to the social anthropologists of the late nineteenth and early twentieth centuries—J. J. Bachofen, Lester F. Ward, Robert Briffault, Erich Neumann—these feminine figures existed before the patriarchal civilizations in a time of matriarchy when the generative powers ruled the intellectual. In this early time the universe was conceived as having an organic origin from the World Egg rather than an intellectual beginning in the Word of the Father. Earth herself was a mother—the Great Mother, *Ge* or *Gaia*—and she contained within herself all good and evil: birth and death, youth and age, pleasure and pain. She brought forth her sons, supported and directed their existence, and when they died, took them back into the womb from which they had come. In her fertile spring she inspired man to grow and when that growth evolved to the intellectual as well as the physical, she continued her inspiration as he imaginatively adapted her spring-like aspect to symbolize his intellectual goal, the as yet unattained woman, the Virgin. In that role he named her Muse, Divine Wisdom, Philosophia. But if her inspiration caused destructive ecstasy of the intellect, if she no longer led but drove him, he called her the Witch, Lilith, Circe. She became the Trinity of Virgin, Mother, and Witch, dramatized most vividly in nature by the phases of the moon, the natural phenomenon that Yeats made his central image of the temporal, generative world.

The presence of the feminine Trinity in both the mythological and the psychoanalytical inquiries of the nineteenth and twentieth centuries won the attention of science because of their employment by the creative imagination. C. G. Jung identified the Virgin, Mother, and Witch among the archetypes, the conceptual elements of the unconscious in modern man. For *The Great Mother: An Analysis of the Archetype*, Erich Neumann devised a diagram to show clearly all the prospects of comfort and of terror that the whole female archetype comprises (see p. 27).[14]

Neumann intends his paradigmatic design to be understood as representing a sphere like the earth. The Great Mother is first of all the organic earth. Thomas Taylor, whose translations of the Orphic Mysteries were familiar to Yeats, identified her with the giant female torsos shown rising out of the earth in ancient sculptures and reliefs. She is the material container of all that is born, lives, and dies. The elementary character of "containing" is shown in the center of the diagram. Every man begins life at this point. Branching from this center are the axes of the maternal and virginal aspects of the archetype. Each axis runs in both positive and negative directions. The man born from the elementary round, the womb, will find himself on the axis of the Mother that will take him through first physical, then spiritual or psychological transformation. If the direction given him is positive—if he has a Good Mother like Demeter, who causes the fruits of earth to mature— he will be given independence and nourishment and will be brought to a fruitful maturity. If his Mother is negative—the Gorgon, who turns men to

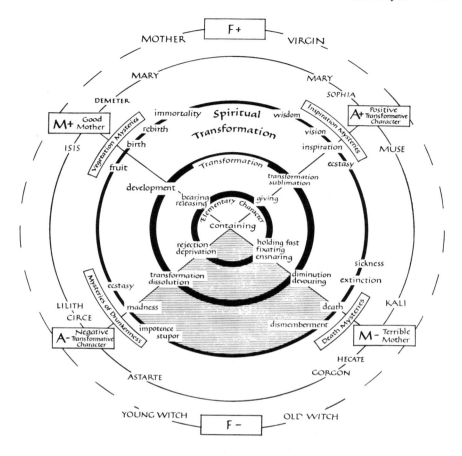

1. Structural Diagram of the Archetypal Feminine

The Great Mother: An Analysis of the Archetype, Erich Neumann, tr. Ralph Manheim, Bollingen Series XLVII. (Princeton: Princeton University Press, 1963), Schema III Used by permission.

stone, or Kali, who devours her young—he will be stillborn physically or mentally or emotionally. But, because the reality represented by the diagram is spherical, he may, while traveling toward one manifestation, meet its opposite; for however positive, releasing, and nourishing the earth may be, she must one day become for every man the grave to which he returns. The Mother who gives birth also lays out the dead. All those who write of the ancient matriarchies stress the element of mourning in those societies, in some of which men in grief donned women's clothes.[15]

The Virgin governs all intellectual and creative development. She transforms positively toward wisdom, vision, and inspiration or negatively toward drunkenness, impotence, and madness. Again the sphere asserts itself in the ancient association of madness with inspiration and in the maxim that a fine line separates genius and insanity. Neumann employs "ecstasy" in double meaning at both ends of the Virgin's axis to indicate how in a breath the Virgin and the Witch can change identities. In "The Seeker," a dramatic poem that Yeats wrote when he was twenty years old, there is a nightmarish interchange of the Virgin-Witch identity. An old knight has followed a sweet-voiced spirit into a wood, believing that it has summoned him with love to reveal to him "joys unhuman." Suddenly the spirit materializes as a bearded witch, whose speech reveals her archetypal ground in the unconscious; she has no self-knowledge and no purpose as the intellect would recognize it:

> *Knight.* I sought thee not.
> *Figure.*   Men call me Infamy.
>   I know not what I am.
> *Knight.* I sought thee not.
> *Figure.* Lover, the voice that summoned thee was mine. (VPy685)

The Mother is found in nature. She seems to have been imposed upon the intellect from without as awakening man personified friendly and unfriendly acts of nature and of human mothers. But the Virgin seems, like her embodiment Athena, to have sprung full-grown from the head of man himself. Since nature, however, does not provide a virgin as she does a mother for every man born, the Virgin is the Person of the feminine Trinity who must be courted.

The coming of patriarchal religions with father-gods, culminating in the West with Christianity, could not eradicate the feminine Presence. Rather, that older Trinity was divided and adapted by Christianity, the Virgin-Mother becoming the Queen of Heaven in association with the masculine Trinity; the Witch becoming a servant of Satan. But in the profane mythology the three females were still One, although often antagonistic facets of the One. The many tales of Virgins poisoned or imprisoned by Witches testify to this identify, as does the recurrence of the old nurse whose wicked advice corrupts her innocent charge. Medieval tales also include interchange of Witch and Virgin within the one woman as in the tale told by Chaucer's Wife of Bath. Robertson's explanation of this particular interchange is that it takes place not in the woman but in the knight's perception of her. When he looks at her with eyes of lust, she is beautiful; when he looks with wisdom, he sees her as the threat of the flesh in its hideousness.[16] But underlying Robertson's Christian interpretation of a Christian story is the fact that man has created in his intellect a dual concept of woman. She symbolizes both good and evil in whatever terms a patriarchal culture constructs. To the Greeks, she could sustain the man in his noble course, as Nausicaa and Penelope sustain Ulysses, or she could drive him to bestiality and self-destruction, as do Circe and the Sirens. In medieval Christianity she carries the dual symbolism of spiritual salvation and lustful damnation, although St. Paul (cited by both Robertson and De Rougemont, who otherwise disagree on the subject of courtly love) declares the sexual stance of Christianity to be unbiased: "There are no more distinctions between Jew and Greek, slave and free, male and female, but all of you are one in Christ Jesus" (Galatians 3:28). In Robertson's view of medieval tales, the witches and beautiful virgins have nothing to do with actual women; in the middle-class understanding of courtly love in the nineteenth and twentieth centuries, actual women were either expected to play the role of the spiritually redeeming Virgin or suspected of being the Witch, usually in her younger, more seductive form of the Enchantress. Indeed, the "glamour girl" of the movies in the thirties and forties derived her title from a word that originally meant a spell or enchantment such as that cast by Keats' "La Belle Dame sans Merci," who left her lover "alone and palely loitering" in a dead landscape. The parallel of the Witch and Satan adds a dimension to the idea of conceding to the Devil the woman who will not play her role of Virgin.[17]

Yeats had no trouble seeing the dual intellectual symbolism of women as a whole since he adhered to no single religious orthodoxy but sought his "infallible church" and the means of its expression in that "fardel of stories, and of personages, and of emotions . . . passed on from generation to generation" (A116) that he accepted in its totality according to the eclecticism taught by his Theosophic and Rosicrucian mentors, who established the position that "the dogmas and symbols of Christianity are substantially identical with those of other and earlier religious systems" and that "the true plan of religious belief is not the objective and physical, but the subjective and spiritual."[18]

A search through the annals of the subjective and the spiritual seems to lead to the ancient juncture of concepts reached by various scholars—Bachofen, Briffault, Neumann, and Jung—through routes of anthropology, mythology, and the unconscious. That the existence of such a juncture is doubted by many is irrelevant to a study of Yeats, who did most firmly believe in its existence. He called it, after Henry More (the Platonist), the *Anima Mundi* or Great Memory and associated it with "Wordsworth's 'immortal sea which brought us hither'" (My346):

> Before the mind's eye, whether in sleep or waking, came images that one was to discover presently in some book one had never read, and after looking in vain for explanation to the current theory of forgotten memory, I came to believe in a Great Memory passing on from generation to generation. (My345)

Yeats's doctrinaire mind demanded that he lay out the dogma for this concept as he had for his "new religion":

> I believe in three doctrines, which have, as I think, been handed down from early times, and been the foundation of nearly all magical practices. These doctrines are:—
> (1) That the borders of our mind are ever shifting, and that many minds can flow into one another, as it were, and create or reveal a single mind, a single energy.
> (2) That the borders of our memories are as shifting, and that our memories are a part of one great memory, the memory of Nature herself.
> (3) That this great mind and great memory can be evoked by symbols. (EI28)

For proof of the existence of a universally shared memory, Yeats cites his success in evoking predetermined images in the minds of certain women by suggesting to them a chosen symbol. The particular symbol and resulting image that he cites in *Per Amica Silentia Lunae* relate again to the archetypal identify of the Virgin-Witch in another of the medieval tales:

> If I wish to 'transfer' a thought I may think, let us say, of Cinderella's slipper, and my subject may see an old woman coming out of a chimney. (My353)

From his fardel of Henry More and those who formed his earlier thinking—Shelley, Spenser, Swedenborg, Boehme, and especially William Blake—Yeats drew his concepts of the feminine and the masculine elements in both the Great Memory and the personal mind. Historically came first the Platonic myth of the original self divided into male and female, each element ever seeking its completion in the other, the foundation of Yeats's effort to resolve the antinomies of existence. Then the metaphor of the Old Testament whereby Yahweh is the lover of Israel as in the Song of Solomon, of which Yeats made use in his own marriage songs; and its parallel in the New Testament whereby Christ is the Bridegroom of His Church. The Gnostic Christians, according to Elaine Pagels, "correlate[d] their description of God in both masculine and feminine terms with a complementary description of human nature (Pagels, *The Gnostic Gospels*, p. 66), a correlation Yeats learned from his Hermetic studies and declared in his "Supernatural Songs." Finally, in Yeats's own time the terms gained at least a quasi-scientific status as psychoanalysts beginning with Sigmund Freud and Otto Weininger delineated what Weininger first called the feminine principle and the masculine principle:

> Man and woman are like two substances which are distributed among living individuals in varying mixed proportions, without the coefficient of one substance ever vanishing. In experience, one might say, there is neither man nor woman, only masculine and feminine.[19]

Among more modern writers, both Ann Belford Ulanov, psychologist, and Lisa Appignanese, literary critic and translator of Weininger, are careful to warn against applying the psychological myths of the sexual principles as standards for judgment of femininity or masculinity in individual women and men. Weininger's "two substances," like the *anima* and *animus*, that Jung later proposed as complements to the ego in man and woman, occur together in all normal human beings. If an individual existed who was totally one or the other, he or she would be actually only half a human being. The fault of the culture that grasped the nineteenth-century idea of courtly love as a rule for middle-class behavior has been just such a mistaken application of these principles in holding up the "all man" and the "all woman" as desirable models. Yeats, for all his dependence on the masculine and the feminine for metaphor, was not guilty of this cultural error.

The masculine principle, however, is that mode of thinking on which Western culture has rested. It clearly distinguishes between the subject and the object, and in dealing with the object, it can be easily "objective." This means that having no sense of participation in the object, it can divide, analyze, organize, modify, and institutionalize the object. In *The Feminine in Jungian Psychology and in Christian Theology*, Ulanov points out that to describe masculine qualities the infinitives of active verbs are required: "to penetrate, separate, take charge, initiate, create, stand firmly and over against, to articulate and express meaning."[20] The masculine works toward bringing the object into stasis, whereby it can be made to balance other objects. The keynotes of this masculine principle are the boundary and the balance. Patriarchal states speak to each other in these terms; their representatives talk of "areas of influence," "parameters of discussion," "limits of indebtedness," "balance of power," and "reciprocal agreements."

The feminine, in contrast, tends to fuse rather than to divide; Ulanov says that feminine qualities are expressed in intransitive verbs of being and nouns. For the pure feminine, subject and object are one, thinking and feeling are identical, Erich Neumann calls the feminine "heart-ego" in contrast to "head-ego."[21] Bachofen defines the feminine as that which sees "nature as expression and source of law."[22] Cyclical like nature, the feminine does not tend to stasis and balance.

Yeats, understanding this conflict, saw the principles functioning historically as do the figures of William Blake's "The Mental Traveler." The poem fascinated Yeats, who said that although it had never been explained, readers of *A Vision* could understand it at once (V189n). For Yeats, Blake was depicting alternating dispensations of time and culture; the *primary* dispensation governed by the feminine, the *antithetical* by masculine. He set out each dispensation with the associations and manifestations that each principle held for him:

> A *primary* dispensation looking beyond itself towards a transcendent power is dogmatic, levelling, unifying, feminine, humane, peace its means and end; an *antithetical* dispensation obeys imminent power, is expressive, hierarchical, multiple, masculine, harsh, surgical. (V263)

A patriarchal culture would by Yeats's definition be *antithetical*. The masculine principle that thinks in boundaries and balances creates a hierarchy of right and restraints including those of sexual roles: the man representing the masculine is expected to be active, objective, intellectually oriented; the woman representing the feminine to be passive, subjective, emotionally oriented. Therefore, to become the Lady of courtly love, the enthroned feminine of the patriarchy, the woman must submit to *antithetical* surgery. She must cut away that in her nature which threatens the masculine. She must become immobile, limited to her pedestal and balanced there.

The desired passivity or immobility of the female is evident in both tales and cultural practices where the confining or cutting-away has typically attached itself to the feet of the female image. Cinderella proves her identity as the Prince's proper consort by having the foot that fits the Prince's slipper. Her stepsisters hack off toes and heels in their anguish to fit in. Male ideas of the enhancement of feminine appeal have traditionally resulted in the deforming of the foot, whether by the binding practiced in China, or the spike heels of Hollywood's glamour queens, or the rigid pink-satin-covered box into which the ballerina must wedge her toes to be balanced on pointe by her male partner. Neumann interprets the emphasis placed upon the buttocks in primitive figures of the Great Mother as marking her sedentary character, the buttocks forming "the antitheses to the feet, the symbols of free movement on the earth."[23] Bachofen says that swiftness is characteristic of the Apollonian sun hero, masculine rival of the moon goddesses:

> Herein lies the root of the often recurring mythological fiction of the Amazonian virgin who races with the hero and is carried off as the prize of his victory.[24]

Where the virgin wins the race, the end of the defeated suitor is decapitation, a symbol of castration, as in the tale of Atalanta. Her story is found in William Morris's *The Earthly Paradise*, which Yeats had read in childhood and again at seventeen. Restrained or "quieted" feet are a striking motif in Yeats's early poetry about women. Throughout "The Rose" and *The Wind Among the Reeds*, he is concerned with the "wandering," "passing," "flashing" feet of the female images. He wants them to be still like those of the pacified queen of "The Cap and Bells" (CP62), who has "the quiet of love in her feet" after her jester has, in one of Yeats's memorable puns, de-capitated himself for her. Even Cathleen ni Houlihan, an image descended from Ireland's legendary Amazonian queens, has "quiet feet" that the men of Ireland adore with kisses (CP79). Yeats extends the same idea in "A Prayer for My Daughter" that she might spend her life like a tree, "Rooted in one dear perpetual place" (CP186)

The masculine drive to bring the feminine principle within boundary and balance becomes a psychological and sociological barter system, of

Alchemical tree

From MS. L. IV, 1, fol. 263, Universitätsbibliothek, Basel.
Plate 110 in Neumann, *The Great Mother* (Princeton: Princeton
University Press). Used by permission.

which the idea of courtly love is one historical expression. As a barter system courtly love requires sacrifice on both sides. In order to bring the feminine under control, to quiet her wandering feet, the masculine must put his real power into her command. He pledges to protect her upon her pedestal and in that pledge gives her symbolic power over him. The symbol of real masculine power is only secondarily the phallic weaponry of sword, spear, and gun with which the patriarchal knight "defends the womanhood" within his boundaries. Behind this dedication of weapons lies the primary symbol of the male genitalia and the bloody rites of the Virgin-Witch goddesses in which frenzied worshippers castrated themselves and flung their organs at the feet of the goddess's image.

Whether through his fardel of ancient stories or through his own unconscious or through both, Yeats found his dark myth. The course of his work follows the course of the reciprocal sacrifice in the barter system between the masculine and the feminine. That course begins in the predominant wildness of the feminine and the material against which the masculine power rises by its superior physical strength until a point of mutual accommodation must be reached. Beyond this point the masculine and the spiritual dominate the feminine and the material. This far J. J. Bachofen described the course of the social contract. He saw matriarchy, or "enthroned motherhood," as the first period of civilization, an era of chastity, restraint, and ceremony followed by patriarchy and preceded by unregulated hetaerism.[25] Hetaerism was presided over by Aphrodite and symbolized by swamp vegetation. Matriarchy, representing "an emancipation from the bonds of crudely sensual animal life,"[26] was ruled by Demeter and symbolized by agriculture. Bachofen compares the era of matriarchy, in which woman "counters man's abuse of his superior strength by the dignity of her enthroned motherhood," to the days of courtly love, especially to the Teutonic *Frauendienst*:

> The matriarchal period is indeed the poetry of history by virtue of the sublimity, the heroic grandeur, even the beauty to which woman rose by inspiring bravery and chivalry in men, by virtue of the meaning she imparted to feminine love and the chastity and restraint that she exacted of young men. To the ancients all this appeared in very much the same light as the chivalric nobility of the Germanic world to our own eyes. Like us, the ancients asked: What has become of those woman whose unblemished beauty, whose chastity and high-mindedness could awaken love even in the immortals? What has become of the heroines whose praises were sung by Hesiod, poet of the matriarchy?[27]

In this same vein comes Yeats's question about the effect of the decadent attitude of the nineties on the enthronement of woman and the middle-class intellectual life that was ordered about it: "How can life be ritual if woman had not her symbolical place?" (A302)

Following matriarchy in Bachofen's outline come two phases of patriarchy, the Dionysian and the Apollonian. The goddess who rises between these phases is Athena, the primal Virgin of the intellect. Her birth completes the process of "purification," to use Bachofen's term, in that it completes the circumvention of the female in the reproduction of the gods. That circumvention had begun with Dionysus, who was conceived in the womb of his mother Semele but removed from her dead body as a six-month fetus and enclosed in the thigh of Zeus to complete gestation. Athena's birth, involving no mother at all, is totally "immaculate conception" by the masculine. Athena brings the patriarchy to its full spiritual realization under Apollo, but her first act is to impose bridle and bit upon the wild horse Sythius. Robertson points out the medieval use of the horse as symbol of sexual passion in the male.[28] Lancelot, for example, climbs on the wagon of the criminal lust after he has lost control of his horse.

Yeats's work follows Bachofen's pattern, beginning in the view of woman first as Enchantress, then as Lady of inspiration. He even made a conscious shift from the Dionysian to the Apollonian when he began to read Nietzsche in 1902, the same year that he rejected the "old high way of love" in "Adam's Curse":

> I think I have to some extent got weary of that wild God Dionysus, and I am hoping that the Far-Darter will come in his place. (L403)

In his cultural quest, Yeats agrees with Bachofen that the enthroned woman is the organizing point of society, particularly of the aristocratic society that Yeats thought produced the best of "passion and precision." But Yeats projected beyond Bachofen. He saw the dominance of the feminine returning in destruction of the aristocratic order. He feared that the purification of the spiritual from the material that Bachofen praises would go so far that the two elements would lose communication with each other and all order would be lost, as he imagines in "The Second Coming":

> Turning and turning in the widening gyre
> The falcon cannot hear the falconer;
> Things fall apart; the centre cannot hold. (CP184)

Anarchy would result in a new birth of the *primary* dispensation that would slouch like a rough beast towards Bethlehem to be born of the unpurified feminine. Yeats's thinking has found, if not an echo, then an antithetical vibration in the thinking of at least one contemporary feminist. In *Beyond God the Father: Toward a Philosophy of Women's Liberation*,[29] Mary Daly advises women that since the ideal of the Virgin-Mother, unachievable in reality, is the only acceptable woman to Christianity, they should return to the matriarchal worship of the Great Mother. Daly defines the Second Coming as the Second Coming of Women.

As age came upon him and he began to fear the second coming of the feminine power in the material of his own body, Yeats took the side of the masculine against the feminine, the intellectual against the generative. He strove to erect "monuments of unaging intellect" only to realize that such an aim was like trying to escape a foul ditch by way of a ladder that has its only footing in the ditch:

> I must lie down where all the ladders start,
> In the foul rag-and-bone shop of the heart. (CP336)

In his last plays on the subject he depicts the masculine pulling the enthroned feminine image down to desecration with a power that survived decapitation. In *The Herne's Egg* he is able to turn the very weapon of comedy that he feared in the nineties against the enthroned woman as he exposes the delusion of a self-proclaimed Virgin-priestess.

Into this darkness, however, come two hopeful suggestions: one is his creation of a Lady of courtly love who exhibits her own creative intellect; the other is a sympathetic appearance of the Great Mother in the old hag Crazy Jane—a character who, above any other he created, seemed real to Yeats. He spoke of her as if she had independent being, calling her "slut" and wishing to be finished with her. She has the passionate and cyclical nature of the Great Mother. It is she who weeps for the poet in his old age and mourns the passing of his intellectual self-recreation as the Celtic hero Cuchulain (CP335). It is as if a pact had been achieved between the intellectual and the generative in which the Mother actually sympathizes with her son's desire to bypass her and create a world of "monuments of unaging intellect." It is not in her nature to allow him to do so, but still she weeps at his failure.

Yeats thoroughly tested courtly love in both his choices: perfection of the life and perfection of the work. In the first, he found it inapplicable; its end proved "as weary-hearted as that hollow moon," whether the woman be lost or won. But in the second it functioned beautifully, falling smoothly into the metaphorical system he had devised for his poetry and his prophecy. It works so smoothly as metaphor that the disillusion and suggestion of sympathy with which it ends give to his work the paradoxical combination of wholeness and incompleteness—of *anagnorisis* and defeat—that characterizes high tragedy.

—2—

Of all the accoutrements of medieval love poetry—knight, lady, and court of love, witch and troubadour—the two that Yeats employs most consistently are the mirror and the enclosed garden. These are understandable choices for him because of their Theosophic and Kabbalistic associations in addition to their mythological and archetypal suggestions. Yeats could find the mirror in both Plotinus and Jacob Boehme as well as in *The Romance of the Rose*, a tale of courtly love to which Rosicrucian commentators give an alchemical interpretation. A. E. Waite, with whom Yeats was associated in the Hermetic Order of the Golden Dawn, quotes Langlet de Fresnoy as saying that Jean de Meung (d. 1316), who wrote by far the greater portion of the *Romance*, was an Hermeticist and had written two treatises on alchemy. Waite cites the speech of Genius in the *Romance* as professing the alchemical *Magnum Opus*.[30] Yeats reveals his familiarity with the *Romance* in his essay on Edmund Spenser, written in October 1902 (EI368). In revising the poems of *The Wind Among the Reeds* (1899) for inclusion in *Poems* (1907), Yeats deleted the names he had originally given the speakers—Aedh, Mongan, Hanrahan, Michael Robartes—and made one speaker, the Lover, as in the *Romance*.

The Lover of *The Romance of the Rose* begins his adventure by entering a garden and seating himself on the rim of a fountain called the Well of Love. He contemplates images reflected in two crystal stones beneath the surface, and like Narcissus, whose pool it is,[31] he sees what he most desires, his own image glorified, and comes in danger of drowning in his own pride:

> The Mirror Perilous it is, where proud
> Narcissus saw his face and his gray eyes,
> Because of which he soon lay on his bier.
> There is no charm nor remedy for this;
> Whatever thing appears before one's eyes,
> While at these stones he looks, he straightway loves.
> Many a valiant man has perished thence;
> The wisest, worthiest, most experienced
> Here have been trapped and taken unawares.[32]

Archetypally, the fountain whose pools form the mirror is woman, the bright, reflecting stones her adoring eyes. Neumann traces her association with gushing underground waters to the female mysteries in the spontaneous flows of blood and of milk. He summarizes:

> The Great Goddess is the flowing unity of subterranean and celestial primordial water. . . . To her belong all waters, streams, fountains, ponds, and springs, as well as the rain. She is the ocean of life with its life- and death-bringing seasons, and life is her child, a fish eternally swimming inside her . . . like men in the fishpool of Mother Church—a late manifestation of the same archetype.[33]

The reflective powers of these waters when still has gathered through the ages an implication that rankles modern women. Virginia Woolf's comment on the traditional female duty of reflecting the man echoes Bachofen's theory of cultural development through enthroned matriarchy:

Women have served all these centuries as looking-glasses possessing the magic and religious power of reflecting the figure of man at twice its natural size. Without that power probably the earth would still be swamp and jungle.[34]

The poet Mona Van Duyn registers more personal impatience with the looking-glass function and the effect it has had upon men. In her poem "Leda" she responds to Yeats's question in "Leda and the Swan" (CP211):

> "*Did she put on his knowledge with his power*
> *Before the indifferent beak could let her drop?*"
>
> Not even for a moment. He knew, for one thing, what he was.
> When he saw the swan in her eyes he could let her drop.
> In the first look of love men find their great disguise,
> and collecting these rare pictures of himself was his life.[35]

And Olivia Shakespear adds that when the reflector herself is glorified by the man, it only means that his aesthetic sense is gratified.

The mirror of Narcissus appears early in Yeats as mutually reflecting mirrors in the hearts of lovers. The image occurs in a vision seen by Red Hanrahan, one of the male characters with whom Yeats had a strong personal association. Taking stock of his life in "The Tower" (1928), Yeats includes Hanrahan as a symbol of his own intellectual confrontation with desires:

> And I myself created Hanrahan
> And drove him drunk or sober through the dawn. . . .
> He stumbled, tumbled, fumbled to and fro
> And had but broken knees for hire
> And horrible splendour of desire;
> I thought it all out twenty years ago. (CP194)

The time in the last line refers to a revision of Yeats's "Stories of Red Hanrahan" made in 1907. The original stories that appeared in *The Secret Rose* of 1897 came from the period of Yeats's Celtic and Hermetic studies into which Maud Gonne was so interwoven in his imagination. Like Hanrahan, who abandons a woman of flesh and blood to follow the vision of a queen of the Sidhe, Yeats was pursuing a Celtic goddess in Maud.

Hanrahan's vision is of a procession of lovers in three groups, after the medieval tradition by which the noble ones who have succeeded in their quest come first and the ignoble who have in some way distorted the quest come last. Such a triple-ranked procession can be found in the Fifth Dialogue of Andreas's *De Amore*, where a women's march in the train of the God of Love gives precedence to the promiscuous over the frigid:

In the first rank, are those most blessed of women who while they were alive knew how to conduct themselves wisely toward the soldiers of love, to show every favor to whose who wished to love, and to give appropriate answers to those who under pretense of love sought love falsely; . . . Those women who follow in the second group and are so pestered by the services of so many men are those shameless women who while they lived did not fear to subject themselves to the pleasure of every man. . . . Those women who follow in the last group, so meanly equipped, going along with downcast faces, without help from anybody and wearied by discomforts of all kinds . . . are those most wretched of all women who while they lived closed the palace of Love to all who wished to enter it.[36]

Each of the groups in Hanrahan's vision represents a facet of courtly love as Yeats had in those years imagined and experienced it. He places the lovers with mirrors in their hearts in the second, somewhat lukewarm group:

They came nearer and nearer, and Hanrahan saw that they also were lovers, and that they had heart-shaped mirrors instead of hearts, and looked in each other's mirrors incessantly pondering upon their own faces. (SR180)

This mutually reflecting love that is totally consumed in itself was lower in Yeats's estimation than the love of those noble lovers in the first group who search together for beauty beyond themselves:

Those that passed the first . . . are the famous lovers of old time . . . and because they sought in one another no blossom of mere youth, but a beauty coeval with the night and with the stars, the night and the stars hold them for ever from the unpeaceful and the perishing, despite the battle and the bitterness their love wrought in the world. (182)

But mutually reflecting love was higher in his estimation than the selfish love that "desired neither to triumph nor to love, but only to be loved." The women who flew from their lovers in this third procession had "beautiful heads full of an exquisite life upon shadowy and bloodless bodies" (180), probably Yeats's most vivid image of his misery and an unconscious recognition of the truth of Maud, with her self-imposed "blinkers," that his mind was not yet ready to admit. That none of the three groups is happy supports Yeats's declaration that acceptance of life as tragic is basic to the romantic attitude.

As his personal quest on the old high way of love failed, Yeats abandoned the Narcissistic mirror. In *Hodos Chameliontos* he relegates it to his early elementary efforts with "all those things that 'popular poets' write off" in "a rhythm that still echoed Morris" (A254). He quotes in illustration from "To the Rose upon the Rood of Time":

Come near, come near, come near—Ah, leave me still
A little space for the Rose-breath to fill,

> Lest I no more hear common things . . .
> But seek alone to hear the strange things said
> By God to the bright hearts of those long dead. (CP31)

He then adds, "I do not remember what I meant by 'the bright hearts,' but a little later I wrote of Spirits 'with mirrors in their hearts'." Already the intellectual gates were beginning to open and he would leave these matters to "become difficult or obscure." He turned back to join the first group in Hanrahan's vision; Maud, insofar as Yeats was concerned, wandered off with the third.

In later works he advised beautiful women that they might

> Live in uncomposite blessedness,
> And lead us to the like—if they
> Will banish every thought, unless
> The lineaments that please their view
> When the long looking-glass is full,
> Even from the foot-sole think it too. (CP174)

He had in mind here their own Unity of Being as well as their partnership with and participation in the masculine principle. A parallel to this admonition of the looking-glass in masculine terms can be found in his perception of intellectual beauty in the flick of the Connemara fisherman's wrist, the fisherman himself becoming an inspiration for poetry in the manner of the love goddess:

> . . . Before I am old
> I shall have written him one
> Poem maybe as cold
> And passionate as the dawn. (CP146)

When Yeats abandoned the second group of Hanrahan's procession with the mirrors in their hearts, it was to pursue the philosophic mirror with the first group. This is the mirror of the Ideal related to courtly love by those who consider it "Platonic." It cannot lead to happiness because it cannot reflect satisfaction with anything in "the unpeaceful and the perishing" creation. Its reflection is instead the burning desire that De Rougement calls Eros in his explanation of courtly love and that he says can be satisfied only by death. This mirror, which Yeats found in Jacob Boehme and Plotinus, is based upon the masculine principle, the creativity of the intellect. Following Plotinus, whom he had read in Stephen MacKenna's translation, Yeats chose Phidias as his symbol of intellectual creativity, placing him above Pythagoras, who turned his intellect to the abstract and ignored the body:

No! Greater than Pythagoras, for the men
That with a mallet or a chisel modelled these
Calculations that look but casual flesh, put down
All Asiatic vague immensities,
And not the banks of oars that swam upon
The many-headed foam at Salamis.
Europe put off that foam when Phidias
Gave women dreams and dreams their looking-glass. (CP322)

Of Phidias, Plotinus had said that he was no mere copier of Nature, as Plato had held of artists, but went "back to the Ideas from which Nature itself derives." The form of his art was "in the designer" before it appeared in the material.[37] In the Theosophy[38] that Yeats studied, however, Plato's very Ideas are themselves reflections in a mirror.

Jacob Boehme explains that the Ground of Nature or the real world begins in the Unground of nothingness where the desire of the inessential will is directed toward the potential fiery essences:

> 7. Seeing that the first will is an ungroundedness, to be regarded as an eternal nothing, we recognize it to be like a mirror, wherein one sees his own image; like a life and yet it is no life, but a figure of life and of the image belonging to life.

> 8. Thus we recognize the eternal Unground out of Nature to be like a mirror. For it is like an eye which sees, and yet conducts nothing in the seeing wherewith it sees.[39]

From the function of the mirror of the Unground, Boehme projects the Theosophic masculine Trinity:

> 15. . . . For the eternal will, which comprehends the eye or the mirror, wherein lies the eternal seeing as its wisdom, is Father. And that which is eternally grasped is wisdom, the grasp . . . passing out of the ungroundedness into a ground, is Son or Heart; for it is the Word of life, or its essentiality, in which the will shines forth with lustre.

> 16. And the going within itself to the centre of the ground is Spirit; for it is the finder, who from eternity continually finds where there is nothing.[40]

The manifestation of the wisdom that the Father utters Boehme calls the Virgin so that the adoration of the feminine as wisdom recapitulates the Narcissistic adoration and becomes a path to the knowledge of God rather than the barren treadmill of self-adoration.

Theosophy also provides an explanation for the third mirror in Yeats's work, the objective masculine consciousness of the Girl in "The Hero, the Girl, and the Fool" (CP216), which tells her that she is no more the incarnation of Beauty than her Hero is of Strength. This mirror of the objective mind Boehme calls External Reason or the "sun-mirror." Functional enough in the real world, it is man's "only by way of loan" and cannot serve his soul's eternal needs:

> 14. External Reason thinks, if the outward eye sees, that is good; there is no other seeing possible. Bad enough forsooth! When the poor soul borrows the external mirror, and must make shift with this alone, where is its seeing? When the external mirror breaks, wherewith will it see then? With the terrible fire-flash in the horror, in the darkness; it can see nowhere else.[41]

In summary, Yeats's message of the mirrors says that the mirror of External Reason should function objectively for truth in terms of the real world, the personal quest. If, however, the External Reason tries to function subjectively, it produces an extravagant romanticism, a Narcissistic mirror, self-deceiving and barren. On the other hand, the soul or imagination must see with its own mirror. If it denies all but External Reason, then in Theosophic terms "it imaginates after earthliness or after the dark world's property."[42] The soul's other choice is to "imaginate" after God's Spirit, which is manifest to the soul in the virgin Wisdom.

But there is a threat in the Theosophical Virgin as well as in the archetypal one. The soul that follows the Virgin toward God's Spirit will be purged in a Theosophical equivalent of the Christian Dark Night of the Soul:

> But if [the soul] desire to plunge into the nothing, into freedom, it must abandon itself to fire; and then it sinks down in the death of the first principle [creation], and buds forth out of the anguish of fire in the light. For when it abandons itself, the eternal will to Nature (which is God the Father) leads it out through fire into himself. . . . Its fire is now become a light and a clear mirror, for it has yielded itself up to Freedom, viz. to God.[43]

—3—

As Yeats discards the mirror of Narcissus for the mirror of the Idea, so too he moves between the gardens of the ruined and the restored Eden. The gardens of courtly love range from the lustful, as in the Garden of Mirth presided over by Idlenesse in *The Romance of the Rose*, to the metaphysical, as in the poetry of Marvell and Donne. Stanley Stewart has shown that the seventeenth-century gardens rest upon the enclosed garden of Solomon and Sheba in *The Song of Songs*. Its theme, "*Hortus conclusus soror mea, sponsa, hortus conclusus, fons signatus*" (4:12), became a canticle for the Vigil of the Assumption of the Blessed Virgin. The enclosed garden and the sealed fountain which the true lover alone can enter symbolize the Virgin-Bride who will become the Virgin-Mother, that combined aspect of the whole archetype which the patriarchal religion has segregated from the Witch. The enclosed area is the elementary round of Neumann's paradigm, the womb and the grave. Bachofen associates the first enclosed fields and walled villages with the rise of agriculture and matriarchy. The garden contains the companion symbols of the female: the fountain, the tree, and the house. The frontispiece of Henry Hawkins's *Partheneia Sacra* (Rouen 1632),[45] with which Stewart illustrates his work, brings the four symbols together in a single unit. The design is Yeatsian in that the garden wall encloses not one but two trees and not the feminine house alone but the phallic tower as well. Mary is "the mystick Rose" of the garden, and Stewart shows how Mary is the garden, tree, and Temple of Solomon. The Christian emblem is paralleled in Neumann's depiction of the Great Mother as Lady of the Plants and of the Beasts, "who governs the animal world and dominates instincts and drives, who gathers the beasts beneath her spirit wings as beneath the branches of a tree."[46]

Yeats referred to the two trees in warning Maud against the destructive passions of the intellect. Biblically, the two trees are the healing Tree of Life and the fatal Tree of Knowledge of Good and Evil, but for Yeats they are more the trees of the Kabbalah, the Tree of Life, whose ascent leads to the knowledge and presence of God, and its demonic, inverted reflection. The first tree, the poet tells his beloved, she has within herself. He urges her to make the feminine inward movement toward it:

> Beloved, gaze in thine own heart,
> The holy tree is growing there; . . .
> The shaking of its leafy head
> Has given the waves their melody,
> And made my lips and music wed,
> Murmuring a wizard song for thee. (CP47–48)

Gazing upon this tree, her eyes "grow full of tender care," but the second tree is a dim mirror reflecting the weariness of the passion-ravaged intellect. Her eyes, mirrors themselves, reflect this mirror:

> There, through the broken branches, go
> The ravens of unresting thought;
> Flying, crying, to and fro,
> Cruel claw and hungry throat,
> Or else they stand and sniff the wind,
> And shake their ragged wings; alas!
> Thy tender eyes grow all unkind:
> Gaze no more in the bitter glass.

"Adam's Curse," Yeats's last statement on his love for Maud before her marriage, implies the fallen garden of Eden. There all beauty, whether of man's art or woman's face, must be wrested from the course of the ruined

Enclosed garden

Henry Hawkins, *Partheneia Sacra* (Rouen, 1632), frontispiece.
Used by permission of the Henry E. Huntington Library and Art
Gallery.

Maud Gonne

Portrait by Sarah Purser
Municipal Gallery of Modern Art, Dublin

and aging creation as Adam is shown in medieval iconography wresting his food from a wasteland:

> . . . It's certain there is no fine thing
> Since Adam's fall but needs much labouring. (CP78)

The poet says,

> . . . A line will take us hours maybe;
> Yet if it does not seem a moment's thought,
> Our stitching and unstitching has been naught;

the beautiful woman, based on Maud's sister Kathleen, agrees,

> To be born woman is to know— . . .
> That we must labour to be beautiful.

After these two kinds of laborious art have been noted with implied approval, the poet delivers his indictment against the third, the art of courtly love:

> There have been lovers who thought love should be
> So much compounded of high courtesy
> That they would sigh and quote with learned looks
> Precedents out of beautiful old books;
> Yet now it seems an idle trade enough.

Love as art alone has failed because it has distorted External Reason subjectively; it has channeled passion into the intellect and denied the body. As a result the lovers have grown "weary-hearted" with the same weariness of misdirected and fruitless passion that is reflected by the second of the two trees.

In a reversal of garden imagery to match the reversal of his personal fortunes, Yeats takes up the Mask of Solomon to celebrate his marriage and enters the rich enclosed garden with his Sheba. The image proved truer in reality for him than it did for Clarence Mangan, of whom Yeats wrote in consistent metaphoric terms in *Irish Fireside* (March 12, 1887):

> A short dream this love affair of Mangan's. Before long between him and his Eden was the flaming cherub and the closed gate.[47]

Yeats's last garden, however, is also in ruins. Unlike the garden of "Adam's Curse," it is not ruined because of abused intellect but simply because it is the garden of the primary world whose nature it is to age and decay. The prophetic old woman Crazy Jane stands under a "blasted oak" that represents her more than it shelters her. She is a female figure not traceable from Yeats's virgins like the Rose and the Countess Cathleen or from the Virgin-Bride Sheba. The early figure of Yeats's that seems to anticipate her is the dying prostitute of "The Adoration of the Magi" (1904). Yeats called the story "half prophecy of a very veiled kind" (L280). It tells how three aged mystics seek to recapitulate the journey of the Biblical Magi to find and adore the Virgin and Her Child. When they find instead a dying prostitute in a shabby room in Paris, they think that they have been deluded by devils; nonetheless, they kneel and adore "one that has been beautiful" (My331). Like the prostitute, Crazy Jane makes no claim to virginal purity or holy wedlock; she has lived the completely female, completely primary life. But she is Virgin in the ancient definition of the independent woman who has lived outside marriage, choosing her sexual partners at will. By her very nature as the independent woman she can never become the woman won and so satiate the poet. She is instead forever his woman lost because she will not be fitted into his myth of courtly love: the enclosed garden and sealed fountain are unknown in nature; they are masculine intellectual constructions which her primary being will not admit.

2

The Personal Quest

My devotion might as well have been offered to an image in a
milliner's window, or to a statue in a museum, but romantic doctrine
had reached its extreme development. (A399)

—1—

When Maud Gonne stepped from her rented hansom before the door of the
Yeats home in Bedford Park, London, she entered the poet's life with "a
sound as of a Burmese gong," the signal of the entrance of an important
figure in a play or of the beginning of a ceremony. She was indeed stepping
into a role already prepared in his imagination:

> I had never thought to see in a living woman so great beauty. It belonged to famous
> pictures, to poetry, to some legendary past. A complexion like the blossom of apples, and
> yet face and body had the beauty of lineaments which Blake calls the highest beauty
> because it changes least from youth to age, and a stature so great that she seemed of a
> divine race. (M40)

Maud arrived in a well-bred Victorian manner with a letter of introduction
to the poet's father John Butler Yeats from John O'Leary, the Fenian leader,
whom Yeats and his son had known in Dublin since 1885. But the poet's
sister Elizabeth (Lolly) saw deeper. It is her diary entry for January 30, 1889,
that sets the date of Maud's arrival:

> Miss Gonne, the Dublin beauty (who is marching on to glory over the hearts of the
> Dublin youths), called to-day on Willie, of course, but also apparently on Papa.[1]

Lolly's cool feminine eye saw that Maud was "immensely tall," and Yeats's
other sister Susan Mary (Lily) noticed that she wore only slippers. Lolly
continues that Maud was "very stylish and well dressed in a careless way"
and that she had "a rich complexion and hazel eyes." She called her
"decidedly handsome" although she could not see Maud's face well because
Maud did not look at her. Lolly Yeats, the younger and homelier of two

daughters in an artist's family that was growing poorer day by day, was impressed enough to record also that Maud had come "in a hansom all the way from Belgravia and kept the hansom waiting while she was here."

Lolly's parenthetical remark may indicate that she feared Maud had come to add her brother's heart to the stepping stones of her fame, for Maud was at the height of her glamour. She lived in a constant shuttle between Dublin and Paris, traveling surrounded by her own piles of cushions and, as Yeats said, "cages of innumerable singing birds."[2] She was stopping for nine days in London on this particular passage.

Yeats admits that "In after years I persuaded myself that I felt premonitory excitement at the first reading of her name"(M40)—in letters that John O'Leary and his sister Ellen had written before Maud's appearance. This admission provides a key to the reading of his *Autobiographies* and *Memoirs*. Denis Donoghue, editor of the *Memoirs*, says of Yeats's method that he

> moves from one person to another, handing each a script, his part in the play. He does not merely enumerate the events of a plot: behind the several scripts, he composes a generation, many lives engaged in a play of history. (M10)

Maud indeed enters like a character in a play whose function is to incite the protagonist to action. Even her descent from the two-wheeled hansom has been foreshadowed and will receive a final echo. In his autobiography Yeats tells how the first girl to excite his imagination, his cousin Laura Armstrong, came upon him when he was eighteen on one of the Howth hills, driving a pony-cart with her red hair blowing loose in the wind, and invited him to get in for a ride. In Crazy Jane's vision of the departure of Cuchulain, the hero rides away with his wife Emer in a two-wheeled carriage. The incitement to action in the episode of Maud derives from her failure to invite him, figuratively, to ride off in the hansom that she kept waiting.

According to Donoghue, Yeats arrived at his plays of history by allowing reverie—"memory under the sweet sway of intuition"(M11)—to dominate logic in their composition. If true, then both the *Autobiographies* and the *Memoirs* are, like his poems and plays, works of art in which the poet's unconscious, where the masculine and feminine principles meet, has its play in the selecting and the ordering of details. In the first part of *Autobiographies*, written in 1914 and called *Reverie over Childhood and Youth*, Yeats presents his parents at the sexual poles of his imagination from the beginning of its development. They become representatives of the intellectually creative masculine principle and the introverted, nature-bound feminine principle.

John Butler Yeats, by far the more consciously influential parent, introduced the enclosed garden and the castle early into his son's imagination. He chose William Morris's "Golden Wings" to read to the child because the poem recalled to him the turrets, gardens, and ponds of Sandymount Castle near Dublin, where he had read law as a young man and in whose shadow his son W. B. was born on June 13, 1865. In the essay Yeats wrote on Morris in 1902, he said that those verses ran in his head for years and became to him "the best description of happiness in the world":

> Midways of a walled garden
> In the happy poplar land
> Did an ancient castle stand,
> With an old knight for a warden. (EI59–60)

John Butler Yeats let his young son know that the castle represented an order of life to be cherished. Sandymount Castle was owned by the Corbet family, to whom the elder Yeats was related through his mother. He never wanted to live in Dublin after the bankruptcy of the Corbets and the sale of the Castle to become a school.

Over the years the father also inculcated in the son the two basic precepts of courtly love: that what a man derives intuitively from a woman's image is of more value to him than what he can glean from her intellect and that love of that image brings out in the lover his highest spiritual qualities. In his Journal of 1909, the year he attempted to reinstate his spiritual marriage with Maud, Yeats records his father's remark on intellect and image in woman: "A man does not love a woman because he thinks her clever or because he admires her, but because he likes the way she has of scratching her head" (M144). In the highly formative four years between 1887 and 1891, his father had said, "There is not more desire . . . in lust than in true love, but in true love desire awakens pity, hope, affection, admiration and, given appropriate circumstance, every emotion possible to man" (A190).

While his father valued an aristocratic social order and pointed out to him its symbols in castle and enclosed garden, Yeats's mother and her family represented the people of the land of Ireland, earthy and mysterious. John Butler Yeats described his wife's family, the Pollexfens of Sligo, as "full of the materials of poetic thought and feeling" in comparison with the Yeatses, who had "knowledge of the art of life and enjoyment."[3] It was a maternal uncle, George Pollexfen, who accompanied Yeats through his occult studies, working horoscopes and making magical and psychical experiments with him. Yeats's maternal background also included the Middletons, who "let their houses decay and the glass fall from the windows of their greenhouses, but one among them at any rate had the second sight"(A17). Yeats was with Middleton cousins at Ballisodare when at the age of eighteen he witnessed the mysterious events that set him off on serious pursuit of Celtic fairy lore

(A76—78). When Yeats was eight years old, his younger brother Robert died at the Pollexfen home in Sligo. He remembered how his mother had heard the death banshee wail the night before.

Yeats's mother, whose actions he describes as "unreasoning and habitual like the seasons" (A167), was always withdrawn from the activities of her husband and children. Equating emotional reserve with good breeding, she taught her young son to feel disgust for the English, who openly kissed at railway stations (A34). Yeats recalls her image as he saw her in his adolescence:

> I almost always see her talking over a cup of tea in the kitchen with our servant, the fisherman's wife. . . . She read no books, but she and the fisherman's wife would tell each other stories that Homer might have told, pleased with any moment of sudden intensity and laughing together over any point of satire. . . . My father was always praising her to my sisters and to me, because she pretended to nothing she did not feel. She would write him letters, telling of her delight in the tumbling clouds, but she did not care for pictures, and never went to his studio to see the day's work, neither now nor when they were first married. (A61–62)

When Yeats visited San Francisco in 1904, he was surprised to meet there an old man who told him that his mother had been the most beautiful girl in Sligo (A19). In the fall of 1887, Mrs. Yeats suffered a paralytic stroke that affected her mind. She lived on, staying in her room until her death in 1900, the responsibility of her daughters. Yeats last remembers her freed from financial worries, happily feeding the birds at the window of her bedroom.

When Yeats was eight, his father read *The Lays of Ancient Rome* to him and continued through his adolescence with readings or retellings of tales from Shakespeare, Chaucer, and Balzac. He gave his son copies of the *Mabinogian* and of Sir Walter Scott's works, *The Lay of the Last Minstrel* and *Ivanhoe*, in which the boy was especially taken by the tale of Gurth, the bold swineherd, who receives a purse of gold from a beautiful veiled lady and then defends it from robbers with his wits. In fairy and folk tales, Willie yearned for beauty and romance. He preferred Hans Christian Anderson to the Grimms "because he was less homely, but even he never gave me the knights and dragons and beautiful ladies that I longed for" (A47). Between the ages of fifteen and seventeen his father gave him Rossetti and Blake. Yeats recalls that at this time he was "charmed" by the third volume of Morris's *The Earthly Paradise* but liked *The Defence of Guenevere* somewhat less. Also at this time Yeats was greatly under the influence of Shelley and Byron, having taken their questing heroes for experimental roles in his youthful search for identity. At this time the Yeats family was living at Howth, an area of cliffs and sea above Dublin, where Yeats wandered by day and night, first collecting insect specimens and then abandoning science for romance:

I still carried my green net but began to play at being a sage, a magician or a poet. . . . When I thought of women they were modelled on those in my favourite poets and loved in brief tragedy, or like the girl in *The Revolt of Islam,* accompanied their lovers through all manner of wild places, lawless women without homes and without children. (A64)

This period saw his sexual coming of age in an incident of almost Edenic innocence and guilt. The guilt was so lasting that in middle age he must justify his narrative "that some young man of talent might not think as I did that my shame was mine alone":

It began when I was fifteen years old. I had been bathing, and lay down in the sun on the sand on the Third Rosses and covered my body with sand. Presently the weight of the sand began to affect the organ of sex, though at first I did not know what the strange, growing sensation was. It was only at the orgasm that I knew, remembering some boy's description or the description in my grandfather's encyclopedia. It was many days before I discovered how to renew that wonderful sensation. From that on it was a continuous struggle against an experience that almost invariably left me with exhausted nerves. Normal sexual intercourse does not affect me more than other men, but that, though never frequent, was plain ruin. (M71–72)

Yeats's account of his sexual awakening in *Reveries,* written for publication, contrasts with the passage in *Memoirs,* intended for his eyes alone.[4] Comparison of the passages will give a view of the poet's mind that explains his choice of "the old high way of love." His private account begins with a justification and proceeds in straightforward terms. His public account replaces the justification with a depersonalized and poetic eulogy of the coming of age that leads away from the physical to the intellectual:

The great event of a boy's life is the awakening of sex. He will bathe many times a day, or get up at dawn and having stripped leap to and fro over a stick laid upon two chairs and hardly know, and never admit, that he had begun to take pleasure in his own nakedness, nor will he understand the change until some dream discovers it. He may never understand at all the greater change in his mind. (A62)

Yeats illustrates here the nineteenth-century middle-class turn of mind that balked at sex unless it could be elevated and turned away from the body. This was the turn of mind that created and delighted in courtly love, wherein the physical became spiritually transforming. On this elevated level he is able to meet the female, a meeting that, prohibited physically, leads to his debilitating masturbation as described in the *Memoirs.* But in *Reveries* he shows how he can participate in the female awakening by envisioning it as expressed in the unconscious, the mystical:

Somnambulistic country girls, when it is upon them, throw plates about or pull them with long hairs in simulation of the poltergeist, or become mediums for some genuine spirit-mischief, surrendering to their desire of the marvellous. (62)

On this level he, too, experiences a "feminine" introversion:

> .... As I look backward, I seem to discover that my passions, my loves and my despairs, instead of being my enemies, a disturbance and an attack, became so beautiful that I had to be constantly alone to give them my whole attention. I notice now, for the first time, what I saw when alone is more vivid in my memory than what I did or saw in company. (62–63)

This intellectual, imaginative emphasis and this introversion provide the foundation of his choice of the old high way of love for public utterance and of his long patience with "spiritual marriage" in his private life. The introversion would grow into the appreciation of feminine awareness shown in his female personae, and later in his life it would become the female consciousness that he confessed to Dorothy Wellesley:

> My dear, my dear—when you crossed the room with that boyish movement, it was no man who looked at you, it was the woman in me. It seems that I can make a woman express herself as never before. I have looked out of her eyes. I have shared her desire. (L868)

The intellectual and imaginative emphasis caused the division of women for Yeats into those he liked and those he loved. The division was a conscious one and lasting, for Lady Gregory remembered his saying to her,

> We never love the woman we like, or like the woman we love, for she whom we like gives us peace, and she whom we love gives us unrest.[5]

Associating friendship with peace and love with unrest gave each of these terms a special meaning in Yeats's application of them. Friendship was an intellectual relationship to him, and love an imaginative one. The prime qualification for friendship was that the woman be noncompetitively intelligent, and the prime qualifications for love that she be beautiful and have the gift of drama, for love with Yeats was a ritual, a continual role-playing in which masks were donned and changed on either side. The women Yeats liked were women won, but the women he loved were women lost so that the imagination would remain stimulated. In Yeats's interpretive complexity, however, the same woman could be both liked and loved, won and lost. Florence Farr and Olivia Shakespear fall into this double category for different reasons. The first had too strong a dramatic sense of her own to respond to his rituals; the second made love too natural, too like friendship. Both remained friends of the poet for life.

Of his relations with women in his early twenties, Yeats speaks of calling on various women friends about tea time both for the meal, since he was very poor at the time, and for the conversation. He felt safe in discussing with these women thoughts that he felt he could not "bring to a man without meeting some competing thought', " but apart from these exchanges he was "timid and abashed" around women. (A152–53). He continues with an account filled with his youthful awkwardness and repression:

> I was sitting on a seat in front of the British Museum feeding pigeons when a couple of girls sat near and began enticing my pigeons away, laughing and whispering to one another, and I looked straight in front of me, very indignant, and presently went into the Museum without turning my head towards them. (A153)

However Yeats may have grown more at ease with women through the years, his attitude did not change toward the mental nature he sought in them. In middle age and marriage he wrote,

> May God be praised for woman
> That gives up all her mind,
> A man may find in no man
> A friendship of her kind
> That covers all he has brought
> As with her flesh and bone,
> Nor quarrels with a thought
> Because it is not her own. (CP144)

What he is expecting is that the woman will receive, internalize, and complement the idea that he lays before her. Such intellectual activity agrees with the explanation of "passivity" in women that the Freudian psychologist Helene Deutsch gives—"activity directed inward."[6] Yeats states it, however, in organic metaphor, as if intellectually the woman is still fulfilling her biological role of receiving the man's seed and building a material body upon it. The organic metaphor had not come to him from marriage; he had applied it years earlier to his friend Arthur Symons:

> He could listen as a woman listens, never meeting one's thought as a man does with a rival thought, but taking up what one said and changing [it], giving it as it were flesh and bone. (M87)

An understanding of Yeats's habitual transference of the physical to the intellectual and imaginative gives increased clarity to the lines addressed to his ancestors in reference to his childlessness and to the poetry that he was inspired to write by his love for Maud. The lines were written in middle age as the reality and significance of the physical world were finally manifest to him:

> Pardon, old fathers, . . .
> Pardon that for a barren passion's sake,
> Although I have come close on forty-nine,

I have no child, I have nothing but a book
Nothing but that to prove your blood and mine. (CP99)

Yeats followed organic metaphor by analyzing his own creative process in sexual terms. As the working of the feminine mind is internally complementary and responsive, waiting to receive the intellectual germ from the masculine as if by impregnation, so the masculine mind of the creative man first behaves in a female manner. It receives a germ from the external world and sets about to give it new form:

> An idle man has no thought. A man's work thinks through him; on the other hand, a woman gets her thought [*] through the influence [**] of a man. Man is a woman to his work, and it begets his thoughts. (M232)

---

*"which may yet be original" deleted.
**"will" deleted.

Yeats passionately desired the union of male and female minds, for from that union came both visions and verse. He sought psychic complementation from Maud Gonne, Olivia Shakespear, and his wife in addition to numerous female mediums and fellow occultists. As a poet he seemed especially happy to have a woman poet simultaneously working on the same subject that he was pursuing. To Katharine Tynan, with whom he had his first prolonged "intimate exchanges of thought" in correspondence, he suggested both the Irish tale of Countess Kathleen O'Shea and the Biblical story of the Magi as material just as he himself was beginning to work with them (L93,129,152–54). Toward the end of his life, he entered into a similar relation with Dorothy Wellesley, who composed a parallel ballad to his "The Three Bushes."

Yeats's friendship with Katharine Tynan is a pure example of his intimate exchange with a woman he liked. He met her in 1885 and began their correspondence when he moved to London in 1887. She was four years his senior, a devout Catholic who disapproved of seances and spiritualism, and a farm-bred girl. She was, however, feminine as Yeats understood the term, receptive, noncompeting. "I write to you," he told her, "as if writing to myself" (L83). He complimented her work but clearly implied a distinction between the work of a woman poet and that of a man:

> Your best work—and no woman poet of the time has done better—is always where you express your own affectionate nature or your religious feeling, either directly or indirectly in some legend. (L98)

In 1887 she had published more than he, yet Yeats assumes a tutorial tone with her. In one instructional letter he reveals that he expects women do have some reality in their lives apart from their appearance to men and that for him *The Idylls of the King* expressed that reality:

> I have been thinking about the women of the poets. . . . Do you not think there is considerable resemblance between the heroines of all the neo-romantic London poets; namely, Swinburne, Morris, Rossetti and their satellites? For one thing, they are essentially men's heroines, with no separate life of their own; in this different from Browning's. Tennyson's are, I believe, less heroic than any of the others and less passionate and splendid but realised, as far as they go, more completely, much more like actual, everyday people. Witness *Mary Tudor* and the aristocratic young ladies in the *Idylls of the King*. (L46)

If Katharine Tynan was a woman writer who met Yeats's approval, George Eliot was one who did not. In her Yeats saw "a fierceness hardly to be found but in a woman turned argumentative" (EI102). In 1887 he wrote to Frederick Gregg, a friend from high school, listing objections that center on the intrusion of the intellectual upon the intuitive in Eliot, of "head-ego" appearing where he would expect "heart-ego":

> She understands only the conscious nature of man. His intellect, his morals—she knows nothing of the dim unconscious nature, the world of instinct. . . . In *The Spanish Gypsy* there are seven arguments of about fifty pages each. This is the way she describes passion. (L31)

In *Reveries* Yeats recalls how his father settled the problem of George Eliot for him once for all: "She disturbed me and alarmed me, but when I spoke of her to my father, he threw her aside with a phrase, 'Oh, she was an ugly woman who hated handsome men and handsome women', and he began to praise *Wuthering Heights*" (A88).

Behind the intimate exchanges of thought with Katherine Tynan, some personal involvement seems to have been developing, at least on her part. She must have bridled at his enthusiasm over Maud Gonne, for he writes on March 21, 1889:

> Who told you that I am 'taken up with Miss Gonne'? I think she is very good-looking and that is all I think about her. What you say of her fondness for sensation is probably true. I sympathise with her love of the national idea rather than any secondary land movement, but care not much for the kind of Red Indian feathers in which she has trapped out that idea. We had some talk as to the possibility of getting my 'Countess O'Shea' acted by amateurs in Dublin and she felt inclined to help, indeed suggested that attempt herself if I remember rightly. I hardly expect it will ever get outside the world of plans. As for the rest, she had a borrowed interest, reminding me of Laura Armstrong without Laura's wild dash of half-insane genius. (L116–17)

—2—

Laura Armstrong was the object of Yeats's first love affair. He met her in the year after he left high school while his family was still living in the Howth hills where he played at being Athanase or Alastor. She was a distant cousin through the aristocratic Corbet connection. She was his own age, red-haired, and a woman lost from the onset because she was already engaged when Yeats met her. Beautiful and dramatic, she exhibited the restlessness of mind that would later appear in his fictional Margaret Leland of *John Sherman* (begun in 1887 and published in 1891) and that would fascinate and trouble him in Maud Gonne:

> She was a wild creature, a fine mimic and given to bursts of religion. I had known her to weep at a sermon, call herself a sinful woman, and mimic it after. (A76)[7]

Yeats wanted to play at romance in the mode of the Spenserian pastoral. Perhaps it was Laura's gift for mimickry that led her to enter wholeheartedly into it, even to the assumption of pastoral names, as her only surviving letter to him indicates. It is dated August 10, 1884, from her house at 60 Stephen's Green, Dublin:

> My dear Clarin, What can I say to you for having been so rude to you—in not being at home when you called and I had asked you? I am really very sorry about it. I hope you will forgive me. It so happened that I was positively obliged to go out at the hour I had appointed for you to come but it was only to a house quite close here—and I had told our maid to send me over word when you *came*—she did so (but I find since it was just before you *went*!) and I was rising to leave the room—I looked out of the window and to my great disappointment saw my Clarin leaving No. 60. It was too bad—and I am indeed sorry I missed you. I like your poems more than I can say—but I should like to hear you read them. I have not nearly finished them. Could you come some afternoon—and read a little to me—I shall be in all Tuesday afternoon. *I promise*! so can you come? I should have written to you sooner but I have been away from home. Pray excuse my silence. Trusting to see 'the poet'—! and with kind regards.
>
> Believe me
Ever yours
'Vivien' (L117)

The name "Vivien" comes from Yeats's first play, "Time and the Witch Vivien," that he wrote for Laura to act in her drawing room and that might, just possibly, have been inspired by her difficulties with time as revealed in her letter. The name "Clarin" resembles those of the Spenserian shepherds in his first published play, "The Island of Statues" (*Dublin University Review*, 1885). Subtitled "An Arcadian Faery Tale," it leans heavily upon Spenser. The enchantress in it was inspired by Laura, whom Yeats credits with turning his mind to the theatre (L118).

Yeats says that he never spoke of his love to Laura because of her engagement but that he wrote her "some bad poems and had more than one sleepless night through anger with her betrothed" (A76). An unpublished lyric of this period that Allan Wade says was almost certainly written for her is couched in the terms of courtly love, complete with wandering poet:

A double moon or more ago
  I writ you a long letter, lady,
  It went astray or vexed you, maybe,
And I would know now yes or no.

Then dying summer on his throne
  Faded in hushed and quiet singing;
  Now winter's arrow's winging, winging,
And autumn's yellow leaves are flown.

Ah we poor poets in our pride
  Tread the bare song road all our summer,
  To wake on lips of some newcomer
'A poor man lived here once and died.'

How could we trudge on mile by mile
  If from red lips like quicken berry,
  At odd times to make us merry,
Came nowise half of half a smile?

And surely therefore would I know
  What manner fared my letter, lady,
  It went astray or vexed you, maybe,
A double moon or so ago. (L117–18)

Laura figures in at least one of Yeats's published poems, "A Dream of Death." One of his earliest poems on Maud, it was written, Bradford says, in December 1891. Maud, ill with fatigue from her fight against evictions of Irish peasants, had refused to see Yeats in Dublin and fled to France to recuperate. The epitaph that ends the poem compares her to Laura:

I dreamed that one had died in a strange place
Near no accustomed hand;
And they had nailed the boards above her face,
The peasants of that land,
Wondering to lay her in that solitude,
And raised above her mound
A cross they had made out of two bits of wood,
And planted cypress round;
And left her to the indifferent stars above
Until I carved these words:
She was more beautiful than thy first love,
But now lies under boards. (CP42)[8]

Having brought Laura into his letter to assuage Katharine's distress over his being "taken up with Miss Gonne," Yeats next seems to feel that the relation with Laura needs an explanation, and he gives one that is the essence of courtly love and of his own relationship with women:

Do not mistake me, she is only as a myth and a symbol. Will you forgive me for having talked of her? She interests me far more than Miss Gonne does and yet is only as a myth and a symbol. (117–18)

A love affair in a mythic mode with one woman and intimate exchanges of thought with another could run simultaneously for Yeats because he ran them on separate and parallel tracks of the creative and the analytical intellect. His friendship with Katharine Tynan ripens in letters after his meeting with Maud. In October 1889, he asks permission to address her as "Katey." On her part, familiar cards come into play after the introduction of Miss Gonne. Katharine promptly plans a visit to England, seeing other friends but letting Yeats know that she is available for an invitation: "Best news I have heard this long time," he replies on May 9 (L126). She plays hard-to-get with her letters, and by mid-December 1889 he is pleading, "*Write to me Write to me Write to me*" (L142). The following December he sends her his photograph. In early summer 1891, he visits her in Ireland and leaves his razor strop behind. He has some difficulty describing it so that she will recognize it to send after him. In August he visits her again and again leaves his strop. In a letter of July 1891 she mentions the name of H. A. Hinkson to him. Hinkson is the barrister-novelist that she will marry in 1893; but if mentioning his name is a warning to Yeats, he is too involved with his new rush of pity for Maud Gonne to heed it. After that summer their long correspondence begins to fade. By December 1891 it is Yeats who has failed to write.

He had moved well into his second phase with Maud. In his first enchantment he had thought, "What wife could she make, . . . what share could she have in the life of a student?" (M42–43); now he saw himself as her protector: "I no longer thought what kind of wife would this woman make, but of her need for protection and for peace" (M45). He was deeply involved and suffering fits of depression. He confesses this to Katharine as his reason for not writing: "I try to keep my black moods out of my letters by keeping my letters out of my black moods" (L187).

Although she was young and sufficiently unchallenging of Yeats in their discussions of poetry, Katharine Tynan lacked the qualification of beauty. He could make of her neither the symbol of the Witch nor the symbol of the Virgin. He did, however, make an effort under pressure of his high ideal of love and courtly gallantry:

I had gathered from the Romantic poets an ideal of perfect love. Perhaps I should never marry in church, but I would love one woman all my life. I wrote many letters to Katharine Tynan, a very plain woman, and one day I overheard somebody say that she was the kind of woman who might make herself very unhappy about a man. I began to wonder if she was in love with me and if it was my duty to marry her. Sometimes when she was in Ireland, I in London would think it possible that I should, but if she came to stay, or I saw her in Ireland, it became impossible again. (M32)

Unlike Katharine, the actress Florence Farr had the requisite beauty, but she infuriated Yeats by refusing to maintain her role. Although as a fellow member of the Hermetic Order of the Golden Dawn, she complemented his interest in the occult and although she pleased him by speaking his verse to the dulcimer, he characterized their relationship as "an enduring friendship that was an enduring exasperation" (A122).[9] Yeats met her in 1890 when she took the leading part in John Todhunter's poetic pastoral play, *A Sicilian Idyll*. Yeats had encouraged the writing of the deliberately romantic piece and was delighted with Florence's "impassioned delivery" of the verse. In Yeats's eyes she had three great gifts: "a tranquil beauty like that of Demeter's image near the British Museum reading-room door, and an incomparable sense of rhythm and a beautiful voice, the seeming natural expression of the image" (A121). "And yet," he complains,

> There was scarce another gift that she did not value above those three. . . . She would dress without care or calculation as if to hide her beauty and seem contemptuous of its power. If a man fell in love with her she would notice that she had seen just that movement upon the stage or had heard just that intonation and all seemed unreal. If she read out some poem in English or in French all was passion, all a traditional splendor, but she spoke of actual things with a cold wit or under the strain of paradox. . . . I used in my rage to compare her thoughts, when her worst mood was upon her, to a game called Spillikens which I had seen played in my childhood with little pieces of bone that you had to draw out with a hook from a bundle of like pieces. A bundle of bones instead of Demeter's golden sheaf!

Wit and paradox were, in Yeats's view, especially destructive of the power of the beautiful woman. They had no place in the ritual of love because they were an encroachment of intellect into image; they made ritual impossible because the role-player in stepping outside the role in order to comment wittily upon it left it empty and "all seemed unreal." The beautiful woman's role was to stay within the image and give it truth, for he had the unshakeable faith of Morris's Pygmalion that, if the image is right, its reality will naturally follow, just as Florence Farr's beautiful voice followed as the "natural expression of the image."

Wit and paradox, too, express the objective, the comic view of life. Yeats had declared that "we begin to live when we have conceived life as tragedy" (A189). The tragic conception induces a high spiritual serenity, and he sought through the stability of ritual to maintain such a serenity throughout the Decadence of the 1890s. In *The Tragic Generation* he speaks of his friends, particularly the members of the Rhymers' Club, as having been taught by Rossetti and Pater "to walk upon a rope, tightly stretched through serene air," only to find themselves in their day trying to keep their feet "upon a swaying rope in a storm" (A302–03). The storm was stirred by the turn of the popular attitude from the high seriousness of beautiful and lofty things to a spirit of objectivity, of comedy. Yeats saw that the romantic world in which he had spent his boyhood was dying:

> In 1895 or 1896, I was in despair at the new breath of comedy that had begun to wither the beauty that I loved, just when that beauty seemed to have united itself to mystery. (A333)

In denying high seriousness, comedy not only withered beauty but also destroyed the excitement of imaginative desire that was for Yeats at this time and for years to come the entire body of love. Yeats labeled comedy "a kind of frozen passion, the virginity of the intellect" (A332), and said that it marked the man who had exhausted "sin in act" as opposed to the saint, who was responsible for the knowledge but not the act of sin (A332). Among his contemporaries, Yeats thought Aubrey Beardsley most representative of that frozen passion:

> I see in his fat women and shadowy, pathetic girls, his horrible children, half child, half embryo, in all the lascivious monstrous imagery of the privately published designs, the phantasms that from the beginning have defied the scourge and the hair shirt. . . . There is no representation of desire. Even the beautiful women are exaggerated with a thwarted or corrupted innocence. (A331)

Yeats goes so far as to associate the rise of comedy with the progress of Beardsley's own illness:

> As the popular rage increased and his own disease increased, he became more and more violent in his satire, or created out of a spirit of mockery a form of beauty where his powerful logical intellect eliminated every outline that suggested meditation or even satisfied passion. (333)

Yeats confessed that his romantic celibacy of the 1890s made him "exceedingly puritanical" (A334). He was prissy enough to walk about at the opposite end of the room when his friends showed certain pictures, and some of them obviously enjoyed teasing him with tales of their exploits. He says that he put his youthful ideal of love into the description of Proud Costello ("Of Costello the Proud, of Oona the Daughter of Dermott and of the Bitter Tongue," *The Secret Rose*, 1897):

> He was one of those ascetics of passion who keep their hearts pure for love or for hatred as other men for God, for Mary and for the saints, and who, when the hour of their visitation arrives, come to the Divine Essence by the bitter tumult, the Garden of Gethsemane, and the desolate Rood ordained for immortal passions in mortal hearts. (111–12)[10]

For most of the Rhymers, however, Yeats felt that he could say, "Woman herself was still in our eyes, for all that, romantic and mysterious, still the priestess of her shrine" (302), and he cites a phrase used by Olivia Shakespear's cousin who was one of the Rhymers:

> [Lionel] Johnson's favourite phrase, that life is ritual, expressed something that was in some degree in all our thoughts, and how could life be ritual if woman had not her symbolical place? (320)

The idea of ritual appealed to Yeats both because of his early training to associate security with the hierarchical custom and ceremony of aristocracy and because of his romantic penchant for subjective form. The concepts of Unity of Being and Unity of Culture were already in his thinking, his father having drawn them to his attention in Dante. Their near identity in his mind led him to make a social application of his personal love image that is by a more democratic, individualized standard surprisingly cold and uncomprehending of human emotions:

> I thought that though it might not matter to the man himself whether he loved a white woman or a black, a female pickpocket or a regular communicant of the Church of England, if only he loved strongly, it certainly did matter to his relations, and even under some circumstances to his whole neighborhood. Sometimes indeed, like some father in Moliere, I ignored the lover's feelings altogether and even refused to admit that a trace of the devil, perhaps a trace of colour, may lend piquancy, especially if the connection be not permanent. (A169-70)

The passage is redolent of all the sexist evils from racism to calculated self-interest, but for Yeats at the time of speaking, it must be remembered that all was in the mind—love was ritual and woman was "only as a myth and a symbol." There was no physical body, no passion that could not be chanted to the dulcimer. When Laura Armstrong excited his imagination, her betrothal protected him from descent into the physical. His friendship with Katharine Tynan could not come to physical consummation because the impetus of imaginative excitement was lacking. And for Florence Farr, who would not behave so as to stimulate his imagination to full play, Yeats's widow would one day speak briefly: "'she got bored.'"[11]

This, then, was the poet who fell in love with Maud Gonne and began to create a myth of courtly love about her. He was twenty-three when he met her. Before that meeting he had spent his emotional life in conscious role-playing. He had been taught in childhood that spontaneous physical expression of affection is disgusting. He had experienced his own sexual maturity as a combination of physical shame and imaginative excitement. He could be friends with women who were ready to internalize and complement his ideas, and he had translated this intellectual intercourse into biological metaphor. But his fascination was reserved for those women who "naturally" reflected his romantic concepts of the beautiful, the wild, and the tragic.

—3—

When Laura Armstrong drove up to Yeats in her pony cart and offered him a ride, she appeared to a mind whose concept of woman had been prepared by Shelley and Spenser. Instead of meeting her in reality, Yeats set her into art like theirs wherein she would exist for him as myth and symbol, and he could confront her symbolically rather than face the awful adventure of the flesh with her himself. George Bornstein points out how Yeats derived his idea of Intellectual Beauty passing through the world ("The Rose of the World," CP36) from Shelley's "The Witch of Atlas"[12] and also cites an interpretation of Yeats's reading of that poem by F. A. C. Wilson which emphasizes the Witch's "purified, 'sexless lover.'"[13]

Despite the Spenserian pastoral setting of their correspondence, Laura seems to have come into Yeats's imagination as pure Witch. He chose his name for her—Vivien—from the legend of Merlin and his Witch Vivien that he had known from childhood in the *Mabinogion* and later in Chrétien de Troyes, whose version of it Yeats includes in the mysteries of courtly love that mark the 15th phase of the current era in *A Vision* (V286). The figure of Merlin appealed to Yeats, who had wanted to be a magician since he had had *The Lay of the Last Minstrel* read to him in childhood. It alternated with sage and poet as his favorite role in his imaginative adolescence, and not long after his friendship with Laura he would explore its possibilities seriously as an initiate of the Order of the Golden Dawn. Yeats could not have begun his mythopoesis of love at a point where the masculine and the feminine are more directly opposed. The Witch is the threatening opposite of the Virgin-Bride; the magician represents the conscious knowledge in which the masculine principle glories, the power to manipulate nature. There is no contract, no mutual surrender of power between them, only a contest.

In the legend, however, the magician Merlin is defeated by the witch. When Yeats set out his first contest of the masculine and feminine powers in the brief play he wrote for Laura "Time and the Witch Vivien" (1884), he replaced Merlin with the person of Time—"wrinkled squanderer of human wealth." Only Time itself could have the victory over the feminine figure associated, in spite of all her enchanting power, with a world subject to time and death, a world Yeats would later call the *primary* and generative, over against the *antithetical* world of the poet's creation, a world of timeless order. The play presents an easy forshadowing dream of the intellectual struggle that dominates Yeats's last works in oftentimes nightmarish imagery.

The single scene of the play begins with Vivien self-enthralled before the mirror in its primitive form of the fountain. The similarity to the opening of *The Romance of the Rose* is by inversion in which the woman studies her reflection in the symbol of her nature, the generative source. In his mature volume *The Winding Stair* (1933), Yeats allows his female persona to explain a woman's fascination before a mirror:

> If I make the lashes dark
> And the eyes more bright
> And the lips more scarlet,
> Or ask if all be right
> From mirror to mirror,
> No vanity's displayed:
> I'm looking for the face I had
> Before the world was made. (CP266)

For young Laura there is no need for aids in mascara and rouge. Her power is manifest in her youthful beauty:

> *Vivien (looking down into the fountain).* Where moves there any beautiful as I,
> Save, with the little golden greedy carp,
> Gold unto gold, a gleam in its long hair,
> My image yonder? (*Spreading her hand over the water.*)
> Ah, my beautiful,
> What roseate fingers! (*Turning away.*) No; nor is there one
> Of equal power in spells and secret rites.
> The proudest or most coy of spirit things,
> Hide where he will, in wave or wrinkled moon,
> Obeys. (VPy1279)

Time enters. He is deceptively little and light. Vivien offers first to buy his hour-glass, then to gamble with him for it. She throws the dice and loses, but she remains confident:

> Come to the chess, for young girls' wits are better
> Than old men's any day, as Merlin found. (1281)

She keeps turning the hour-glass on its side, but Time rights it, reminding her that she has no control of that. He checkmates her and she dies.

But the pat defeat of the Witch by Time did not satisfy Yeats. He sensed the eternal element in the feminine that in a few years would find expression in his "Rose of the World" (December 1891),[14] and he depicted that eternal essence of the Witch in a longer play, *The Island of Statues* (1885), where he shows the essence reincarnating from generation to generation of beautiful women. He also introduces a new element: the sacrifice of the male as necessary to that reincarnation. Two shepherds in the play kill each other in a duel for a shepherdess who is in love with a nobleman and has given them no encouragement. They are merely entranced by her beauty. The fact that Yeats had given himself a shepherd's name—Clarin—in correspondence with Laura at the time of the writing of this play indicates his association with the blindly inspired shepherds. The association displays the turn of his imagination toward the tragic role for himself. Although it is true that Laura was betrothed when Yeats met her, it is also evident that she was very willing to flirt. A more positive young man might have made her break her engagement, but Yeats took no chances with this possible turn of affairs. He knew just what he wanted from their relationship—the material of imaginative tragedy—and managed to get just that and nothing more.

The death of the shepherds introduces a motif of death or castration that endures throughout Yeats's myth of love. It is the end always of the man enthralled by beauty. Of his personal love quest it is easy to say that this theme expresses the virginal poet's fear of sexual initiation or—as an exclusively archetypal interpretation would have it—that he was particularly sensitive to the threat of the devouring female. Philosophically, the poet is more concerned with the generative world's destroying his carefully built order of intellect, and beyond that, the fear of the female remains, grounded in Yeats's Theosophical and Rosicrucian studies, as the only gateway to knowledge. Theodor H. Gaster cites "the widespread notion that sexual intercourse can convey the qualities of the one partner to the other" and explains that intercourse of divinity with a human being is therefore taboo "lest the divine thus become human and the human divine."[15] The idea of sharing divine knowledge through intercourse is explicit in Yeats's "Leda and the Swan" (CP211) and implicit in all his love poems and especially in his late plays.

The fate of his male figures seems also to be the poetic equivalent of the temporary impotence he suffered when his imagination was centered on the beauty of a woman who stirred his desire. On the occasion of his first proposal to Maud, in 1891, Yeats had such an experience. Maud had told him of her dream in which they had been brother and sister in a previous life, and buoyed by this intimacy, he proposed:

> That evening, but a few minutes after we had met, [I] asked her to marry me. I remember a curious thing. I had come into the room with that purpose in my mind, and hardly looked at her or thought of her beauty. I sat there holding her hand and speaking vehemently. She did not take away her hand for a while. I ceased to speak, and presently as I sat in silence I felt her nearness to me and her beauty. At once I knew that my confidence had gone, and an instant later she drew her hand away. (M46)

Yeats was thirty-one when sexual initiation did come. After a year of discussion and consultation with trusted friends, Yeats and Olivia Shakespear moved into rooms at the Woburn Buildings, but on their first night together, he was "impotent from nervous excitement" (M88):

> A week later she came to me again, and my nervous excitement was so painful that it seemed best but to sit over our tea and talk. I do not think we kissed each other except at

the moment of her leaving. She understood instead of, as another would, changing liking for dislike—was only troubled by my trouble. My nervousness did not return again and we had many days of happiness. It will always be a grief to me that I could not give the love that was her beauty's right, but she was too near my soul, too salutary and wholesome to my inmost being. (M88)

Yeats goes immediately from this account into an association that it had for him, a passage on desire from *The Notebooks of Leonardo da Vinci*:

All our lives long, as da Vinci says, we long, thinking it is but the moon that we long [for], for our destruction, and how, when we meet [it] in the shape of a most fair woman, can we do less than leave all others for her? Do we not seek our dissolution upon her lips?

Da Vinci, speaking of "the hope and desire of . . . returning to primal chaos"[16] hints at the nature of the Great Mother archetype, but he does not relate it to woman. Yeats does.

In *The Island of Statues*, the fountain does not reflect as a mirror the mere image of woman's power as beauty, but it represents a restless discontent of the feminine within itself, a longing for polarity with the male. Almintor finds the shepherdess Naschina bored with the adoring shepherds and tries to interest her in his love by describing a forest setting where they might go together. There, he says,

> By day and night a lonely fountain sings,
> And there to its own heart for ever moans. (1229)

But Naschina will not move; she chooses passivity. She had rather be alone like the fountain and moan to herself as it does. In place of the fountain, Yeats introduces the garden as reflector of the effects of woman's power. The first garden of the play is the Edenic "gracious woodland" of the shepherds. Naschina disrupts the peace of that garden by her petulence. She inspires the shepherds to duel and sends Almintor on his fatal quest.[17] The woodland hunter is too passive for her. Passivity is her role; he must enhance it by moving to the opposite pole of action:

> I weary of your songs and hunter's toys.
> To prove his love a knight with lance in rest
> Will circle round the world upon a quest,
> Until afar appear the gleaming dragon-scales;
> From morn the twain until the evening pales
> Will struggle. Or he'll seek enchanter old,
> Who sits in lovely splendour, mail'd in gold,
> And they will war, 'mid wondrous elfin-sights:
> Such may I love. (1230)

When Yeats had Naschina in her passivity describe the active ideal of the masculine principle and then declare that only "such may I love," he created his first Lady of courtly love.

The play is coltish with strained rhymes achieved by painfully inverted sentences. The characters are flat reproductions from Spenser, and Freudian imagery abounds. The questing knight of Naschina's dreams pounds away "with his lance in rest," that is, raised, positioned for the tilt; Almintor goes to seek a flower that is "within a cloven rock dispart / A scarlet bloom" (1252). In only a few years Yeats would want it forgotten; nevertheless, in January 1889, he was delighted that Maud Gonne had read a fragment of it in the *Dublin University Review*. She hated Naschina but "altogether favoured the Enchantress" (L106).

The Enchantress reigns over a garden that is doubly enclosed. It is on an island, surrounded by the feminine presence of the sea, and is itself behind a gate of brass. The garden is filled with seekers after the "goblin flower," who are now turned to statues for their audacity. They have met the evil Virgin, who like Medusa has turned them to stone. The symbolism of the stone and the statue in Yeats's work is complex. He liked to think of beautiful women as statues and designated Phidias as the true creator of beauty and order in Western civilization by his correction and depiction of mutable human form in stone. But stone is only beautiful when it receives its form from an artist who expresses in it his vision of intellectual beauty. In contradistinction, the personality that yields to intellectual passion, especially intellectual hatred, becomes an obstruction, a stone to trouble the stream of life. The woman who gives herself to intellectual passion becomes, instead of a statue, a terrible stone doll:

> Women, because the main event of their lives has been a giving of themselves, give themselves to an opinion as if [it] were some terrible stone doll. We take up an opinion lightly and are easily false to it, and when faithful keep the habit of many interests. We still see the world, if we are strong of mind and body, with steady and careful eyes, but opinions become as their children or their sweethearts, and the greater their emotional nature the more do they forget all other things. They grow cruel, as if [in] defence of lover or child, this is done for something other then human life. At last the opinion becomes so much a part of them that it is as though a part of their flesh becomes, as it were, stone, and much of their being passes out of life. . . . Women should have their play with dolls finished in childish happiness, for if they play with them again it is amid hatred and malice. (M192)

The Enchantress's act of turning seekers after the flower to stone is not individually or rationally done; it is her blind nature to guard the flower. The Enchantress reveals to Naschina, who has come in search of Almintor disguised as a boy, that the flower can be safely picked only by a shepherdess for whom some living thing has been willing to die. But she further reveals that she would destroy that shepherdess before she could pluck the flower because the existence of the Enchantress depends upon the security of the blossom within its cloven rock. The image, whether consciously or unconsciously in Yeats, suggests *virgo intacta*, the high prize of courtly love and archetypally the Virgin as symbol of the unattained, inspiring goal. The division of the feminine between her whose existence depends on withholding the flower and her whose desire is to give it appears again in Yeats's last romantic poem, the ballad "The Three Bushes" (CP193), in which the Lady, like the Enchantress, cannot exist without her chastity.

The irrational nature of the Enchantress is stressed by her declaration that she would foil the shepherdess by destroying her rational powers:

> E'en then, before her shepherd hair
> Had felt that island breeze, my lore
> Had driven her forth for ever more
> To wander by the bubbling shore,
> Laughter-lipped, but for her brain
> A guerdon of deep-rooted pain,
> And in her eyes a lightless stare. (1247)

Naschina, pretending it a whim, wants an appeal sent out that someone should die for her:

> . . . bid some attendant sprite
> Of thine cry over wold and water white,
> That one shall die, unless one die for her.

Although Naschina's understood intention is to save Almintor, the selfish wording of this cry may have been what made Maud hate her. As spoken, it sounds a mere test of woman's power and her privilege of survival under the rules of patriarchy. Or the hateful act may have been Naschina's triumphant shout at the Enchantress when spirits bring word of the deaths of the duelling shepherds: "I am mightier now than thee."

In the interim between Naschina's cry for a sacrifice and the announcement of the spirits, the Enchantress falls in love with the disguised shepherdess. She courts her in the very terms of proffered rest that Yeats would later address to Maud in his repeated proposals. It is also an invitation to the restful stasis and passivity of the enclosed garden:

> My words were all: 'O whither, whither, whither
> Wilt roam away from this rich island rest?
> I bid thee stay, renouncing thy mad quest.'
> But thou wouldst not, for then thou wert unblest
> And stony-hearted; now thou hast grown kind,
> And thou wilt stay. All thought of what they find
> In the far world will vanish from thy mind,

> Till thou rememberest only how the sea
> Has fenced us round for all eternity. (1248–49)

The Enchantress makes it clear that this garden is a place of perfect peace where no emotions disturb the tranquillity. There is no joy as well as no sorrow: "For peace and laughter have been seldom friends." Yeats was, therefore, always aware that the excitement engendered by love destroyed peace, but from the beginning he also knew that there was no creative drive in peace. That love could make the world a narrow pound when he achieved his own long-sought garden must have come as no surprise to him. Read in the light of this understanding, his youthful statement that we begin to live when we have conceived life as tragedy is not a romantic burbling but an analytical assessment of the nature of the impetus to poetry that he desired.

At Naschina's triumphant shout, the Enchantress begins to pine. She warns Naschina, who will now take her place, of what becoming the Eternal Feminine means:

> Well nigh immortal in this charmed clime,
> Thou shalt outlive thine amorous happy time,
> And dead as are the lovers of old rime
> Shall be the hunter-lover of thy youth.
> Yet ever more, through all thy days of ruth,
> Shall grow thy beauty and the dreamless truth,
> As an hurt leopard fills with ceaseless moan,
> And aimless wanderings the woodlands lone,
> Thy soul shall be, though pitiless and bright
> It is, yet shall it fail thee day and night
> Beneath the burden of the infinite. (1253)

The Enchantress disappears into oblivion as a spirit sings:

> A man has hope for heaven,
> But soulless a faery dies.

Left alone, Naschina realizes that her former life is over; all that she had known in the woodland is "As figures moving mirrored in a glass." She knows that a touch of the goblin flower upon his lips will restore Almintor to life, but she is wracked by the question of whether he will be more or less miserable alive on the island. Naschina wakens him first, then the other statues, who identify themselves as lovers who lived in the days of Carthage, Camelot, and Troy, each the era of an Enchantress. They realize that they will stay forever on the island, and Almintor declares Naschina queen "within the charmed ring." Then the moon rises and its light shows that among the group Naschina alone is shadowless. She is the new Enchantress; she has lost her soul and with it her hope of heaven.

Yeats left no record of how he parted from Laura Armstrong or whether she ever married her fiancé, but he did remember her at least into the early years of his involvement with Maud, and the plays that he wrote for her show that even before he had firmly chosen to follow poetry over painting, he had rehearsed the ritual and selected the elements with which he would construct his mythopoesis of love: the ritual consisting of the sublimation of the physical to the imaginative wherein the incarnation of the Feminine is accompanied by the sacrifice of the male; the elements consisting of the mirror, the enclosed garden, the flower, the stone. He was ready to begin his variations and, months before he saw Maud Gonne, had already chosen his next myth and symbol from the story of the Countess Kathleen O'Shea.

—4—

Five years after Laura had extended her invitation to ride in her cart, Maud ordered her hansom to wait in front of Yeats's house. In those five years Yeats had matured artistically and had added Theosophy and Celtic folklore to the background of his reading from Spenser and Shelley. He had read Blake and Swedenborg and Boehme; and he had begun to fit his findings into the overall pattern of thought that would one day become his *Anima Mundi*. His concept of feminine beauty as evidence of eternal enchantment fitted the growing pattern, but his self-concept was changing. His role of Arcadian shepherd had disappeared with adolescence, and his role of magician had evolved into his serious study of magic in the occult. He was facing the immediate practical choice between writing and painting for a vocation, and both his father and his esteemed friend John O'Leary were urging him to write. His father was especially relieved that his son tended to poetry and not to the hack journalism that in his aristocratic view no man could follow and call himself a gentleman. The decision was in effect made. In the five years Yeats had not sold a painting, but he had written and published a great deal for one so young. Besides *The Island of Statues*, he had another play in print, *Mosada* (1886), and several poems, mostly on Celtic themes. He had edited *Poems and Ballads of Young Ireland* (1888) and *Fairy and Folk Tales of the Irish Peasantry* (1888), in recognition of which he had become London's authority on fairy lore.[18] At his father's suggestion he had written the draft of a novel, *John Sherman*. His most important work, the long poem *The Wanderings of Oisin*, in which the hero is led away by a fairy-enchantress, appeared in January 1889, the month of Maud's arrival.

It is probably this activity that brought Maud to his door since she had for some months set herself to meet the leaders of the rising generation in Ireland, but in her accounts of their meeting, which do not agree in time or place with Yeats's, Maud consistently speaks of him as an art student and specifies his paint-stained fingers and clothes. Her arrival was a decisive point, if not in his deciding that he would be a poet, then in his deciding what kind of poet he would become. He wanted her to think of him as a writer, but just what kind of writer was not firm in his mind. He was swayed by what he judged her tastes to be. She told him she had wept over the scene between Naschina and the Enchantress. She invited him to dine in her rooms in London where he saw Hugo's *Les Contemplations* and Swinburne's *Tristram of Lyonesse*, which contains a tribute to Hugo, lying on her table. He leapt to the idea that she would respond to him if he declared that he wanted to become "an Irish Victor Hugo": "It was natural to commend myself by claiming a very public talent, for her beauty as I saw it in those days seemed incompatible with private, intimate life" (M41). The time of his enchantment had begun. He would be her troubadour.

Yeats introduced the role of troubadour, the court poet who is ritually in love with his queen of whom he sings, into an Irish tale that he traced to Léo Lespès's *Les Matinées de Timothé Trimm* (VPy170-72). It is the story of a countess called Ketty O'Connor in Lespès but later Kathleen O'Shea, who saves the peasants of famine-stricken Donegal with money she receives from the sale of her soul to the devil. The original was intended to be told during Lent. It has an interesting combination of Christian and pagan themes in that the countess both redeems the souls of peasants who had sold them to the devil for food and at the same time restores the land to fertility by her death. Yeats believed the tale far older than Christianity:

> I have no doubt of the essential antiquity of what seems to me the most impressive form of one of the supreme parables of the world. The parable came to the Greeks in the sacrifice of Alcestis, but her sacrifice was less overwhelming, less apparently irremedial. (VPy170)

The material could have been selected with Maud in mind since she had just come to London from her first activities in Donegal, but Yeats's letter to Katharine Tynan on November 14, 1888, reveals his previous plans to develop it "in some more elaborate way than a ballad perhaps" (L94). Nevertheless, Maud fell naturally into Yeats's image of an Irish heroine, as she fell into the image of a woman of the Sidhe for the peasant who saw her in her green dress.

Yeats explains that her beauty gave her a power over the people not only because it suggested freedom and joy but also because

> there was an element in her beauty that moved minds full of old Gaelic stories and poems, for she looked as though she lived in an ancient civilization where all superiorities whether of the mind or the body were a part of public ceremonial, were in some way the crowd's creation, as the entrance of the Pope into St. Peter's is the crowd's creation. (A364)

Of that Gaelic or Celtic view of woman to which Maud so strongly appealed, J. Ernest Renan said:

> No other [race] had conceived with more delicacy the ideal of woman, or been more fully dominated by it. It is a sort of intoxication, a madness, a vertigo. Read the strange *Mabinogi of Peredur*, or its French imitation *Perceval le Gallois*; its pages are, as it were, dewy with feminine sentiment. Woman appears therein as a kind of vague vision and intermediary between man and the supernatural world.[19]

The role of the Countess Cathleen makes that vague vision more concrete. Such was the goal in art that Yeats had devoted himself to accomplishing (A188).

Yeats wrote more versions of this play than of any other. The *Variorum Edition* contains the complete first version that appeared in September 1892 as *The Countess Kathleen* and the version published in 1895 but dated 1892, in which the name is spelled *Cathleen*. A comparison of the dedications to Maud indicates the emotional storms through which Yeats was passing. The first version fills the entire title page (VPy3):

THE COUNTESS KATHLEEN
An Irish Drama
*

I Dedicate
this play
to
my friend,
Miss Maud Gonne,
at whose suggestion
it was
planned out and begun
some
three years ago.
*

"*The sorrowful are dumb for thee.*"
The Lament of Morian Shehone for Mary Bourke.

That was in Yeats's period of enchantment. By 1895 the play had become "but the symbolical song of my pity" (M47). Yeats and Maud had quarreled in the summer of 1893, and the new dedication had shrunk:

'The sorrowful are dumb for thee'
Lament of Morian Shehone
for Miss Mary Bourke
TO
MAUD GONNE

In *The Poetical Works of William B. Yeats* of 1907, the entire dedication is omitted. Yeats had not seen Maud since her marriage in 1903. But in *The Collected Works in Verse and Prose* of 1908, the dedication "To Maud Gonne" returned and remained.

The figure of the Countess is more symbol than character. At first she is merely fated, without personal motivation, like the characters in a medieval morality play. Even at her most fully developed point in 1901, she symbolizes an attitude toward the world. At the beginning of his work, Yeats saw character as a problem in his women. In *The Trembling of the Veil* he remembers being "encouraged by Congreve's saying that 'passions are too powerful in the fair sex to let humour' or as we say character, 'have its course'" (A191–92), and in his Journal he agrees with Balzac, who, he says, found it necessary to deny character to his great ladies and young lovers that he might give them passion. "What beautiful woman," he asks, "delights us by her look of character? That shows itself when beauty is gone. . . . Beauty consumes character with what Patmore calls 'the integrity of fire'" (M189).

Yeats separates the Countess from human generations by giving her in the mythological manner a deaf old woman as stepmother and saying nothing of her antecedents. The fact that an old inn is named for her implies a long tenure in the title, yet she is young. The wall of her enclosed garden is breached by evil ones who have come to buy the souls of the starving peasants. The tree of her sorrow is the Weeping Willow of the World, named Eri for Erin. Her eternal essence is declared by a Heavenly Spirit after she has died to redeem the souls of her people:

> She gave away her soul for others—God,
> Who sees the motive and the deed regards not,
> Bade us go down and save her from the demons, . . .

And she comes to share the image of the Beloved of the Lover in "The Rose of the World":

> . . . the red rose by the seat of God,
> Which is among the angelic multitude
> What she, whose body lies here, was to men. (VPy164–68)

The story is interspersed with references to Maud herself. Although Yeats had seen little of her between January 1889 and July 1891,[20] he did know the highlights of her public activities, and he worked what he knew into the play, including a theological opinion Maud had cited in a pamphlet drafted with James Connolly for distribution among peasants of Kerry during the potato blight of 1897–98. Entitled "The Rights of Life and the Rights of Property," it contained quotations on the ownership of the fruits of the earth from Pope Clement I, Pope Gregory the Great, Cardinal Manning, and St. Thomas Aquinas, who had replied to the question "Is it lawful to steal on the plea of necessity?" that if the need be plain and pressing then the man may relieve his distress out of the property of another, taking it either openly or secretly.[21] This pamphlet, as Maud dates it, comes too late for Yeats to have used for reference in *The Countess Kathleen*; however, in Donegal in 1888–1890 she had led defiance of the turf laws and eviction procedures. She may have spoken of the theological rulings to Yeats then, or he may even have suggested them to her. However the matter came to Yeats's knowledge, he has Kathleen, when she is informed in an early scene that the peasants have robbed her storehouses, reply,

> Yet learned theologians have laid down
> That he who has no food, offending no way,
> May take his meat and bread from too-full larders. (64)

In the intimacy of the summer of 1891, Yeats read the unfinished play to Maud and saw her moved at the passage from Kathleen's deepest depression when the evil ones explain to her that the God-fearing peasants sell their souls not only from fear of starvation for themselves and their children but also

> . . . because there is a kind of joy
> In casting hope away, in losing joy,
> In ceasing all resistance, in at last
> Opening one's arms to the eternal flames. (108)

Yeats's idea of such loss of a woman's soul, begun in *The Island of Statues*, fixed itself to Maud. Remembering her emotion at the reading he thought what a burden of responsibility she carried:

> I told her after meeting her in London I had come to understand the tale of a woman selling her soul to buy food for a starving people as a symbol of all souls who lose their peace, or their fineness, or any beauty of spirit in political service, but chiefly of her soul that had seemed so incapable of rest. (M47)

His fear for her soul is recalled in his late poems, "A Bronze Head":

> But even at the starting-post, all sleek and new,
> I saw the wildness in her and I thought
> A vision of terror that it must live through
> Had shattered her soul; (CP329)

and "The Circus Animals' Desertion":

And then a counter-truth filled out its play,
The Countess Cathleen was the name I gave it;
She, pity-crazed, had given her soul away,
But masterful Heaven had intervened to save it.

I thought my dear must her own soul destroy,
So did fanaticism and hate enslave it.
And this brought forth a dream and soon enough
This dream itself had all my thought and love. (CP336)

Kathleen's "young bard" Kevin tells her tales of magical escapes drawn from Celtic lore. His purpose is to induce her, as Yeats attempted to induce Maud, to "cast off this cloud of care." Kathleen calls the stories "wicked words" as if, like Maud, she wore mental blinkers to avoid distraction from her purpose.

Kevin is a minor, self-deprecating representation of his creator. When he comes to offer his own soul to the devil-merchants, they read out his worth from their record books. It is Yeats's self-assessment in the days before he met Maud:

A man of songs—
Alone in the hushed passion of romance,
His mind ran on sheogues, and on tales
Of Finian labours and the Red-branch kings,
And he cared nothing for the life of man:
But now all changes. (134)

The merchants, however, cannot touch Kevin's soul for it is sheltered by the soul of the Countess. In his only other appearance, Kevin rushes in to snatch the fatal deed of sale before Kathleen can sign it, but after announcing a vision he has had of the final triumph of God over Satan, he simply drops the deed and allows two peasants who have become henchmen of the merchants to lead him away. Unhindered, Kathleen signs the deed. Just before her death, a young peasant reports that Kevin is wandering in the woods, occasionally placing his ear to the ground to listen to the activities of the wood demons. An old woman declares that "love had made him crazy."

Both Kevin and the more independent Aleel of the later versions of *The Countess Cathleen* are effeminate figures although as revisions progressed Aleel moved toward masculinity. In 1899 he was played by Florence Farr in the tradition of the English pantomime in which the Principal Boy is played by a woman, the tradition that produced Peter Pan. Both Kevin and Aleel are far weaker than the Countess and totally ineffectual in advising or protecting her. Each bard does, however, have his moment of power, but it is power derived from his service to the Countess. It is as if her spirit possesses them as the Holy Spirit possessed the early Christian Apostles. Her spirit in

Aleel causes his gaze to fill the devil-merchants "with shaking and a dreadful fear."

As *The Countess Cathleen* is a more fully developed play, so Aleel is a more fully developed character. Cathleen says that she found him singing and playing his stringed instrument at the edge of the wood. She took him for her guide, but he was too given to prophecy, too "wrapped up in dreams of terrors to come" (CPy7) to be of any help. Aleel does have spirit enough to answer peasants who challenge him with the cheekiness of the courtier who is secure in the favor of his patroness. He is aggressive enough to be slightly wounded by one of the merchants, and although like Kevin he does not prevent the Countess's signing away her soul, he offers more resistance to those who take him from the scene. His madness, staged rather than reported, takes on the weight of prophecy couched in Celtic allusions. With his gift of second-sight, the mystery that Yeats called "mostly a woman's privilege" (A185), he narrates for the audience the invisible struggle of angels and demons for the soul of Cathleen. He seizes one of the angels and holds him until he describes Cathleen's reception in Heaven.

In the revision of 1901, Yeats added what he called "the love scene" between Aleel and the Countess. Aleel, appearing more decisive and masculine than elsewhere in the play, urges Cathleen to bring her immediate household and flee with him to live in the hills until the trouble is past. Prostrating himself before her, he begs,

> Let Him that made mankind, the angels and devils
> And dearth and plenty, mend what He has made,
> For when we labour in vain and eye still sees,
> Heart breaks in vain. (CPy27)

Aleel says the message to flee came to him in a vision of a figure walking in fire with birds flying about his head. This is the figure of Aengus Mac Og, the Celtic god of love, who appears frequently in *The Celtic Twilight* and in one of Yeats's early poems about Maud, "The Song of Wandering Aengus" (CP57). Aleel insists that the figure is angelic and should be obeyed, but Cathleen says it is not angelic, not within the Christian point of view that she comes more and more to represent as the play is revised:

> No, not angelical, but of the old gods,
> Who wander about the world to waken the heart—
> The passionate, proud heart—that all the angels,
> Leaving nine heavens empty, would rock to sleep. (27)

Their debate becomes increasingly a debate of religion, probably reflecting Maud's conversion to the Church of Rome in the late 1890s. Cathleen has taken a vow to the Blessed Virgin:

Do not hold out to me beseeching hands.
This heart shall never waken on earth. I have sworn,
By her whose heart the seven sorrows have pierced,
To pray before this altar until my heart
Has grown to Heaven like a tree, and there
Rustled its leaves, till Heaven has saved my people. (27)

At this Cathleen both "becomes" the feminine tree and exhibits the masculine trait of devotion to an external idea. She is concerned with delineation of abstract good and evil. Aleel is aware of the other world represented by the woods and the nature demons as an alternative to the Christian world in which abstract good and evil struggle but he urges the feminine pattern of retreat for survival. Cathleen seems strong in her masculinity, but when Aleel turns to leave saying that he has "overdared" in his plea, she confesses,

                    If the old tales are true,
Queens have wed shepherds and kings beggar-maids;
God's procreant waters flowing about your mind
Have made you more than kings or queens; and not you
But I am the empty pitcher.

And she adds,

. . . you shall hear wind cry and water cry,
And curlew cry, and have the peace I longed for. (28)

Cathleen makes the ultimate surrender of woman to the patriarchal or *antithetical* order. In acknowledging that "God's procreant waters" flow in Aleel's mind, she places intellectual creation above *primary* creation as represented by the queens and shepherds, kings and beggar-maids, and herself as woman. She yields to Aleel the female water symbol, procreant and flowing, while her water symbol, the pitcher, is dry. Having developed his feminine nature, Aleel has become complete; having developed her masculine nature, Cathleen has lost all. In depicting the complete—or in the Jungian term "individuated"—human being, Yeats seems to have overlooked the example of the strong female knights in Spenser. Women designed to praise the characteristics of Elizabeth I could hardly have their masculine principle frustrated or atrophied. For his idea of androgyny Yeats later cited the Greeks, writing to Dorothy Wellesley, "Have you noticed that the Greek androgynous statue is always the woman in man, never the man in woman? It was made for men who loved men first" (L875).

The scene between Aleel and Cathleen is consistent with what Yeats had later to say about the destruction of the woman's soul in intellectual hatred and all the warnings in "A Prayer for My Daughter" of how she can destroy the gifts that are hers from nature. But contrasted with his actual feelings between his proposal to Maud in 1891 and their quarrel in 1893, as recalled in *Memoirs*, the scene is constructed upon wish-fulfillment. In actuality Yeats was suffering from a sense of his own incompleteness compared with Maud:

> It had come to seem as if the intimacy of our minds could not be greater, and I explained the fact that marriage seemed to have slipped further away by my own immaturity and lack of achievement. One night when going to sleep I had seen suddenly a thimble, and a shapeless white mass that puzzled me. The next day on passing a tobacconist's I saw that it was a lump of meershaum not yet made into a pipe. She was complete; I was not. (M63)

The question of relative completeness between himself and Maud rises again in "The People," which Yeats wrote in January 1915.[22] Speaking of his irritation with the ordinary, unromantic Irish people—an irritation heightened by his trip to Urbino, where he considered the highest aristocratic culture to have had its seat—Yeats recalls a conversation with Maud in which she speaks from her experience with the common people when she was most like the Countess Cathleen. Yeats complains that he would have liked always to choose his company and the scenery that pleased him most as a poet:

> Thereupon my phoenix answered in reproof,
> 'The drunkards, pilferers of public funds,
> All the dishonest crowd I had driven away,
> When my luck changed and they dared meet my face,
> Crawled from obscurity, and set upon me
> Those I had served and some that I had fed;
> Yet never have I now nor any time,
> Complained of the people.' (CP149)

In reply Yeats turns again to the question of whether "head-ego" or "heart-ego" makes the more complete person. The Jungian answer is, of course, neither ego of itself can be complete, but Yeats again finds in favor of Maud. The qualities he here attributes to himself and to her are the qualities that Cathleen and Aleel represented in their debate, but they are here presented in the masculine mode of objective analysis instead of the feminine mode of subjective ("I am the empty pitcher") judgment:

> All that I could reply
> Was: 'You, that have not lived in thought but deed,
> Can have the purity of a natural force,
> But I, whose virtues are the definitions
> Of the analytic mind, can neither close
> The eye of the mind nor keep my tongue from speech.'

But the emotional response essential to a "love scene" is here supplied by the masculine speaker," . . . because my heart leaped at her words, / I was abashed, and now they come to mind / After nine years, I sink my head abashed."

At the end of their love scene Cathleen sends Aleel away, asking him to compare the task she has set for him—to leave her to her vow—with those tasks assigned by the ladies of the old love stories. The list she recites recalls Naschina's speech in *The Island of Statues* although to a different purpose:

> There have been women that bid men to rob
> Crowns from the Country-under-Wave or apples
> Upon a dragon-guarded hill, and all
> That they might sift the hearts and wills of men,
> And trembled as they bid it, as I tremble
> That lay a hard task upon you, that you go,
> And silently, and do not turn your head.
> Good-bye; but do not turn your head and look;
> Above all else, I would not have you look. (28)

Aleel leaves. The scene would have been more poignant had Yeats edited the rest of the play so that Aleel would not see Cathleen alive again.

Following Cathleen's confession of emptiness, the last lines she says seem pathetic, and Yeats may have intended them to be read so since Cathleen moves directly to the act that—but for the grace of God—would damn her soul. But read in the light of the tradition of courtly love and of Yeats's real assessment of Maud's completeness, as well as of the redemption of Cathleen's soul, the lines do not have to be pathetic at all. Courtly love always begins with looking. The vision of incarnate Beauty is the enchantment in the mirror of Narcissus and the arrow that Cupid shoots through the eye into the heart. Cathleen's instruction to Aleel not to look back at her protects him from being reinfected with love. That she should give such instruction makes her dominant in the scene because she is not only assuring Aleel's freedom but relieving herself of responsibility for the effect of her beauty. She is breaking the deceptive mirror for him.

Aleel breaks a mirror himself at the end of the play, but does so in an acceptance of tragedy and a return from order to chaos. He snatches the mirror that the old woman has held over Cathleen's face to test for any hint of breath and flings it to the ground, saying,

> I shatter you in fragments, for the face
> That brimmed you up with beauty is no more;
> And die, dull heart, for she whose mournful words
> Made you a living spirit has passed away
> And left you but a ball of passionate dust. (48)

As he begins to curse all nature and time, lightning flashes and thunder rolls. The peasants fear that he will call down destruction upon them, but the second sight comes upon him, and he sees the return of chaos in reenactment of battles from Celtic myth:

> Angels and devils clash in the middle air,
> And brazen swords clang upon brazen helms.
> Yonder a bright spear, cast out of a sling,
> Has torn through Balor's eye, and the dark clans
> Fly screaming as they fled Moytura of old. (49)

The scene is "lost in darkness" while an old man's voice shouts that the Almighty has "blotted out the world." The entire scene, apocalyptic imagery foreshadowing the "blood-dimmed tide" that overwhelms the "ceremony of innocence" in "The Second Coming," can be compared to the breaking of the mirror of External Reason in Boehme's Theosophy, a breaking of Creation followed by "the terrible fire-flash in the horror, in the darkness." But as the soul of the Countess is redeemed, so is Creation; a "visionary light" breaks the darkness, and the angels guarding the gate of Heaven appear. The angel Aleel forces to speak reports that the earthly virgin has been received by the Heavenly One:

> . . . she is passing to the floor of peace,
> And Mary of the seven times wounded heart
> Has kissed her lips, and the long blessed hair
> Has fallen over her face. (50)

The restoration of order to Creation is the result of the restoration of the female figure, woman again in her "symbolical place." The ritual enacted is that of the Atonement in Christian theology—with the major change of substituting female figures for both God the Son and God the Father. Erich Neumann cites a parallel from the East in the tale of the goddess Kwan-Yin, who "hears the cry of the world" and sacrifices her Buddhahood for the sake of the suffering, an expression, he says, of the matriarchal goddess without the patriarchal overlay of the West that he calls "abstract and hostile to nature."[23]

Charges of heresy were leveled at *The Countess Cathleen* on its first production in 1899, but the point of accusation was not the female figure but the question of the justification under any circumstance of selling one's soul. It remained for Yeats's friend George Moore to publish a pamphlet called *Souls for Gold!* (London, 1899) attacking Yeats for suggesting that Irish women would barter their souls. Yeats responded that the pamphlet was either "sheer dishonesty" or else the product of delirium in Moore, who was undergoing some religious trauma of his own at the time. His question in rebuttal, "Has not every living truth, like every living man, an infinite number of forefathers?" (M120), refers the theme of the play to the fardel of traditions from which he drew all his themes. Yeats had, however, experienced an insight from the uproar: "In using what I considered traditional symbols I forgot that in Ireland they are not symbols but realities." The awakening in his mind of the difference between the poetic symbol and the everyday reality was also beginning to apply to his understanding of women.

—5—

Yeats was moving rapidly toward his rejection of courtly love as personal pursuit. Ten years had passed since his *Countess Kathleen*, and the play and been revised from a morality play centered on a saintly image to a symbolical song of pity for a woman who he was certain would destroy her soul in external activism to a drama that, whether Yeats wished it to or not, vindicated the completeness that he had been compelled to recognize in Maud Gonne. In one more year he would write "Adam's Curse" and declare the hollowness of his experience with "the old high way of love."

But two unresolved elements remained. One was Yeats's establishment of his own posture as poet within an aristocratic order. The other was the impulse toward self-destruction on the part of his male figures, an impulse that intensified with the male's effort to achieve unity with the female, or in Yeats's phrase, to "solve the antinomies" that male and female represented.

The aristocratic order that Yeats sought is the object of his cultural quest, but it affects the works rising from his personal quest by giving them the frame of courtly love and by opening the traditional door of the courtier for his presence in them. Yeats's roles as bard, jester, and courtier reveal him kneeling in the corner of his love poems as he noticed the patrons of medieval paintings kneeling in the corners of compositions full of saints and madonnas (A116). Besides having the rank of attendant or servitor, those self-images of the poet are placed lower than the female even in the physical scale, as when Aleel kisses Cathleen's hand and she responds with a benedictional kiss upon his forehead. Especially in the poems of *The Wind Among the Reeds* the Lover lies or desires to lie under the hair of his beloved, and he lays down his dreams for her to walk upon. The latter sentiment is the theme of the poem that Yeats liked to introduce in his public readings as the "formula for losing a woman":

> Had I the heavens' embroidered cloths,
> Enwrought with golden and silver light,
> The blue and the dim and the dark cloths
> Of night and light and the half-light,

I would spread the cloths under your feet:
But I, being poor, have only my dreams;
I have spread my dreams under your feet;
Tread softly because you tread on my dreams. (CP70)

The introductory remark must surely have puzzled those in Yeats's audience for whom love meant the offering of lavish gifts, material or spiritual, and the search for a woman who was worthy to receive them and capable of understanding them—in other words, the courtly lovers in the audience. And they must have been even more puzzled when Yeats presented the companion-piece to this lovely poem. It was titled "The Cap and Bells," and he called it the formula for successful wooing. It makes much more explicit the irony, from the masculine view, of the woman's values, of what she wants most to have of all that a man can offer. The poem opens the depth of the question that underlies all Yeats's intellectual juggling of mirrors, gardens, bards, and queens, and it presents the image that unifies all that he had to say on the subject.

"The Cap and Bells" begins as what can now be recognized as a Yeatsian set-piece: the servant, whose only purpose is to amuse, standing in the still—dead?—garden, spatially inferior—looking up at the queen's window. He makes his first offering of his soul, then of his heart. When these are refused, he proffers the ancient sacrifice demanded by the Earth Mother:

'I have cap and bells,' he pondered,
'I will send them to her and die'. (CP62)

This gift achieves his bliss in the taming of her hair and the quieting of her feet. Read with the irony with which he introduced it, the poem seems to vindicate locker-room judgment—"what they want is your balls"—and to leave the masculine and feminine more separated than reconciled, a physical union of the crippled with the unconscious.

The garden of the jester and the queen demonstrates the extreme antithetical outcome of the Garden of Eden. In that first garden the patriarchal hierarchy was at its simplest, the man at the head and the woman as his "helpmeet," his companion. The relationship, although centered on the masculine, was still structured from the cooperation of two whole human beings. Eve had an intellect and an independent, conscious power of choice, for it was to these capabilities that the Serpent appealed. In the garden of "The Cap and Bells," the analytical creativity of the masculine principle has operated to the extreme of reducing each figure to one aspect of its whole nature and establishing a much more divisive hierarchy so that the aspects are alienated from one another. All inspiration is settled in the passive queen, who can close the windows and doors of her house; all striving in the jester, who yearns for access to the queen's house. The isolation of the two characters reduces the theme to its essentials as in two of Yeats's last plays, *The King of the Great Clock Tower* (1934)—which has a king, a queen, and a stroller—and its revision *A Full Moon in March* (1935), which has only the queen and the stroller reduced to a swineherd. Yeats said that he made the simplifications to achieve greater intensity (VPy1311).

"The Cap and Bells" was written in 1893, the beginning of Yeats's first long separation from Maud. It appears in *The Wind Among the Reeds* (1899) with a note explaining that it is a dream told just as the poet saw it and that, while it had always meant a great deal to him, it had not always meant quite the same thing. There is small wonder that the meaning varied over these six years. In 1893 Yeats had had the experience of proposing to Maud and being refused, but his sexual innocence was still such that he knew only how to give a "brother's kiss" (M86). In 1896 he had lost his virginity with some difficulty. In 1897 he had faced the full revelation of Maud's life with Millevoye and the children she had borne to him while he, Yeats, had played at being Lancelot in exile until he had wanted to scream his frustration alone in the woods at Coole. Then in 1898 he had been spiritually married to Maud in a binding relationship that stopped short of the "final solace," as did the "pure love" of the Middle Ages.[24] And in 1899 he had finally accepted Maud's refusal to appear on stage in the role of the Countess Cathleen over which he had toiled for ten years. In 1902 he wrote of the hollowness of the "old high way of love." In February 1903, Maud married John MacBride, and in November of that year Yeats began his American tours on which he introduced "He [The Lover] Wishes for the Cloths of Heaven" and "The Cap and Bells" as formulas for losing and winning women. A sense of comedy was invading his imagination and, as he had foreseen earlier in the 1890s, threatening the symbolic place of woman. The meaning of "The Cap and Bells" at this time seems to have been a comic and cynical understanding of the Victorian cliché that "pure love" would demand of a man the best that he had in him.

The fact that the poem had its beginning in a dream opens it to the psychoanalytic reading as the surfacing of a fear of castration. Most of the critics who mention the poem seem satisfied with that comment, but Harold Bloom goes on to point out that the poem is a dream version of the memorable symbol of the Decadence of the 1890s, the dancer with the severed head.[25] Among Beardsley's designs it was the one Yeats had thought uncharacteristically beautiful. Yeats made this connection of the symbols himself in his notes to the two late plays in which stroller or swineherd is decapitated but continues to sing to his queen (VPy1311). Curtis Bradford applies the interpretation of castration directly to Yeats's relationship with Maud: "Either Yeats was unable to offer Maud Gonne his cap and bells, or, more likely, she was unable to accept them."[26]

At least one example of an articulate severed head can be found in a Celtic war legend, but considering the dream in archetypal figures leads, as Yeats also said in his notes to the plays, to "the mother-goddess and the slain god" and to the rites of the cults of those mother-goddesses like Cybele and Artemis in which frenzied male worshippers castrated themselves and threw their bleeding genitalia upon the goddess's statue. Esther Harding describes the rites of Cybele, which from 900 B. C. took place around the twenty-fourth of March, Yeats's full moon in March. After castration the men became eunuch priests, longhaired and dressed in women's clothes. Similar ceremonies honored Syrian Astarte, Ephesian Diana, Ashtoreth (Ishtar), and Hecate. Above her numerous breasts, Diana's statue is decorated with a necklace of testicles.[27] The poem can be read, therefore, in depth beyond that of Freudian fear of castration, an interpretation which seems to call for a Devil-take-her conclusion from any rational man. "The Cap and Bells" has no such ending. It concludes with a scene of mutual acceptance. It can be read as a confrontation and exchange with the Virgin, not at all gentle, meek, and full of grace but as Yeats would later call her, "fierce."

The self-castration of the jester is a more explicit development of the symbolic act that began with the bard Kevin, who tears the strings of his lute before offering his soul to the devil. His act is his response to the spiritually transforming power of his Lady:

> The face of the Countess Kathleen dwells with me, The sadness of the world upon her brow—
> The crying of these strings grew burdensome,
> Therefore I tore them—see—now take my soul. (VPy1136)

The jester's cap and bells and Kevin's lute signify their means of imaginative expression as well as sexual power. In a single gesture they yield their creative potency both physically and intellectually. Aleel, the stronger character, destroys not his lute but the mirror that represents the illusion that demands sacrifice. His assumption of the feminine principle in addition to his masculine nature makes him stronger than the other two; having "God's procreant waters" in his own heart, he can break the illusion that he must sacrifice himself to attain that power from a woman.

After his sacrifice Kevin wanders off in ineffectual madness, putting his ear to the ground to hear the demons at work and communicating nothing from the experience. With Aleel and the jester Yeats seems to have become more convinced of the Theosophical idea that confrontation with the Virgin, while it may demand sacrifice, also carries reward. Aleel's eyes are opened when he surrenders the hope of possessing Cathleen; he sees and can communicate how she through all the tumult is finally possessed by God and His Mother. The jester realizes an even greater reward in coming to peace with his queen. Having received his cap and bells, she also accepts his heart and soul and then returns them to him, articulate as they had not been before his surrender of them. Of the two characters, however, Aleel seems to represent the true solution for Yeats. The poem of the jester became an amusing showpiece for the public, but the play *The Countess Cathleen* stands out in Yeats's final assessments of his life's work where the poem is unmentioned (CP336). More importantly, the recognition of the feminine principle developed within the male poet, that is foreshadowed in the character of Aleel, becomes a conscious aspect of Yeats's own personality in his later years when his verse is at its strongest, most "masculine" quality.

"The Cap and Bells" moves from purely Celtic background to admit elements of classical mythology. The queen rising in her pale night-gown is a moon-like image. The owls in her garden are not the human-headed demonic birds of Celtic lore that appear in *The Countess Cathleen* but real owls, the owls of Athena that represent her as Lady Wisdom. The poem also draws upon the image of hair and feet that are motifs of the feminine throughout *The Wind Among the Reeds*. Jeffares has counted over twenty-three references to hair in the book and says that these convey "a sense of languorous abandonment."[28] The hair has also been called the hair of Shelley's wild Maenads. It might also be likened to the hair of Beardsley's women that snakes its way into his whole design. But Yeats associates it with the hair of the Sidhe, who "journey in whirling winds, the winds that were called the dance of the daughters of Herodias in the Middle Ages, Herodias doubtless taking the place of some old goddess. . . . They are almost always said to wear no covering upon their heads, and to let their hair stream out" (WAR65–66). In *The Celtic Twilight* Yeats reports that a young seer had described a faery to him as "a shining, winged woman, covered by her long hair" (37). Hair is an erotic image to the poet:

> Beloved, let your eyes half close, and your heart beat
> Over my heart, and your hair fall over my breast. (CP60)

> O curlew, cry no more in the air, . . .
> Because your crying brings to my mind
> Passion-dimmed eyes and long heavy hair
> That was shaken out over my breast. (60)

But it also provides a hypnotic protectiveness like a return to the womb when the female image offers it:

> The shadowy blossom of my hair
> Will hide us from the bitter storm. (58)

Then the ordering or arranging of the hair, which the woman does instinctively, symbolizes creative order, for which the poet must consciously labor:

> Fasten your hair with a golden pin,
> And bind up every wandering tress;
> I bade my heart build these poor rhymes:
> It worked at them day out, day in, . . .

> You need but lift a pearl-pale hand,
> And bind up your long hair and sigh;
> And all men's hearts must burn and beat. (61)

Once his cap and bells have been offered and accepted, the jester—in a manner poetically comparable to Yeats's life in spiritual marriage to Maud—becomes a kind of eunuch priest admitted to the divine presence and embued with the divine knowledge. After the sacrifice of his own potency, the order he had previously thought and dreamed comes to exist for him. His soul had become wise by thinking of the quiet feet of the Good Virgin and his heart sweet by dreaming of her hair folded into flower-like order. United with his queen, he finds that she truly fulfills his intellectual and imaginative ideal. Having turned over his creative power to her intuitive wisdom, he achieves Unity of Being and can create in its perfect assurance.

The jester says that he will send his cap and bells and die, but the death seems philosophical, as in the death and rebirth of Christianity. Yeats gives his explanation in "The Queen and the Fool" from *The Celtic Twilight*:

> What else can death be but the beginning of wisdom and power and beauty? and foolishness may be a kind of death. . . . Wisdom and beauty and power may sometimes, as I think, come to those who die every day they live, though their dying may not be like the dying Shakespeare spoke of [*Macbeth*, IV, iii, 109–111?]. (My115–16)

In the late plays the victory of the jester becomes both more physical and more generative as accomplished by the stroller and swineherd. By their deaths they manage to pull the queen from her throne and to impregnate her, thereby assuring their survival in the only way the primary world knows.

Yeats's figure of the jester or fool is of Celtic origin. He is the same Aengus Mac Og who appears to Aleel in the dream and urges him as the angel urged St. Joseph to take his Virgin and flee the evil times. He is the old Irish god of love, poetry, and ecstasy, who changed four of his kisses into birds that accompany and identify him as in Aleel's dream. Unlike Cupid or Amor, who only causes mortals to fall in love, Aengus suffers from passion himself. His existence is spent in pursuit of Edain, a mortal made immortal by his love but kept from him by human jealousies and subjected to shape-changings that range from fly to human to swan. In one story of Aengus's never-ending pursuit of Edain, the two fly off together as white swans joined by a golden chain. This image seems to have been in Yeats's mind when he wrote of "The White Swans at Coole"—lines that betray his own weary-heartedness with spiritual love:

> Unwearied still, lover by lover,
> They paddle in the cold
> Companionable streams or climb the air;
> Their hearts have not grown old;
> Passion or conquest, wander where they will,
> Attend upon them still. (CP129)

Aengus was the object of early magical evocations by Yeats and his friend AE, to whom the god sent his messenger as a fool dressed in white. AE saw him in a mystical version of the traditional setting of courtly love:

> . . . a white fool in a visionary garden, where there was a tree with peacocks' feathers instead of leaves, and flowers that opened to show little human faces when the white fool touched them with his cockscomb, and he saw at another time a white fool sitting by a pool and smiling and watching images of beautiful women floating up from the pool. (My115)

On a visit to Coole, probably in 1897 or 1898, AE saw the white jester about the corridors of the house (M125). Although the jester was not visible to Yeats, he believed that he had evoked him by his continual efforts at this time to evoke the old Celtic gods for the preparation of rites for the projected Castle of Heroes. He wrote to AE asking him to make a sketch of the white fool when next he saw him:

> Aengus is the most curious of all the gods. He seems both Hermes and Dionysus. He has some part perhaps in all enthusiasm. I think his white fool is going to give me a couple of lines in *The Shadowy Waters*. . . . (L324)[29]

Yeats said of *The Shadowy Waters* (1900) that its subject is "the whole story of the relation of man and woman in symbol" (L324) but admitted in notes included in the *Variorum Edition* that the play was "so overgrown with symbolical ideas" as to become "obscure and vague" (340). It can best be described as a dream of wish-fulfillment in which the hero Forgael uses magic to convince his queen Dectora that he is the resurrected lover for whom she grieves—her wish-fulfillment—and that they are in an eternal golden net of love. Under his spell of music, she turns from demanding his death to crown him with her own coronet and to cover him as the Queen covered the Jester with her flowing hair so that he will "gaze upon this world no longer" (CP426). It is a graphic enactment of love realized in death as well as of the creative intellect using its magical power suicidally to achieve its own submersion under the dual feminine symbols of hair and sea. George Harper says that the play "records the spiritual marriage of Yeats and Maud" and fittingly marks the "water-shed in Yeats's life" that occurred with Maud's marriage to John MacBride and with Yeats's disillusionment with the Order of the Golden Dawn, which had been the center of his Hermetic and Rosicrucian studies for over a decade.[30]

—6—

In April 1902, Maud Gonne appeared with great success in *Cathleen ni Houlihan* as the Old Woman who lures a young man away from his bride to become her lover, that is to fight for Ireland in the revolution of 1798. Representing the land itself, the Old Woman is clearly the Great Goddess as Mother. Yeats became familiar with the Great Mother through his researches into the Eleusinian Mysteries in 1897–98. He and Maud had studied together John Rhys's *Celtic Heathendom*[31] and Yeats had read Thomas Taylor's dissertation on *The Eleusinian and Bacchic Mysteries* as well as his translations of *Iamblicus on the Mysteries of the Egyptians, Chaldeans, and Assyrians* and of *The Mystical Hymns of Orpheus*, and probably Fraser's early works.

Yeats took the name Cathleen ni Houlihan from James Clarence Mangan's poem "Kathleen-Ni-Houlahan," written in the 1840s, and applied it to the traditional figure of the Shan Van Voght or Poor Old Woman who has lost her four green fields, the four ancient provinces of Ireland—Munster, Leinster, Ulster, and Connaught. The Poor Old Woman herself is, according to Professor Brendan P. O'Hehir, "one of a myriad avatars of the same person or goddess" who is originally "mana or totem of a cattle-based ancient culture."[32] Yeats's Cathleen says that she has never married but has had many lovers who have died for her. Beyond the immediate patriotic application, these lovers reappear in the slain gods of the plays *The King of the Great Clock Tower* and *A Full Moon in March*. The Old Woman promises immortality to the young men who follow her:

> They shall be remembered for ever,
> They shall be alive for ever,
> They shall be speaking for ever.
> The people shall hear them for ever, (CPy86)

but no spiritual transformation occurs and no spiritual gifts are bestowed. A primary figure not easily adaptable to antithetical courtly terms, the Old Woman enters the lives of the people as an irresistible force; the bridegroom follows her as if enthralled. Her eternal essence is established when a young boy who sees her leave the house reports that he saw no old woman but "a young girl, and she had the walk of a queen" (CPy88).

The play is a significant incident in the tug-of-war between Yeats and Maud in that she had obdurately refused to play his Countess Cathleen, his intellectual idealization of her, but succeeded handsomely when he let her have her own head in this primary role.

Yeats did attempt to return to the courtly mode once more in *The Player Queen*, which he began shortly after his reunion with Maud in Paris in June 1908, when she offered to renew their spiritual marriage. For Maud's sake Yeats tried to return to the old harness of self-denial. On November 9, 1909, he wrote in his Journal: "An ideal of love: To love with all desire and yet to be as kind as an old man past desire" (M235).

Like *The Countess Cathleen*, this play was ten years and more in the writing. It represents the evolution of the poet's feelings from his renewed attempt at spiritual marriage, which seemed to work much better for Maud on this second trial than for him, to his final proposal in 1917, and his arrival at the conclusion that Maud was more his child than his sweetheart.[33] This change of attitude parallels the change from enthrallment to pity in 1891 except that it carries recognition of a real failing in Maud, who was now in her forties. The genuine sadness of this recognition may have been the element that prevented Yeats from maintaining the high seriousness necessary to a work of courtly love. His own growing analytical trait led him to think objectively of Maud's condition rather than to experience it passionately, as he would have before 1903:

> I wasted the best working months of several years in an attempt to write a poetical play where every character became an example of the finding or not finding of what I have called the Antithetical Self; and because passion and not thought makes tragedy, what I made had neither simplicity nor life. I knew precisely what was wrong and yet could neither escape from thought nor give up my play. At last it came into my head all of a sudden that I could get rid of the play if I turned it into a farce; and never did I do anything so easily, for I think that I wrote the present play in about a month; and when it was performed at the Stage Society in 1919 I forgot that it was my own work, so completely that I discovered from the surprise of a neighbor, that, indignant with a house that seemed cold to my second act (since much reformed), I was applauding. If it only could have come into my head three years earlier. (Notes to edition of 1922, VPy1761)[34]

What remains of the courtly element in the final version of this play centers on an unhappy young queen, a recluse who has a unicorn for a lover. Just before he began *The Player Queen*, Yeats had finished revising a play based on Nietzsche's statement, "Where there is nothing, there is God." He had entitled the revision *The Unicorn from the Stars* (1908). The unicorn of that play is a symbol of Christ, of tireless, virginal strength. It was, in addition, a sacred Rosicrusian symbol for Yeats. To find it suddenly in a prose farce is surprising. *The Player Queen* also makes sport of other subjects that Yeats treated with great seriousness—the end of the Christian era, reincarnation, and the transmigration of souls. It is as though Yeats had reached a saturation point intellectually and emotionally, and in order to pick up these themes again with serious intent, he had to play the fool with them at this point. He still had in his imagination the example of Aengus, the holy fool. One more time before his death he would treat these concepts comically, but *The Herne's Egg* of 1938 would be tinged with bitterness, as *The Player Queen* is with relief.

The plot of the play is how the real queen escapes the wrath of her subjects, who want a ruler more human than she, and achieves the cloistered life that she wants by giving her throne to a young actress whose ambition has made her a bad wife to her actor husband. Among the characters, who have more numbers than names—Septimus, Octema, Nona, Decima—are distributed several attitudes of mind toward a single subject in the manner Yeats had early established in his novels *John Sherman* and *The Speckled Bird* and in his personae Michael Robartes, Owen Aherne, and Red Hanrahan. Septimus, an actor-poet, is very like Yeats. The women can be arranged in a hierarchy of ambition that for each except Nona involves a withdrawal from the world and hence a kind of self-destruction. Octema, who does not appear in the play, is a saint on the order of the Countess Cathleen except that her sanctity, instead of benefiting others as Cathleen's did, consists of remarkable feats of self-mortification. Beloved of a beautiful prince, she shut herself away from him in a tower on a mountain. The real queen desires to emulate Octema. She allows only the unicorn to make love to her and settles for a convent instead of a tower. Decima, the player queen, displays the childishness that Yeats saw in Maud in comic petulance until she ascends the queen's throne. Then donning the laughing mask of Noah's sister who drowned because she ignored his warnings, Decima banishes her former fellow-players in a willful but poignant speech:

> A woman player has left you. Do not mourn her. She was a bad, headstrong, cruel woman, and seeks destruction somewhere and with some man she knows nothing of; such a woman they tell me that this mask would well become, this foolish, smiling face! (CPy430)

Nona, the plain, steady, sensible actress, also has ambition. She would like to be Septimus's wife. She is already his lover. When Decima flaunts poems Septimus has written to her as guarantee of his passionate bondage to her, Nona reveals that Septimus wrote them in bed, not alone pining for Decima, but in bed with Nona, using her shoulder as writing table and her spine to tap out the rhythm. The revelation differentiates between the real woman with whom the poet has a full sexual and personal relationship and the ideal woman who is his myth and symbol. The differentiation at long last is laudable, but the castigation of Decima overlooks the fact that her head-strong childishness is the very product of the role that the patriarchal culture teaches women to play.

The details of the composition of the poems on Nona's shoulder and spine parody Yeats's own expressive mannerisms when composing verse:

> That one with the fourteen verses kept me from my sleep two hours, and when the lines were finished he lay upon his back another hour waving one arm in the air, making up the music. I liked him well enough to seem to be asleep through it all, and many another poem too—but when he made up that short one you sang he was so pleased that he muttered the words all about his lying alone in his bed thinking of you, and that made me mad. So I said to him, 'Am I not beautiful? Turn around and look.' O, I cut it short, for even I can please a man when there is but one candle. (CPy413)

This confession occurs in the second act that Yeats himself applauded. Nona has Septimus's good at heart in all things and puts her energy and practical sense into saving his acting company. Her loyalty and her humor reflect the personality of George Yeats, whom the poet married during his struggle to write the play. George seems never to have succumbed to jealousy; of all people she would have known best whether Maud still held her husband in thrall or whether, like Decima, she remained in his memory with the other beautiful and lofty things he had known "only as a myth and a symbol."

—7—

There is no record of Georgie Hyde-Lee's alighting into Yeats's life from a two-wheeled carriage. In the winter of 1911–12, Olivia Shakespear invited him to visit her brother Mr. Tucker and his wife, a former Mrs. Hyde-Lees. A few months later Yeats visited the Tuckers a second time and met Mrs. Tucker's nineteen-year-old daughter, whom Joseph Hone describes as having a keen sense of criticism and humor, naturalness, and practical ability.[35] Curtis Bradford's description of her only a year or two before her death coincides with Hone's: "I had a first impression of generosity, wit and great intelligence combined with eccentricity and a somewhat malicious enjoyment of the human comedy" (Hone. p. 306). She was interested in music and literature. She also became interested in Hermetic studies, for Yeats sponsored her membership in the Stella Matutina, successor to the Order of the Golden Dawn. Their courtship was low-keyed. Yeats was involved in a liaison with "an unmarried woman past her first youth"[36] and continuing his involvement with Maud. His proposal to George was almost off-hand. On September 19, 1917, having been rejected by Maud and her daughter Iseult, Yeats wrote to Lady Gregory:

I am going to Mrs. Tucker's in the country on Saturday or Monday at latest and I will ask her daughter to marry me. . . . I shall however make it clear that I will still be friend and guardian to Iseult. (L633)

They were married at the Harrow Road register office in London on October 20, 1917. Within a short time after their marriage, the prosaic quality suddenly changed. It was not that Yeats fell passionately in love with his wife or that marriage became an ecstatic experience to him. George was never exciting enough to become also threatening, to become a potential "fierce virgin," but she did prove capable of an uncanny union of mind with him.

On October 29, while they honeymooned at the Ashdown Forest Hotel in England, Yeats wrote again to Lady Gregory: "There has been something very like a miraculous intervention" (L653). Saying that she felt that something was to be written through her, George got a piece of paper and, talking all the while to Yeats so that her thoughts could not affect what she was writing, she put down a message that he interpreted as meaning that all was well with Iseult, over whom he was concerned. The "intervention" on the fourth day of their marriage (V8) was the beginning of a period of years during which George spent hours at a stretch responding to questions that Yeats posed first in automatic writing, then in mediumistic speaking.[37] This material went to make up Yeats's system of human history, personality, and afterlife published as *A Vision* first in 1927, then revised in 1938. In addition, George was Yeats's best secretary, typing draft after draft as he worked habitually through many revisions of his poems and longer works. She handled his business correspondence and oversaw the publication of his books, reading proofs with him and making corrected copies for his files.

At the same time she gave him an environment that was in his words "serene and full of order" (L634). Just as Laura Armstrong and Maud Gonne had taken up roles in Yeats's imagination, George took up a role in the plan of life that he envisioned. On May 16, 1917, with no idea who would live in it with him, Yeats purchased a Norman tower on what had been an outlying area of the Gregory estate, Coole Park, near Gort in County Galway. The land had been taken from the estate by the Congested Districts Board for redistribution among the people, but no one wanted the tower with its two adjacent cottages, all in ruins. Yeats bought it for thirty-five pounds and called it lovingly and almost reverently his "castle." George plunged enthusiastically into its restoration. Curtis Bradford says that she put far more of her own resources into it than Yeats's dedicatory plaque implies:

I, the poet William Yeats,
With old mill boards and sea-green slates,

And smithy work from the Gort forge,
Restored this tower for my wife George;
And may these characters remain
When all is ruin once again. (CP188)

The tower, by its proper name Thoor Ballylee, posed its own challenge to George's maintenance of order and serenity in the poet's life. It is located at the bank of a small river that frequently inundated the ground floor. George's daughter Anne remembers how the family would flee to the upper floors when the flood came and how, when the waters receded, her mother would descend first to clean out the mud and worms before Yeats came down.[38] Bradford summarizes George's contribution to the poet's life:

> George Yeats was his wife, mother of his children, favorite medium, interior decorator, cook, amanuensis, secretary, gardener, and business manager. She was the impresario who kept the show on the road.[39]

But the expression with which he closes his account of his acquaintance with Mrs. Yeats betrays his own understanding of the woman's place at the center of order in the life of the creative man. The last two sentences together make the point:

> I recalled the immense intellectual gusto with which she still faced the world. It seemed to me that George Yeats, too, loved life as passionately as had the great artist she had served.

In his opinion of George's place in Yeats's life, Jon Stallworthy strikes the same note: "Literature owes more to Georgina Hyde-Lees, whose automatic writing provided Yeats with the framework for most of the finest poems of his last twenty years, than to Maud Gonne."[40]

Although Yeats's marriage was an uncommonly good one, the marriage experience brought his theories down to earth. Marriage had been his symbol of the resolution of the Kantian antinomies, and as with all his symbols, he wished to prove that one magically demonstrable in the real world. In the same letter of 1899 in which he asked AE to sketch the white fool for him, Yeats, "spiritually" married, comments authoritatively on a symbol that AE has seen:

> It may be merely a symbol of ideal human marriage. The slight separation of the sun and moon permits the polarity which we call sex, while it allows of the creation of an emotional unity. (L324)

In January 1909, during his first efforts at renewal of the spiritual marriage, he made an entry in his Journal that reveals the antithetical extreme to which he had been forced by Maud's insistence that their love have no physical consummation:

> It seems to me that love, if it is fine, is essentially a discipline, but it needs so much wisdom that the love of Solomon and Sheba must have lasted for all the silence of the Scriptures. In wise love each divines the high secret self of the other and, refusing to believe in the mere daily self, creates a mirror where the lover or the beloved sees an image to copy in daily life. (M144–45)

Nine years later Yeats found the love of Solomon and Sheba a proper image for his marriage with its rare partnership of mind and body. By that same play of choice and chance that made Maud so perfectly the Celtic ideal with her great height and appleblossom-pale complexion, George's exotic appearance fitted her to be Yeats's Sheba.[41] Yeats could write of her as "that Arab lady," with "Arab eyes," and "dusky face." His delight in her darker coloring follows a change in his view of woman as myth and symbol to woman as wife and companion. In youth, imagining the proper woman to be the beloved of an artist, he had idealized Grecian features that roused Classical associations in his mind—Maud was Helen and Pallas Athene, Olivia Shakespear was Diana, and Florence Farr was Demeter, but he had a more physical taste for vivid coloring. He noted in his private diary that Olivia had skin, "a little darker than a Greek's would have been and her hair was very dark" (M72). He described George in a letter to his father as having "red-brown hair and a high colour which she sets off by wearing dark green in her clothes and earrings, etc."[42] Yeats called George's beauty "barbaric" in a verbal description to Iseult Gonne.[43] Francis Stuart, the novelist who married Iseult, remembers George as having bronze hair, sea-green eyes, and a Roman nose—appearing across the dinner table at their home in Merrion Square, Dublin, as "a candle-lit ikon." This was the appearance that Yeats made into the "dusky face" of the "Arab lady" who played Sheba to his Solomon.

After physical consummation had taken its natural part in his marriage, Yeats tried to bring into his old ideal roles that combination of eroticism and innocence that the metaphysical poets celebrated as essentials of love in *The Song of Songs*. But Yeats was not successful in bringing them together. Unlike the metaphysical poets, he had been molded by a Puritan age. The description of lovemaking in "Solomon and the Witch" (CP174) and "Solomon to Sheba" (136) cannot be called erotic. It might instead be called "censored" or veiled by abstract allusions, as when Solomon replies to Sheba's cry of love:

> . . . A cockerel
> Crew from a blossoming apple bough

Three hundred years before the Fall,
And never crew again till now.
And would not now but that he thought,
Chance being at one with Choice at last,
All that the brigand apple brought
And this foul world were dead at last. (175)

The passage starts with promise of passionate excitement but loses it when the abstractions Chance and Choice are brought in, demanding the attention of the intellect. Both poems are, in fact, more intellectual exchanges than love poems, and in the light of the rest of Yeats's attitude toward the primary, generative world, the last line reveals his underlying desire for a triumph of the intellect over the "foul" body. The body is "foul" because what the brigand apple brought to Adam and Eve was the knowledge that they were going to die. "Foul" would become a more and more prominent word in Yeats's verse as his own death approached. Knowledge of death affects the union of love because it is the knowledge that no matter how joyous the physical union, it cannot be permanent; therefore, it does not solve the antinomies of time and identity. In the preface to both editions of *A Vision*, Yeats has his philosophical persona Michael Robartes say,

> The marriage bed is the symbol of the solved antinomy, and were more than symbol could a man there lose and keep his identity, but he falls asleep. That sleep is the same as the sleep of death. (V52)

Sheba, in the poem, cries out, "O! Solomon! let us try again." Her faith is in the body, but Yeats's ultimate disappointment in the physical pursuit gives understanding in aftersight to his willingness to listen to such pleas as Maud made when she wrote to him after an astral union with him in 1909. She tells of a second dream, a sequel to the dream of union, in which they talked happily of the wonderful spiritual event she had just described. But Yeats, in the dream, says that it would serve to increase physical desire, and Maud is troubled: she wants to maintain the spiritual union beside which, in her estimation, the physical is a pale shadow.[44]

Yeats discusses the innocence of love in the enclosed garden in a poem that excludes the erotic by having as its subject not his wife but his infant daughter and the hypothetical bride that she will one day be. In "A Prayer for My Daughter" (CP185), the symbol of innocence is the rooted tree, inseparable from complete passivity. Stanley Stewart agrees that in the metaphysical poets there is overwhelming evidence that passivity is the proper attitude for the Bride.[45] He quotes St. Teresa: "The Lord is giving her the fruit from the apple-tree. . . . He picks it and cooks it and almost eats it for her."[46] In addition to likening her to "a flourishing hidden tree," Yeats prays further for his daughter's innocence and passivity in terms of her social environment:

> And may her bridegroom bring her to a house
> Where all's accustomed, ceremonious. (187)

Other lines make it clear that his intent is to keep her safe from the raging passions of the intellect, which he associates with the unenclosed streets:

> For arrogance and hatred are the wares
> Peddled in the thoroughfares.

As Maud's image hovers over the poem like a Jungian shadow, a threatening possibility for the infant daughter's development, so the streets in which she pursued her activist role seem to hover in Yeats's mind as the antithesis of the garden. He had told how Maud "hurled the little streets upon the great" in the earlier poem "No Second Troy" (December 1908, CP89). The image reflects a central assumption of nineteenth-century middle-class courtly love: The lady in the streets, for whatever purpose she is there, is no lady. At best she is an object of pity with no man to take care of her. At worst she is in the streets to lure men to sin or to encroach, as Maud did, into men's affairs.

Yeats's use of the verb "recovers" in speaking of the radical innocence of the soul after all hatred is driven hence implies a return to a previous innocent state. This element of recovery or cleansing of Sheba is present also in the metaphysical interpretation of *The Song of Songs*. Sheba complains, "I am blacke, but comely, (O ye daughters of Jerusalem)." She has been burned black, according to the Patristic consensus, because representing "man's desolate state," she has been subjected to the rays of the sun of God's Justice.[47] In the shade of the tree in the garden she will be sheltered from pure justice and supposedly will regain her proper color. Says Origen,

> That blackness for which you now reproach me will be
> banished from me so completely, that I shall be
> counted worthy to be called *the light of the world*.[48]

In his motif of purification that parallels the metaphysical allegory of Sheba, Yeats would bring his lady in from the streets and enclose her like a tree within his garden wall. There she will experience true self-realization as if by an existential revelation:

> Considering that, all hatred driven hence,
> The soul recovers radical innocence
> And learns at last that it is self-delighting,

Self-appeasing, self-affrighting,
And that its own sweet will is Heaven's will;
She can, though every face should scowl
And every windy quarter howl
Or every bellows burst, be happy still.

The passage about the soul's finding that its will is Heaven's will is not the solipsism it has been called and most certainly not a frustrated poet's sentimental expression of the ego-centricity that he would accept in a pampered woman. Yeats knew that his Unity of Being, fully realized, would be an unconscious, unquestioning state. Absorbing the whole personality, it would leave no place for a separate consciousness that would give it differentiation. The soul that achieved Unity of Being would have that "purity of a natural force" that he recognized in Maud Gonne and that made her seem complete in his eyes although he was unhappy with the direction he saw her force taking.

The sermon Yeats seems to be preaching to women can be read as his own pursuit. Unity of Being, which resembles that interiorization of sensitivity that Helene Deutsch calls the essence of the feminine, led Yeats in his early twenties to reject the externally oriented revolutionary path that would have taken him closer to success with Maud by making him more masculine in the manner of Millevoye and MacBride. He turned instead to seek Unity of Culture for Ireland. What he sought for the nation is close to what he sought for his daughter. He looked for the external identity of Ireland in her internal myth and folklore. He saw this distinction from other nations as far more important and far more lasting than mere political independence. That independence indeed was meaningless to him unless it could mean freedom to pursue Unity of Culture.

But the sermon preached to women in "A Prayer for My Daughter" departs from Yeats's own pursuit of Unity of Being in that the woman is to come to rest in the garden as the masculine speaker does not. Yeats's intent differs, for example, from that of the metaphysical poet Andrew Marvel, whose garden is furnished with images similar to Yeats's:

When we have run our Passions heat,
Love hither makes his best retreat.
The *Gods*, that mortal Beauty chase,
Still in a Tree did end their race.
Apollo hunted *Daphne* so,
Only that She might Laurel grow. . . .

The speaker in Marvell's poem does desire passivity in the garden for himself:

My Soul into the boughs does glide:
There like a Bird it sits, and sings.

But Yeats's soul is not the linnet that the wind can never tear from the leaf. The experience of his garden is wholly for the woman and her soul. Yeats was not seeking spiritual rest; he was seeking intellectual fulfillment. For all his attention to the female image and his recognition of the feminine within himself, Yeats was always a masculine poet. His unending desire was to create in the external male fashion that which in his art would parallel the *magnum opus* of the alchemists whom he had read. He had begun by discovering the eternal essence of the Virgin-enchantress in his early love ritual with Laura Armstrong. Having portrayed this essence in the courtly and mythological modes through half a lifetime and having made his ultimate magical evocation by the marriage symbol, he was still unsatisfied. He wanted to isolate and purify that eternal essence. In this poem he attempts to isolate it in the organic image of the linnet. This is his supreme effort in line with his courtly dream of finding his quiet Virgin in a real woman, in organic, *primary* material. Following this linnet would come in 1930 the golden bird of the Byzantine smithies, a bird that was purely inorganic, a "monument of unaging intellect." In the time of his own failing health and his attempt at rejuvenation through the Steinnach operation, this *antithetical* bird could

   . . . scorn aloud
In glory of changeless metal
Common bird or petal
And all complexities of mire or blood. (CP243)

The comparison with "common bird or petal" recalls the linnet and certainly the appleblossom, not the intellectual Rose, that were his organic emblems of perfection in woman.

His disappointment in the creation of the Ideal from organic material resulted not only from the aging and death inseparable from nature but also from its satiation, from what Shelley called "love's sad satiety." Yeats shortly found that the woman lost was a more compelling symbol than the woman won. He allowed Michael Robartes to explain:

"Love contains all Kant's antinomies, but it is the first that poisons our lives. Thesis, there is no beginning; antithesis, there is a beginning; or, as I prefer: thesis, there is an end; antithesis, there is no end. Exhausted by the cry that it can never end, my love ends; without that cry it were not love but desire, desire does not end." (V40)

Because desire cannot end, Yeats resurrected Maud as his phoenix (CP149). In the volume of poetry published in the second year of his marriage (*The*

Wild Swans at Coole, 1919) appear poems based severally on the conflicting currents of Yeats's view of women. In "Solomon to Sheba," he has discovered, having achieved love with as devoted a wife as any man has ever had, that

> There's not a thing but love can make
> The world a narrow pound. (136)

But in "On Woman" he praises God for the women who, like his wife, can give up all their minds to receptivity of the man's ideas. Yet he wrote at least five poems—"Her Praise," "The People," "His Phoenix," "Broken Dreams," and "A Deep-Sworn Vow"—that celebrate the untamed glory that Maud had been.

Evidence from this volume shows that Maud had indeed displayed the wisdom of the Virgin in her understanding of Yeats at the time of his proposal to her before her marriage to MacBride. The statement with which she closed did prove oracular. As she recalls it, Yeats began with an invitation to the garden:

> "Oh Maud, why don't you marry me and give up this tragic struggle and live a peaceful life? I could make such a beautiful life for you among artists and writers who would understand you."

> "Willie, are you not tired of asking that question? How often have I told you to thank the gods that I will not marry you. You would not be happy with me."

> "I am not happy without you."

> "Oh yes, you are, because you make beautiful poetry out of what you call your unhappiness and you are happy in that. Marriage would be such a dull affair. Poets should never marry. The world should thank me for not marrying you."[49]

3

The Cultural Quest

My medieval knees lack health until they bend,
But in that woman, in that household where
Honour had lived so long, all lacking found. (CP317)

—1—

Coexistent with Yeats's search for Unity of Being was his search for Unity of Culture, both Unities depending upon a unifying image. For Yeats the image of the first was the perfect sexual union; for the second it was the figure of the Good Mother as the point around which society is ordered. Just as Yeats found the myth and symbol of Unity of Being in the mode of courtly love that nineteenth-century scholars had inferred from the literature of the twelfth, thirteenth, and fourteenth centuries, he found the image for his second quest in terms of the courtly service of the Renaissance. As he cast the woman he loved in the role of Jean de Meun's Rose, so he sought a culturally unifying feminine image in the role of Castiglione's Duchess of Urbino.

He achieved his great success in the cultural quest in realizing for himself an aristocratic life that derived its order from a woman. The woman was Isabella Augusta Persse, Lady Gregory. The daughter of a distinguished family of the Protestant Ascendancy that Yeats associated with Shakespeare's Percys, she married a British diplomat, Sir William Gregory of Coole Park, County Galway. She was his second wife and some years younger than he, yet she stepped into his establishment smoothly and proved herself capable of the traveling, the entertaining, and the demanding protocol of her husband's position. She had one son, whose death in the Royal Flying Corps of World War I Yeats commemorated in several poems that echo Elizabethan courtliness. One poem refers to young Major Gregory as "Our Sidney and our perfect man" (CP131); the other, "Shepherd and Goatherd" (140–43), eulogizes him in a pastoral "like that Spenser wrote for Sir Philip Sidney" (L646).

Sir William died in 1892, and Lady Gregory met Yeats in August 1896 when he was staying with Edward Martyn at Tullyra Castle neighboring Coole. She invited Yeats to spend a few days that summer at Coole, and he made his first entrance to the estate riding on an outside car through the famous avenue of sheltering trees, a most feminine, mothering image. Lady Gregory was forty-four; Yeats thirty-one. The next year she took a flat in Queen Anne's Mansions, Westminster, where Yeats visited her, and with Edward Martyn they began plans for the Irish National Theatre, now popularly known as the Abbey. From 1897 until he married, Yeats spent part of every summer at Coole; then shortly before his marriage he purchased Thoor Ballylee, his "castle" located like a fief at the edge of the Gregory estate.

Lady Gregory was a woman of mythical proportions in the eyes of some who saw her relationship to Yeats. Oliver St. John Gogarty said that "her lunar encirclement of Yeats made his friends moonstruck."[1] Walter Starkie calls her first a mother and second an Egeria (the water goddess who advised the early Roman king Numa Pompilius); he saw Yeats caught until his marriage in conflict between Helen (Maud) and Egeria.[2] Some conflict is evident in Maud's account of how Lady Gregory asked her whether she intended to marry Yeats:

> It did not seem exactly her business, and I had answered rather shortly that we were neither of us the marrying sort, having other things which interested us more; and I had thought she seemed rather relieved.[3]

Maud's dislike of Lady Gregory went to her deepest level of feeling, the political. She accuses Lady Gregory of inviting the literary members of John O'Leary's group to her home not because of her interest in Gaelic literature but to "draw them away from too vehement expression of Irish Independence." In contrast Yeats says that Lady Gregory's favorite phrase whenever contemplating a new project was, "We work to add dignity to Ireland" (A456). Maud so much enjoyed watching Lady Gregory and Miss Annie Horniman, the wealthy English patroness of the theatre, compete for Yeats that she departed from the time-frame of her autobiography to include this interlude that took place in the years following her marriage to MacBride with which her book ends:

> Miss Horniman had the money and was willing to spend it, but Lady Gregory had the brains. They should have been allies for both stood for art for art's sake and deprecated the intrusion of politics, which meant Irish freedom; instead they were rivals; they both liked Willie too well. Lady Gregory won the battle; Miss Horniman's money converted the old city morgue into the Abbey Theatre, but it was Lady Gregory's plays that were acted there. Miss Horniman brought back Italian plaques to decorate it but Lady Gregory carried off Willie to visit the Italian towns where they were made and Willie's national outlook underwent a complete change. There would be no more poems against English kings' visits.[4]

As for Lady Gregory, she urged Yeats to marry after a woman announced that she was pregnant by him in 1914. She introduced him to several suitable young women but did not sponsor Miss Hyde-Lees, having spoken to her only once before she and Yeats were married.[5]

Corinna Salvadori credits Lady Gregory's mothering with the actual physical preservation of the poet who was in desperately poor health when he first visited Coole.[6] He was so run down that he could scarcely dress himself in the mornings. Lady Gregory ordered a cup of soup taken to his room when he was wakened. She had rugs laid over the carpets in the halls leading to his room. When Yeats was at Tullyra Castle working with George Moore on the play *Diarmuid and Grania*, Lady Gregory sent Moore written instructions that Yeats was not to go more than two hours without food—"a glass of milk, or, a cup of beef-tea in the afternoon, and half an hour after lunch he was to have a glass of sherry and a biscuit."[7] Moore also remembers how Lady Gregory showed him the back drawing-room at Coole that she had set aside for Yeats's writing: "I admired the clean pens, the fresh ink, and the spotless blotter; these were her special care every morning." Moore places Lady Gregory in the grand tradition of the supportive female by noting that instead of writing novels herself, "she had released the poet from the quern of daily journalism."[8] He is right about the release she provided Yeats, but he overlooks the plays and books of folklore that she did write.

Lady Gregory was Yeats's patron in every medieval and Renaissance sense. In *Dramatis Personae, 1896–1902*, he recalls the formative years of the Irish theatre and carefully notes her gifts and benefits to the project and to himself. Besides the large parcels of food and wine sent to him at Woburn Buildings, she supplied furniture, curtains, "a great leather arm-chair" that George Yeats still had when Bradford called on her, and cash:

> One night when she and the other guests had gone I found twenty pounds behind my clock. I went to see her and tried to return it. "You must take this money," she said. "You should give up journalism. The only wrong act that matters is not doing one's best work." . . . From time to time from that on she gave me money. I was not to consider it a loan, though I might return it some day if well off. When I finished my first lecture tour in the United States, the winter of 1903–4, I tried to return it, but she said: "Not until I think you have enough money to feel independent." . . . Four or five years later she consented. I asked how much; she said, "Five hundred." It was a shock to find I owed so much. (A408)

Her patronage had its disciplinary edge: when Yeats's health improved, he felt indolent, and she set him a schedule with specific hours for writing and for letters. He comments, "I doubt if I should have done much with my life but for her firmness and her care" (A377).

In his accounting of debts to Lady Gregory, Yeats also mentions that her great collection of folklore provided him material for essays that brought ten or fifteen pounds from monthly reviews. Her research in tales and in the Kiltartan dialect—"the idiom of the peasant who speaks in English and thinks in Gaelic"⁹—was a real contribution to Irish knowledge and to the inspiration of both Yeats and John Millington Synge. In 1907 Yeats revised his stories in *The Secret Rose* with Lady Gregory to "put the Irish" on them. It began as part of her mothering, a therapy of interest and exercise— walking across fields from cottage to cottage of the estate tenants—designed to lie "'very light upon the mind'" of the sick man. George Moore remembers that it was Lady Gregory who entered the stifling cottages in summer while Yeats sat in the shade and fanned himself. But her research began to have value in her eyes for its own sake. Without neglecting her new responsibility for Yeats or her old responsibilities to the estate or to her son, who was seventeen and already away at school when Yeats arrived, she became a prototype of the contemporary woman whose mind begins to open and grow after she has fulfilled and passed the time of her biological and social domestic roles.

Yeats records how as a younger woman she had "written two or three articles, such as many clever fashionable women write, more recently had edited her husband, Sir William Gregory's, *Autobiography* and *Mr. Gregory's Letter-Box*, a volume of letters to Richard Gregory, Irish Under-Secretary at the beginning of the nineteenth century" (A456). But he saved his admiration for the adult character of her later writings—character in a woman obviously being no longer a problem for him when the woman's beauty was not essential to her symbolic role:

> Sometimes in her letters, in her books when she wrote ordinary English, she was the late-Victorian woman turning aside from reality to what seems pleasing, or to a slightly sentimental persiflage as to a form of politeness . . . but in her last years, when speaking in her own character, she seemed always her greater self. (A456–57)

Lady Gregory did not play the Victorian woman turning aside from reality when she took up the challenge of the professor at Trinity College who described ancient Irish literature as "'silly, religious, or indecent'" (456); she thought her work necessary for the dignity of Ireland.

Not only her devotion to research but also her creativity surprised Yeats. From the beginning he had assumed that her contribution to the Irish theatre would be financial: "Neither she nor we thought her a possible creator. And now all in a moment, as it seemed, she became the founder of modern Irish dialect literature." Yeats's assessment that her comedies have "merriment and beauty" (380), which he calls an unusual combination, agrees with the terms of "A Prayer for My Daughter":

> Nor but in merriment begin a chase,
> Nor but in merriment a quarrel.

And he adds that her two volumes of Irish heroic tales[10] function where woman has her great mythological ability; they "may do more than other books to deepen Irish imagination" (A380). He could applaud her work because it was concrete: Irish identity embodied in a heroic tale; the sound of an Irish voice in a written sentence. It was such art for art's sake that Maud despised; her art for propaganda's sake was the "old bellows full of angry wind" that he described in the poem for his daughter. Not being an assertion of abstract opinion—"something other than human life"—Lady Gregory's work did not became her stone doll. It enriched her; it did not absorb her. It had nothing to do with hate. She must have provided a dramatic contrast in Yeats's mind at the time of his reunion with Maud, for in his Journal of 1909 he seems preoccupied with hatred and its effects upon the one who hates.

Yeats's analogy for hatred is again castration, the same image as that for coming to terms with the Virgin in the works of his personal quest. The difference is that the castration of hatred is of the intellect, and act in the *antithetical* world where it equals breaking the mirror of External Reason. Instead of putting the *primary*, generative energy into the service of the creative intellect, it literally, "cuts off" the creative power of the intellect:

> The political class in Ireland—the lower-middle class from whom the patriotic associations have drawn their journalists and their leaders for the past ten years—have suffered through the cultivation of hatred as the one energy of their movement, a deprivation which is the intellectual equivalent to the removal of the genitals. Hence the shrillness of their voices. They contemplate all creative power as the eunuchs contemplate Don Juan as he passes through Hell on the white horse. (M176)

Yeats liked the analogy so much that he wrote what he had said to Lady Gregory (March 8, 1909, L525) and made it the central image of his poem, "On Those that Hated 'The Playboy of the Western World,' 1907" (CP109). Yeats makes the same substitution of male parts that the medieval poets did following the Biblical tradition:[11] the eunuchs in Hell crowd to stare on Juan's "sinewy thigh."

In a later Journal entry Yeats pursues the idea that hate may be an evocation that can work "beyond the senses" to alter events, particularly to render sterile:

> Certain individuals who hate much seem to be followed by violent events outside their control. Maud Gonne has been so followed always. . . . Certainly evocation with symbol has taught me that much that we think of as limited to certain obvious effects influences the whole being. A meditation on sunlight, for instance, affects the nature throughout, producing all that follows from the symbolical nature of the sun. Hate must, in the same way, make sterile. . . . Hatred as a basis of imagination, in ways which one could explain even without magic, helps to dry up the nature and makes the sexual abstinence, so common among young men and women in Ireland, possible. This abstinence reacts in its turn on the imagination, so that we get at last that strange eunuch-like tone and temper. (M176–77)

In Yeats's mind culture was the specific that could rid the intellect of hate. "Culture," he wrote in his Journal, March 1909, "is the sanctity of the intellect" (M179), and again pleased with the thought, repeated it to Lady Gregory in a letter, explaining that he was thinking of the profesional revolutionaries of Ireland ("men like Griffith"), who, lacking culture, could renounce external things in behalf of their cause but could not renounce envy, revenge, and jealousy (L525). He pursued the idea throughout his Journal entries of that spring:

> All empty souls tend to extreme opinions. It is only in those who have built up a rich world of memories and habits of thought that extreme opinions affront the sense of probability. All propositions, for instance, which set all the truth upon one side can only enter rich minds to dislocate and strain, if they can enter at all, and sooner or later the mind expels them by instinct. (M151)

> A mind without traditional culture, moral or literary, is only powerful in hate. A clever man unhelped by a synthetic social ideal, or the remnant of it which lives on as culture in certain social regions, becomes an executioner. (181)

He calls the culture of a society a "synthetic" ideal, that is, an ideal made up of parts, the unity of which can, he says, be "defined and evoked by Unity of Image" (A269). The synthesis of parts, the Unity of Culture, can be so fully achieved that the literature, for example, "though made by many minds, would seem the work of a single mind" (254). Yeats had from his earliest association with the Young Ireland movement sought to bring the Irish writers to agree with him upon an image to unify modern Irish culture. In those days his idea of image had come from the Middle Ages. Then, in April 1907, Lady Gregory took him on a tour of northern Italy, the seat of the Renaissance. Hone tells how Yeats had gone doubting into this area because he had thought of the Renaissance as the shattering of Medieval unity.[12] At Urbino, however, Yeats found his unifying image of the Renaissance, not in Duke Ercole, who built the silver-and-gold palace with its magnificent library and its theatre devoted to Plautus, but in the "wise Duchess" who presided over all.

Culture had been itself feminine to Yeats because the cultured individual, in his earlier definition of the term, receives and reflects, deliberates and discriminates. He sees himself "face to face with what is permanent in the world" and his "soul becomes a mirror, not a brazier." Yeats prefers the education of Oxford University, where Pater's ideal of culture produces "feminine souls," to the education of Dublin that produces pedants for whom the world remains external, in the spirit of masculine detachment and abstraction. He cites Newman's definition of culture as "wise receptivity" and says that "culture of this kind produces the most perfect flowers in a few high-bred women" (M159–60). The culture of the Renaissance differed from

Yeats's earlier ideal in that it was not founded so much upon self-knowledge as upon knowledge of some other self, "Christ or Caesar." Because of the feminine matrix that the Duchess provided, the more external, more masculine culture could flourish. The new view of culture combined with his admission of the hollowness of merely spiritual love and his discovery of the uses of comedy to bring about a mid-life transition for Yeats.

Lady Gregory had introduced him to Castiglione's *The Book of the Courtier* as she read to him in the summer evenings of 1904, that bleak year when Maud was MacBride's wife and having her child by him. Yeats was especially receptive then; his Countess Cathleen gone, he needed a new myth and symbol for his own unifying image. In "The People," written eleven years after those evening readings, Yeats lays the two images side by side for comparison: his memory of Maud, who had lived in deed rather than thought like a natural force, and his vision of the Duchess, who created a house of intellectual delights:

> . . . I might have lived,
> And you know well how great the longing has been,
> Where every day my footfall should have lit
> In the green shadow of Ferrara wall;
> Or climbed among the images of the past—
> The unperturbed and courtly images—
> Evening and morning, the steep street of Urbino
> To where the Duchess and her people talked
> The stately midnight through until they stood
> In their great window looking at the dawn;
> I might have had no friend that could not mix
> Courtesy and passion into one like those
> That saw the wicks grow yellow in the dawn. (CP148–49)

Even reconciliation with Maud could not satisfy him in his new role of Renaissance courtier. She could never represent a finely balanced masculine order. Yeats was no longer being merely personal; he spoke of his new quest in broader cultural terms: "Perhaps we may find in the spectacle of some beautiful woman our Ferrara, our Urbino. Perhaps that is why we have no longer any poetry but the poetry of love" (M156). For this quest he adjusted his interpretation of beauty away from the apprehension of the eternal essence in a beautiful physical body to appreciation of that essence manifest directly in mind or soul:

> In what toils, in what life, in what war of the Amazons did women, whose beauty is more than the promise of physical pleasure and an easy path to get it, win their beauty? For Castiglione says, speaking the high Urbino thought, that all such beauty 'is the spoil and monument of the victory of the soul'. (M157)

In Sir Thomas Hoby's translation, which Lady Gregory read to Yeats, Castiglione says even more specifically, "Beautie . . . with her light over-commeth the darknesse of the bodie."[13]

As Yeats's courtly mode moved into the Renaissance, the cultural symbol of the house replaced the natural symbol of the pool or fountain as mirror of the feminine presence and reflector of intellectual ideal. Even his introduction to Lady Gregory's house was a step out of the "medievalism of William Morris" that made him at first reject the heavily ornamented gold frames around pictures in the drawing room. It was the "rich world of memories and habits of thought" that he came to prize in the house:

> . . . here many generations, and no uncultivated generation, had left the images of their service in furniture, in statuary, in pictures, and in the outline of wood and of field. I think I was meant not for a master but for a servant, and that it has been my unhappiness to see the analytic faculty dissolve all those things that invite our service, and so it is that all images of service are dear to me. (M102)

Her house was Lady Gregory's passion when Yeats met her and became more so as it took its place in the public life of Ireland. Yeats attributed her concern to "her own strange feudal, almost medieval youth" that gave her a "sense of feudal responsibility, not of duty as the word is generally understood, but of burdens laid upon her by her station and her character, a choice constantly renewed in solitude" (392–95). He seemed most struck by the combination of pride and humility in her character. He believed that her ability to interpet the heroic tales of ancient Ireland had its roots in "her inherited sense of caste, her knowledge of that top of the world where men and women are valued for their manhood and their charm, not for their opinions" (A456).

Coole Park became an especial concern of Yeats when it was threatened first by Irish land reform and later by the death of the heir and the aging of Lady Gregory. In relation to the first threat Yeats asks,

> How should the world be luckier if this house,
> Where passion and precision have been one
> Time out of mind, became too ruinous
> To breed the lidless eye that loves the sun? . . .
>   Although
> Mean roof-trees were the sturdier for its fall,
> How should their luck run high enough to reach
> The gifts that govern men, and after these
> To gradual Time's last gift, a written speech
> Wrought of high laughter, loveliness and ease? (CP93)

In relation to the second he celebrates the house in years just preceding Lady Gregory's death in 1932. He places his own timid-hearted portrait among the men who gathered at his Duchess's court:

I meditate upon a swallow's flight,
Upon an aged woman and her house. . . .
Great works constructed there in nature's spite
For scholars and for poets after us,
Thoughts long knitted into a single thought,
A dance-like glory that those walls begot.

There Hyde before he had beaten into prose
That noble blade the Muses buckled on,
There one that ruffled in a manly pose
For all his timid heart, there that slow man,
That meditative man, John Synge, and those
Impetuous men, Shawe-Taylor and Hugh Lane,
Found pride established in humility,
A scene well set and excellent company.
They came like swallows and like swallows went,
And yet a woman's powerful character
Could keep a swallow to its first intent. . . . (CP238)

Yeats has so founded his courtly myth of the Duchess upon Lady Gregory that when she fell ill in 1909, he rehearsed his role of grieving courtier in his Journal. The imagery of the house remained in his thinking, for he wrote that the "thought of losing her is like a conflagration in the rafters. Friendship is all the house I have" (M161). But the Mother image also flashed through his thoughts in something of a hallucination:

I did not recognize her son's writing at first, and my mind wandered. . . . I thought my mother was ill and that my sister was asking me to come at once: then I remembered that my mother died years ago and that more than kin was at stake. She has been to me mother, friend, sister and brother. I cannot realize the world without her—she brought to my wavering thoughts steadfast nobility. (160–61)

When Lady Gregory herself wrote on February 6 to say that she had "'very nearly slipped away,'" he found his mind still obsessed by the words of *The Courtier*:

All Wednesday I heard Castiglione's phrase ringing in my memory, 'Never be it spoken without tears, the Duchess, too, is dead.' . . . and I felt all his sorrow as though one saw the worth of life fade for ever. (M163)

When Lady Gregory died in May 1932, Yeats's reaction was deep and genuine. He could not write verse for several months. It was as though he had written more of the truth than he had known when he said, "I cannot realize the world without her," for she had been the unifying image of culture for him.

It was at the Royal Court of Sweden on December 10, 1923, that the course of Yeats's imaginative role of courtier crossed the path of reality,

"Chance being at one with Choice" again as it had in his marriage. The following day he thanked the Swedish Royal Academy for selecting him to receive the Nobel Prize for Literature, saying,

> When your King gave me medal and diploma, two forms should have stood, one at either side of me, an old woman sinking into the infirmity of age and a young man's ghost. I think when Lady Gregory's name and John Synge's name are spoken by future generations, my name, if remembered, will come up in the talk, and that if my name is spoken first their names will come in their turn because of the years we worked together. I think that both had been well pleased to have stood beside me at the great reception at your Palace, for their work and mine had delighted in history and tradition. (A553–54)

Yeats recapitulated some of his own history in those two royal days that he recounted in *The Bounty of Sweden* (1924). When a "very beautiful, stately woman" asked him a question about his psychical research, he began an analytical, factual answer but suddenly dropped away from the level of intellectual exchange to his old worship of the eternal essence of Beauty in the living woman. His closing phrase of the account recalls the passing feet of the Rose of the World:

> Then I stop ashamed, for I am talking habitual thoughts, and not adapting them to her ear, forgetting beauty in the pursuit of truth, and I wonder if age has made my mind rigid and heavy. I deliberately falter as though I could think of nothing more to say, that she may pass upon her smiling road. (A542)

Then, as he was later informed to his delight, he distinguished himself by his courtly manners before the Royal Family. After receiving his medal from the King, Yeats first glanced at the face of the Princess Margaretha, in whose impassive beauty he saw "that final consummate strength which rounds the spiral of a shell" (540), and then walked with great dignity, backwards, up a flight of five steps in adherence to the court etiquette that he had never rehearsed except in his imagination. It was years later that he heard that members of the Royal Family had singled him out from the other prize winners as the one with the manners of a courtier.

Yeats records how his meditations while waiting to be presented at the Court reception ran on the courtly service of women. He thought how the Irish had always been good lovers of women and had served only one abstract cause, the political entity of Ireland, personifying it as a woman. He compared the service of woman to the service of a Court and pictured to himself the exiled Irish nobility of the seventeenth century awaiting at a Court the woman's smile or frown that would determine their future in a foreign land. That picture of proffered service led him to a kind of self-explanation:

> I . . . thought that there were men living, meant by nature for that vicissitude, who had served a woman through all folly, because they had found no Court to serve. (545)

But after thought of folly, his mind came to rest upon Lady Gregory and Urbino, the Court that she had made real to him:

> Then my memory had gone back twenty years to that summer when a friend read out to me at the end of each day's work Castiglione's commendations and descriptions of that Court of Urbino where youth for certain brief years imposed upon drowsy learning the discipline of its joy, and I remembered a cry of Bembo's made years after, 'Would that I were a shepherd that I might look down daily upon Urbino'. (545)

—2—

Having meditated upon the similarity between service of woman and service of a Court, both of which can give concreteness to the abstract cause, Yeats recited to himself what he could remember of Ben Jonson's address to the Court that he served, couched in the feminine archetypal terms of water and mirror:

> Thou art a beautiful and brave spring and waterest all the noble plants of this Island. In thee the whole Kingdom dresseth itself and is ambitious to use thee as her glass. Beware then thou render men's figures truly and teach them no less to hate their deformities, than to love their forms. (A545–46)

Woman's place in patriarchal culture therefore stood in Yeats's mind as it had stood in Jonson's and in Bachofen's: woman was to serve as man's reflector, guide, and reminder of his highest intellectual and spiritual potential. If she had a beautiful body, as did Maud Gonne and Florence Farr, she could be a visual and physical inspiration to man the creator; if not, she could like Lady Gregory achieve that beauty which is the spoil of the victory of the soul and become his intellectual inspiration. She could become enthroned motherhood in the sense of the *primary* world's offering itself to be shaped and interpreted by the *antithetical* ideal. The proper attitude of *primary* woman toward *antithetical* artistry is expressed in Yeats's particular terms of sculpting or doll-making. The doll-maker's wife, who has proved her primary function by producing a living child from her own body, sets her own creation aside to sympathize with the antithetical dream of her husband, whose designs seek a perfection beyond the primary world:

> A doll in the doll-maker's house
> Looks at the cradle and bawls:
> 'That is an insult to us.'
> But the oldest of all the dolls, . . .
> Out-screams the whole shelf: . . .
> 'The man and the woman bring
> Hither, to our disgrace,
> A noisy and filthy thing.'
> Hearing him groan and stretch
> The doll-maker's wife is aware

Her husband has heard the wretch,
And crouched by the arm of his chair,
She murmurs into his ear,
Head upon shoulder leant:
'My dear, my dear, O dear,
It was an accident.' (CP124)

Yeats, a doll-maker himself, cries out against the discord and decay of the generative world in a poem addressed to the Rose:

All things uncomely and broken, all things worn out and old,
The cry of a child by the roadway, the creak of a lumbering cart,
The heavy steps of the ploughman, splashing the wintry mold,
Are wronging your image that blossoms a rose in the deeps
    of my heart.

The wrong of unshapely things is a wrong too great to be told;
I hunger to build them anew and sit on a green knoll apart,
With the earth and the sky and the water, remade, like a casket
    of gold
For my dreams of your image that blossoms a rose in the deeps
    of my heart. (54)

For all the beautiful *antithetical* compliment of having the earth and the heavens remade into a golden casket fit to contain her beauty, the *primary* woman knows that such remaking will alienate her from the world in which her archetype of birth and death functions. That which seems to be offered in tribute to her is really an unnatural demand placed upon her. Service *of* woman is really the *antithetical* interpretation of service *by* woman. Under the *antithetical* deference, the *primary* conflict seethes.

William Blake, from whose poem "The Mental Traveller" Yeats derived his prototypal masculine and feminine, depicted that conflict as alternate dominance of the forces. First a Woman Old takes the male Babe and

. . . nails him down upon a rock,
Catches his shrieks in cups of gold.

She binds iron thorns around his head,
She pierces both his hands & feet,
She cuts his heart out at his side
To make it feel both cold & heat.[14]

But as the Babe grows into his strength the Woman grows younger to become "Virgin bright" over whom the male dominates:

Then he rends up his Manacles
and binds her down for his delight.

> He plants himself in all her Nerves,
> Just as a Husbandman his mould;
> And she becomes his dwelling place
> And Garden fruitful seventy fold.

Pursuing his antithetical way, the masculine figure transforms all "the gems of the Human Soul" into the inorganic:

> The rubies & pearls of a lovesick eye,
> The countless gold of the akeing heart,
> The martyr's groan & the lover's sigh.

But from nature new energy springs in form of a Female Babe who drives the man from his house, and the archetypal images of the female which he has redesigned to his own use disappear:

> The Cottage fades before his sight,
> The Garden & its lovely Charms.

Under her reign Blake's land of Beulah, the land of generation, reappears until the frowning masculine energy is reborn and the Woman, now grown old,

> . . . nails him down upon the Rock,
> And all is done as I have told.

So runs the alternating pattern similar to that which underlies the system of historical gyres and cones that Yeats called *A Vision*. The alternating gyres or spiral movements represent the basic rhythm of human existence and can apply in any duration of time to any human situation, individual or collective, but the major duration with which Yeats is concerned is the Great Year or era of two thousand solar years. In the chapter "Dove or Swan" (V267–300), he analyzes the Great Years of Christianity and the Grecian era that preceded it.

The Great Years are themselves alternately *primary* and *antithetical*, and each is divided into *primary* and *antithetical* millenia. Each Great Year and each millenium also passes through twenty-eight developmental stages that Yeats calls the Phases of the Moon, giving his entire system a foundation in the feminine lunar terms as well as in feminine, or internalized, thinking since the system is, as he states it to be, another myth and symbol, an imaginative reconstruction of the objective, external events of history.

Being feminine, these phases and the Great Years that they compose cannot depict a mathematical, mechanistic theory of history such as would delight the masculine principle. Their success does not exactly reproduce the past because all movements are under spiritual direction from what Yeats calls the *Thirteenth Cone*, or the sphere. Again the terms are feminine, thirteen being, according to Robert Graves, the number of the White Goddess, his name for the eternal feminine, because thirteen lunar months fill the masculine solar year. Yeats's alternative term, the "sphere," corresponds to Neumann's Great Round. That directing sphere, which is simply "There," is the ultimate Unity of all Being, perhaps in itself the spawning-ground of new Chaos to be followed by new Creation:

> There all the barrel-hoops are knit,
> There all the serpent-tails are bit,
> There all the gyres converge in one,
> There all the planets drop in the Sun. (CP284)

Finally, the source of the system is feminine, not archetypally or mythologically, but quite directly. Yeats derived it from the quantity of automatic writing that his wife did in the early years of their marriage. According to the spirits who spoke through her, the material revealed was to provide him with a new metaphorical system for his poetry. His analytical masculine drive had to work over the material twice before he was satisfied with its order.

Under the influence of the *Thirteenth Cone*, each Great Year must be a reversal of the previous one and must resume all past eras. It proceeds on the order of Blake's poem with a *primary* dispensation rising out of the feminine principle, an irrational revelation symbolized by woman and bird and accompanied by the collapse or destruction of the existing *antithetical* dispensation:

> A civilization is a struggle to keep self-control, and in this it is like some great tragic person, some Niobe who must display an almost superhuman will or the cry will not touch our sympathy. The loss of control over thought comes toward the end; first a sinking in upon the moral being, then the last surrender, the irrational cry, revelation—the scream of Juno's peacock. (V268)

Yeats pictured the progressions of phases and the rising and falling of the feminine and masculine principles as conical motions he called "gyres." They are analogous to winding staircases, such as the stone stairs at Thoor Ballylee for which he named one of his later collections (*The Winding Stair and Other Poems* of 1933), except that the gyres are in constant flux of widening and closing and widening again as phases and principles change or reverse themselves.

The Great Year of Greece that reached its secular, *antithetical* apex in the fifth century B.C. began in the *primary* irrational act of divine annunciation to Leda, her impregnation by Zeus in the form of a swan and the resulting birth of children whose destinies led to the event that gave a unifying image to Greek culture, the Trojan War:

A shudder in the loins engenders there
The broken wall, the burning roof and tower
And Agamemnon dead. (CP212)

Yeats believed that this generative act also signaled the end of the preceding Great Year whose culture had turned *antithetical* and had achieved all that it could, or was destined to, by the determination of the *Thirteenth Cone.* Of that culture, to which he had assigned the scream of Juno's peacock as starting signal, he admits that he had no full concept:

. . . and when in my ignorance I try to imagine what older civilisation that annunciation rejected I can but see bird and woman blotting out some corner of the Babylonian mathematical starlight. (V268)

Similarly, when the Annunciation was made to the Blessed Virgin Mary—into which scene the Medieval painters insisted on introducing the Dove of the Holy Spirit although the Third Gospel specifies the Angel Gabriel as the messenger—a careful system of masculine intellect was overthrown. In the five hundred years before the birth of Christ, the secular philosophers of Greece had imposed a system of intellectual unity on the old religion that had turned *antithetical*, hierarchical, and multiple, or polytheistic. "Plato thinks all things into Unity," says Yeats (V262–63), but the advent of Christ undoes intellectual structure and initiates a new *primary* religious dispensation that begins in intellectual chaos of blood and miracle:

The Roman Empire stood appalled:
It dropped the reins[15] of peace and war
When that fierce virgin and her Star
Out of the fabulous darkness called . . .
Odour of blood when Christ was slain
Made all Platonic tolerance vain
And vain all Doric discipline. (CP210–11)

Yeats's interpretation does not stand alone, for St. Paul himself said that the message of the Crucifixion was "to the pagans madness" (I Corinthians 1:23 in the Jerusalem Bible).

The chart titled "Succession of Primary Dispensations" shows the progression of the Greek and Christian Great Years with the female figures that supplied the unifying images at each change.

Phase I of the Greek era shows Leda at the head of the *primary* religious dispensation and Helen, springing from the creative intellect of Homer, at

2. The Succession of Primary Dispensations

The Greek and Christian Great Years

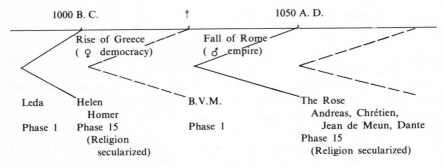

1000 B. C.   †   1050 A. D.

Rise of Greece   Fall of Rome
(♀ democracy)   (♂ empire)

Leda   Helen   B.V.M.   The Rose
          Homer   Andreas, Chrétien,
Phase 1   Phase 15   Phase 1   Jean de Meun, Dante
          (Religion   Phase 15
           secularized)   (Religion secularized)

Solid lines = religious dispensations; broken lines = secular dispensations

the head of the *antithetical* secular dispensation that begins at Phase 15, halfway through the twenty-eight phases that Yeats gave to each Great Year.

The Christian era begins with the Blessed Virgin Mary and becomes secularized when the Rose, the intellectual construction of Jean de Meun, appears representing similar ladies of courtly love created by such other poets as Chrétien de Troyes. Dante's Beatrice, who leads her lover to the presence of the Blessed Virgin, is not so secularized as the Rose, but the ladies who appear in Andreas's *De Amore* are *antithetical* to the point of satirizing love itself.

In every dispensation, Yeats conceives history as operating through four *faculties*. Two of them, the *Will* and the *Creative Mind*, relate to what man does with the external world and ideas. They are therefore the masculine faculties. The other two, the *Mask* and the *Body of Fate*, relate, respectively, to man's view of himself and to his inherited and informing factors and, therefore, are feminine. These faculties are the feminine and the masculine that Yeats associates with the woman and the man of Blake's "The Mental Traveller" (V262).

In a *primary* dispensation, the feminine faculties dominate the Solar cone of the religious and vital aspects of the civilization; the masculine faculties dominate the Lunar, secular and political aspects. In the *antithetical* dispensation the positions are reversed. In the reversal of the Great Year of the Greeks, Plato's Will and Creative Mind put the anti-thetical remnants of Greek religion into order as an act of the intellect in contrast to the act of irrational revelation with which that religion had begun—the annunciation to Leda.

In the diagram on page 117, adapted from the chart in V266, the shaded

3. Phases of the Great Year

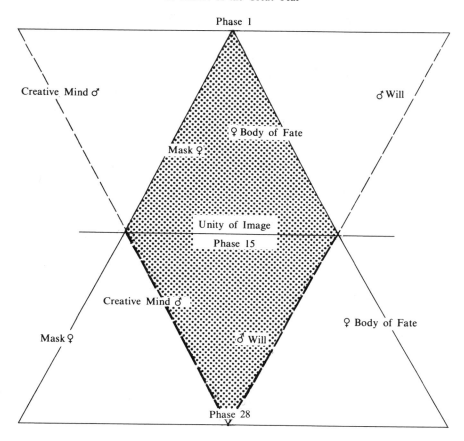

diamond represents the Solar cone of the religious and vital aspects of the era; the hour-glass shape represents the Lunar or secular life of the era. The solid lines trace the movement of the feminine faculties; the broken lines trace the masculine. Phase 1, or the Dark of the Moon, is the phase out of which the feminine revelation comes: for the Christian era, the Annunciation to Mary. Phase 15 is the Full of the Moon at which masculine and feminine, religious and secular are unified in an Image; Yeats set this phase of the Christian era at 1050 A.D. and identified it with the appearance of courtly love. It also coincides with the beginning of the veneration of the Blessed Virgin.

At Phase 15, the Full of the Moon, there is no "human" life because all intellect is transformed into beauty. The body, rendered inorganic through art, becomes totally Mask. The feminine body becomes the perfect mirror, reflecting the masculine ideal. It is the supreme image of beauty as it "embodies" the supreme achievements of the Will and Creative Mind, which have created the idea of beauty (V135–37). Woman has become not only sex-object but entire intellect-object. She is completely the projection of man's mind, his metaphor. As the culture adopts intellectual perfection of face and body—which a few exceptional women like Maud Gonne have by genetic and social accident—as the "norm" for all, millions of women are induced to lead lives of artifice and artificiality striving for what Yeats calls "no human life." The rebellion of women against such a "norm" illustrates the democratic "leveling" force of the secular feminine as Yeats describes it, just as the imposition of the "norm" illustrates the hierarchical secular masculine.

Phase 28 is the phase of the collapse of the era entering the darkness that will produce the next revelation from the feminine, as Yeats asks of the coming revelation that will begin the post-Christian era,

> And what rough beast, its hour come round at last,
> Slouches towards Bethlehem to be born? (CP185)

At Phase 1, the Dark of the Moon, human life again disappears because Will and Creative Mind have been absorbed into the body, which has become the feminine without intellectual form, completely passive, plastic, "dough-like" (183–84): "All that has been knowledge becomes instinct." Yeats is closely supported by the psychologist Esther Harding in his seemingly mystical statement that human life disappears at the Full and the Dark of the Moon.[16] She points out that the masculine principle makes the intellect (Logos) God and increases rational control of nature. In its view, the feminine power (Eros) is daemonic, releasing images from the unconscious, the instinctive. Since the human mind comprises both the conscious and the unconscious, neither pure intellect nor pure instinct can be called human.[17] Harding also makes analogy of realistic and abstract art to masculine and feminine expression, much as Yeats does in prophesying the imminence of Phase 1 from twentieth-century abstract art (V299–300):

> Abstraction which began at Phase 19 will end at Phase 25, for these movements and this science will have for their object or result the elimination of intellect.

As Yeats passed his sixtieth birthday, he moved into a period of longing for "monuments of unaging intellect." Probably because of his age, he took as his ideal Phase 15 of the first Christian millenium rather than Phase 15 of the entire Christian era, the phase of courtly love. His poetic symbol of this phase of intellectual embodiment is Byzantium at the year 560:

> I think if I could be given a month of Antiquity and leave to spend it where I chose, I would spend it in Byzantium a little before Justinian opened St. Sophia and closed the Academy of Plato. (V279)

4. The Great Year of Christianity

This diagram divides the Christian era into its two millenia and shows the entrance of *Creative Mind* and *Will* into religious life at the rise of secular dispensation in Phase 15 of the Great Year. It emphasizes the reversal of principles by which religious life, which begins in the feminine, becomes masculine, and secular life becomes feminine.

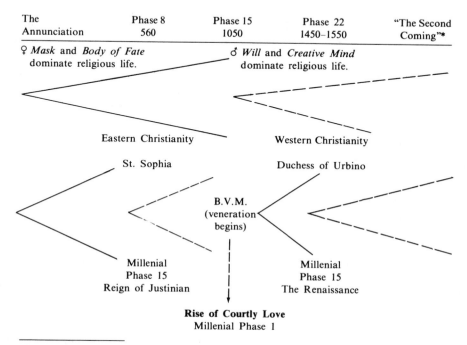

| The Annunciation | Phase 8 560 | Phase 15 1050 | Phase 22 1450–1550 | "The Second Coming"* |

♀ *Mask* and *Body of Fate* dominate religious life.

♂ *Will* and *Creative Mind* dominate religious life.

Eastern Christianity

Western Christianity

St. Sophia

Duchess of Urbino

B.V.M. (veneration begins)

Millenial Phase 15 Reign of Justinian

Millenial Phase 15 The Renaissance

Rise of Courtly Love Millenial Phase 1

*A *primary* religious revelation that will break the secular order. Love will be for "some living person, and not an image of the mind" (V140).

That exact moment in the administration of the Emperor marks the advent of Phase 15 because he removes secular control from masculine Plato, who *thinks* things into Unity, and places it in the feminine image of Sophia, where it is embodied rather than thought. Of the leveling aspects of this Unity in the feminine, Yeats says,

> I think that in early Byzantium, maybe never before or since in recorded history, religious, aesthetic and practical life were one, that architect and artificers—though not, it may be, poets, for language had been the instrument of controversy and must have grown abstract—spoke to the multitude and the few alike. . . . They would copy out of old Gospel books those pictures that seemed as sacred as the text, and yet weave all into a vast design, the work of many that seemed the work of one, that made building, picture, pattern, metal-work or rail and lamp, seem but a single image. (279–80)

The architect of St. Sophia, who gave thought body, corresponds to Phidias, sculptor of Phase 15 of the second millenium of the Greek era. By his idealizing the human body in marble, Phidias is, in Yeats's opinion, the true founder of Western secular civilization. By embodying intellect in his sculpture, he overcame the "vague immensities" of Asiatic art (CP322). In the last stanza of "Byzantium" artists like Phidias, the Emperor's "golden smithies," themselves more intellect than body, meet and re-create the continuously generated images from the sea, the same feminine flood that produced the "many-headed foam at Salamis":

> Astraddle on the dolphin's mire and blood,
> Spirit after spirit! The smithies break the flood,
> The golden smithies of the Emperor!
> Marbles of the dancing floor
> Break bitter furies of complexity,
> Those images that yet
> Fresh images beget,
> That dolphin-torn, that gong-tormented sea. (244)

Phidias not only imposed form on the body, but he also imposed the idea of form into the minds of women, giving them dreams so that they could become the mirrors of those dreams. They could reflect intellectual beauty as Maud reflected it for Yeats, in the body not the mind:

> If . . . her face, like the face of some Greek statue, showed little thought, her whole body seemed a master work of long labouring thought, as though a Scopas had measured and calculated, consorted with Egyptian sages, and mathematicians out of Babylon, that he might outface even Artemisia's sepulchral image with a living norm. (A364–65)

Phase 15 is the phase of Unity of Being and of Culture, for when the image is embued not with its own intellect but the intellect of the artist, worshipper and worshipped become one. When the woman as image is embued not with her own intellect but with the man's, when she "gives up all her mind" (CP144), then the feminine and the masculine are one. But this Unity is, of course, on masculine terms; the opposite, Unity on feminine terms, would produce Phase 1, the Dark of the Moon, where all knowledge is instinct and all form plastic.

In the Unity of Phase 15, which Yeats called the superhuman phase, complexity of life disappears. When it reappears, it has had an *antithetical* revelation. Religion loses its domination; the secular dispensation begins. In Phase 16 Western man realized or came to the opinion that he was not in the unity of God but a separate being from God, from nature, and from other men:

> When the tide changed and faith no longer sufficed, something must have happened in the courts and castles of which history has perhaps no record, for with the first vague dawn of

the ultimate *antithetical* revelation man, under the eyes of the Virgin, or upon the breast of his mistress, become but a fragment. (V285)

Yeats illustrates the effect of the revelation with a comparison of parables:

> A certain Byzantine Bishop had said upon seeing a singer of Antioch, "I looked long upon her beauty, knowing that I would behold it upon the day of judgment, and I wept to remember that I had taken less care of my soul than she of her body", but when in the *Arabian Nights* Harun Al-Rashid looked at the singer Heart's Miracle, and on the instant loved her, he covered her head with a little silk veil to show that her beauty "had already retreated into the mystery of our faith". The Bishop saw a beauty that would be sanctified, but the Caliph that which was its own sanctity, and it was this latter sanctity, come back from the first Crusade or up from Arabian Spain or half Asiatic Provence and Sicily, that created romance. What forgotten reverie, what initiation, it may be, separated wisdom from the monastery and ... joined it to passion? (286)

Yeats says that in the phases immediately preceding and following Phase 15 "the greatest human beauty becomes possible" (V131). In Phase 14 "are born those women who are most touching in their beauty":

> Helen was of the phase; and she comes before the mind's eye elaborating a delicate personal discipline, as though she would make her whole life an image of a unified *antithetical* energy. While seeming an image of softness and of quiet, she draws perpetually upon glass with a diamond. Yet she will not number among her sins anything that does not break that personal discipline, no matter what it may seem according to others' discipline. ... She will wander much alone as though she consciously meditated her masterpiece that shall be at the full moon. ... Is it not because she desires so little, gives so little that men will die and murder in her service? (132–33)

It is significant that women of this phase, who have become so externally passive, so close to being the masculine ideal of courtly love, have truly given up all their minds. Yeats says of the feminine faculties of this phase that the Body of Fate is that of the Child and the chosen Mask is that of the Fool (137):

> One thinks of the "Eternal Idol" of Rodin: that kneeling man with hands clasped behind his back in humble adoration, kissing a young girl a little below the breast, while she gazes down, without comprehending, under her half-closed eyelids. Perhaps, could we see her a little later, with flushed cheeks casting her money upon some gambling table, we would wonder that action and form could so belie each other, not understanding that the Fool's Mask is her chosen motley. (133)

The Fool's Mask, he says, "covers her terror before death and stillness." Culturally fated to remain ever the Child, she cannot cope with death and stillness. Surely from his own experience Yeats comprehended the terrifying emptiness he was describing in these women-idols. The "half-closed eyelids" that he recognized in the Rodin sculpture are those of his own Rose, before whom he had once knelt in adoration:

Far-off, most secret, and inviolate Rose,
Enfold me in my hour of hours; where those
Who sought thee in the Holy Sepulchre,
Or in the wine-vat, dwell beyond the stir
And tumult of defeated dreams; and deep
Among pale eyelids, heavy with the sleep
Men have named beauty. (CP67)

That sleepy emptiness is beauty only because the masculine intellect has named it so. To the woman it is the void of her own alienation, and she fills it with whatever is at hand to grasp. That she does so surprises and dismays the man:

One thinks too of the women of Burne-Jones, but not of Botticelli's women, who have too much curiosity, nor Rossetti's women, who have too much passion; and as we see before the mind's eye those pure faces gathered around the "Sleep of Arthur," or crowded upon the "Golden Stair," we wonder if they too would not have filled us with surprise, or dismay, because of some craze, some passion for mere excitement, or slavery to a drug.[18]

By Phase 16, the women, still beautiful, have been caught up in the rise of *antithetical* secular intellect. They have turned from seeking fulfillment in the passive power of inspiration and have made that power active as a fulfillment in its own right. They have dropped the Mask of the Fool and adopted the Mask of Illusion, which Yeats calls "true" because they have consciously adopted it. Their Body of Fate is no longer the Child but Enforced Illusion. Thus, to be an illusion is the whole conscious thrust of their lives as well as what their environment enforces upon them. They have learned the masculine game and are on their way to becoming dominant players. Their intellect, subordinated to the Body of Fate, becomes cruel and narrow, deforming the Mask so that their masculine faculty, the Will, is blinded to all except its desire until "there is nothing left but the fixed idea and some hysterical hatred" (138).

If Helen, in her Fool's Mask and Child's Body of Fate, uncomprehendingly caused men to die and murder in her service, these women will consciously devote themselves to that same purpose. They will also give themselves to their own destruction. They are untouched by what they do because their alienated intellects can give them no true self-image. The accommodation of feminine and masculine principles is therefore accomplished at the height of courtly love by the provision of boundless illusion in the female to satisfy boundless desire in the male:

Here too are beautiful women, whose bodies have taken upon themselves the image of the True *Mask*, and in these there is a radiant intensity, something of "The Burning Babe" of Elizabethan lyric. They walk like queens, and seem to carry upon their backs a quiver of arrows, but they are gentle only to those whom they have chosen or subdued, or to the dogs that follow at their heels. Boundless in generosity, and in illusion, they will give themselves to a beggar because he resembles a religious picture and be faithful all their lives, or if they take another turn and choose a dozen lovers, die convinced that none but the first or last has ever touched their lips, for they are of those whose "virginity renews itself like the moon." (139-40)

In the phrase that he quotes, Yeats arrives at the ancient pagan definition of "virgin," a woman whose virginity has nothing to do with the Christian ideals of purity or chastity but only with her independent, unmarried status. Harding describes such a virgin as a "one-in-herself woman" who neither remains chaste nor yields to an unwanted embrace. Among the Greek goddesses only the virgins or *parthenai* like Aphrodite and Demeter were really deities. The married goddesses like Hera were really fading manifestations of the Great Mother whose places had been usurped by their male counterparts, now their "husbands."[19] Mortal *parthenai* were often *hierdules* or sacred prostitutes whose union, *hieros gamos*, with priest or stranger representing one of the nature gods insured fertility of the land.[20] The *hieros gamos* was actually a purifying act that insured the virginity of the *parthenos*,[21] a concept carried over into Christianity in the mystical marriages of some of the female saints and in Donne's lines: addressed to the Holy Spirit: "Nor ever chast, except thou ravish mee."

The vestige of *parthenos* in women of Yeats's Phase 16 functions through their adoption of the same abstracting by which men look at women and draw myth and symbol from them. The woman of Phase 16 gives herself to a beggar because of the myth or symbol she sees in him. This yielding to an illusion might be feasible in the real world if it were not for the objectivity that lies at the base of patriarchy. The masculine principle can never participate in the feminine; the woman being outside the man will forever be an object for him to judge. The more she is willing to embody his conscious illusions, the more she loses her own objectivity and the more she becomes inferior in his judgment. Although he may long for her to give up all her mind to him and become a reflector of his own intellect, he can always see her objectively enough to know how she destroys herself in her yielding. While lesser men pride themselves on what fools they can make of women, greater men like Yeats come to admit after all their worship of the embodied intellectual ideal that "indeed, perhaps if the body have great perfection, there is always something imperfect in the mind" (V140).

With the separation of the faculties and the growth of the *primary* secular life that begins in Phase 16, Yeats says that history prepares for "those who love some living person, and not an image of the mind." Then he adds, "As the new love grows the sense of beauty will fade." So it must, for as woman becomes a living person, she ceases to be myth and symbol. In the terms of Blake's alternating dominance, the Female Babe has grown up and has driven the Man from the house:

The Cottage fades before his sight,
The Garden & its lovely Charms.

4

Recapitulation and Critique

Why must those holy, haughty feet descend
From emblematic niches . . . ?

For desecration and the lover's night.

(A Full Moon in March)

When he had less than five years to live, some events of Yeats's life began to recapitulate his earlier relationships with women. With the actress Margot Ruddock he experienced something of the fascination and drive to re-create the object of the fascination that he had known with Maud Gonne and Florence Farr. In Dorothy Wellesley he found a new Duchess and in her home at Penns in the Rocks, Sussex, a new Urbino. But this recapitulation was accompanied by a repudiation of the tenets of courtly love. The repudiation began in the sterility of "spiritual marriage" and in the satiety of real marriage, which although ideal in an earthly sense still had those limitations imposed by reality to which the imagination cannot be subject. Courtly love as myth and symbol of cultural order also proved to have its limits in that the Lady around whom the culture is organized represents only the positive aspects of the Virgin and the Good Mother. As his own age advanced and as he studied his system of Great Years, Yeats became more and more aware of the potency of the negative aspects of the feminine. He had tried to make woman the emblem of perfect stasis in the *antithetical* garden, but he found that as *primary* nature, she was the image of disintegration and Chaos. He had finally learned that the pose of the courtly lover is a double denial. First, the Lover denies the femininity of his own psyche to project those qualitites on his Lady and then to possess them again through possession of her. Second, the Lover denies his Lady the wholeness of her nature, rejecting in her those things which he would for whatever subjective reason not want to make part of himself. The Lover's stance violates even the original myth of the garden, in which it is God and not Adam who creates the woman. Adam does have to give up part of himself in her creation, but when she is brought to him, he recognizes her as the Mother, not as his mirror, and he shortly finds himself because of her expelled from the world of *primary* innocence and forced forever to deal with the *antithetical* abstractions of good and evil.

This is the new view of the myth that appears in Yeats's period of recapitulation and critique. The Lover and his Rose are replaced by the Mother goddess and the slain god. Yeats's youthful romantic poses become poses of madness, extreme asceticism, and what he understood of femininity itself.

—1—

In May 1934 Yeats submitted to the Steinach operation for sexual rejuvenation. Richard Ellmann comments that Yeats's health, which had been unsteady since Lady Gregory's death, remained so after the Steinach procedure but that Yeats did receive a burst of energy and that "his attitude towards his maladies was changed."[1] So also was his attitude toward sex changed. In March 1937 Yeats wrote to decline an invitation from his friend Shri Purohit Swami to lecture in India on what Roger McHugh calls "somewhat unusual" grounds:

> Please tell him [the Swami's master] of the operation I went through in London and say that though it revived my creative power it revived also sexual desire; and that in all likelihood will last me until I die. I believe that if I repressed this for any long period I would break down under the strain as did the great Ruskin.[2]

The new value and even sense of urgency placed upon sexual activity is more than "somewhat unusual." It represents a facing turn not only from his youthful extravagance of romanticism that thought "one woman, whether wife, mistress, or incitement to platonic love, enough for a life-time," but also from the importance he had given the complementary identity of the woman as symbolized in the relationship of Solomon and Sheba. For the rejuvenated Yeats, the identity of the woman was unimportant, emotional joy had all but disappeared, and intellectual appreciation of beauty had become almost peripheral.

The change in Yeats's attitude toward love is well illustrated in his affair with the actress Margot Ruddock.[3] She initiated their meeting by writing to him in September 1934 to ask advice for one of her many projects, the establishment of a poet's theatre in London. He was then sixty-nine; she twenty-seven. Margot resembled Maud in her external orientation to a public life. She also had, as Yeats wrote in the preface of the volume of verse he helped her to publish,[4] "distinguished beauty of face and limb." She was an actress and a poet, and she aspired, as he did, to an immortal achievement. Her "intellectual passion," as he called it, was channeled toward beauty as he had once so greatly wished Maud's to be. In contrast to Maud, Margot won Yeats's interest at first with her intellect instead of her physical presence. In 1889 Yeats had discounted what Maud said, choosing only to see the goddess in her. In 1934 he was won by a word. In her first letter Margot used "trueness" rather than "veracity," the word other admirers used, to describe his works. He responded, "That you had found this word your own word, made me see you, it was as though I saw your face."[5] His immediate reaction was that she should become his mirror, but a mirror to show him other people's ideas, not to reflect his own: "When I was young I think I wanted to be deceived, but now I want wisdom always or as much as my blind heart permits."[6]

His passionate attachment to her seems to have come and gone quickly. The only published letters that can be called "love letters" occur in October and November 1934: "I see your image always before me, that image of kindness, sweetness, beauty. Should you have to go on tour London will have no charm for me though some other city may have."[7] The last clause may mean that he would follow her on tour. His poem "Margot," sent in a letter but never published, praises her lovely eyes and admits that a great part of his joy in her is the joy in his own rejuvenation:

All famine struck sat I, and then
Those generous eyes on mine were cast,
Sat like other aged men
Dumfoundered, gazing on a past
That appeared constructed of
Lost opportunities to love.[8]

Other lines recall his Rose poems with their hint of transforming power behind half-closed eyes:

When half closed her eye-lid lies
A sort of hidden glory shall
About these stooping shoulders fall.

But the second stanza begins with anxious questions:

O how can I that interest hold?
What offer to attentive eyes?

He seems to have feared a return of the old nervous impotency. He tells her that he awoke in "utter black gloom," thinking "'perhaps after all [a reference to the Steinach operation?] this nervous inhibition has not left me'—I pictured Margot unsatisfied and lost."[9] Then he tells her how George, sensing his low spirits, had arranged an evening for him with "Ireland's chief wit Gogarty," and he had invited still another wit along. Among them they exchanged "Rabelaisian stories of the Dublin slums" for five hours. Yeats explains that such talk is to him what ale and the public house are to her.

The ribaldry that so distressed Monk Gibbon in Yeats[10] seems to have become his practical remedy for the quietus that feminine beauty imposed on him.

Another practicality robbed their liaison of romantic elegance. Yeats instructs Margot to write to him at his home in Dublin because "my wife knows that we work on the theatre project. It is more natural if you write there."[11] Later he reassures her: "Write here and as you will, there will be no accidental opening."[12]

Even as his passionate interest began to wane, he viewed her more and more as an object of art. He took her to Edmund Dulac to learn to speak and to Frederick Ashton to learn to move. He began to revise her poetry and introduced the plan of her reading his works to the zither as Florence Farr had read them to the dulcimer. He rewrote the first song in *The King of the Great Clock Tower* so that it referred to her charms, again her eyes, and promised that he would add lines to the part of the silent queen for her to speak, but that change was never made. He thought Margot resembled Decima in *The Player Queen*—another association with Maud—but when Nancy Price produced the play at the Little Theatre in October 1935, she cast Margot in the lesser role of the true queen, and Yeats did not interfere. He did manage, however, to have Margot read in three of his four broadcasts on the BBC in 1937 in spite of some criticism of her work, and he included seven of her poems, with his revisions, in *The Oxford Book of Modern Verse* (1936), which he edited.

But his letters become only friendly from 1935 while she continues to sign, "I love you darling," a phrase he had not written to her. Her letters give forewarning of the breakdown that occurred in mid-May 1936 when she followed him to Majorca in order that, in her words, "Yeats will tell me if I am a good poet, Shree Purohit Swami if I have a right to live."[13] When she arrived at 6:30 in the morning, Yeats was not prepared to answer. He had not looked at the sheets of poems she continued to send in various letters even after he had told her to stop writing verse because her technique was getting worse. While he hastily read, she wandered away in bedroom slippers borrowed from the Swami and the next day went to visit friends in Barcelona. There, as Yeats recounted to Olivia Shakespear, she

> went mad, climbing out of a window, falling through a baker's roof, breaking a kneecap, hiding in a ship's hold, singing her own poems most of the time. The British consul in Barcelona appealed to me, so George and I went there, found her with recovered sanity sitting up in bed at a clinic writing an account of her madness. It was impossible to get adequate money out of her family, so I accepted financial responsibility and she was dispatched to England and now I won't be able to afford new clothes for a year. (L856)

Yeats had certainly behaved decently, but his last remark shows him personally detached from the pathos of Margot's madness. When he returned to England after her breakdown, he did not see her. He feared a scandal which the newspapers, encouraged by Margot's publicity-seeking husband, seemed about to start, and he told Olivia in the same letter,

> When I am in London I shall probably hide because the husband may send me journalists and because I want to keep at a distance from a tragedy where I can be no further help.

Then he adds his plans for a characteristic flight to the woman who had become the center of cultural order for him since Lady Gregory's death: "I am going to Lady Gerald Wellesley's, and shall go as soon as possible."

When Margot was permanently committed at the end of 1937, a year of seeming recovery during which Yeats continued enough interest in her to include her in his broadcasts, he was saddened; but her illness never became the passionate concern Maud's soul-destroying intensity had been. His real detachment did not, however, prevent his imaginative myth-making. In "A Crazed Girl" he adds Margot to his list of "beautiful lofty things." He sees her as heroically defiant in her madness, removed from the ordinary as Maud had been when she stood taller by her whole arrogant head than the crowd that day at Howth station:

> That crazed girl improvising her music,
> Her poetry, dancing upon the shore,
> Her soul in division from itself
> Climbing, falling she knew not where,
> Hiding amid the cargo of a steamship,
> Her knee-cap broken, that girl I declare
> A beautiful lofty thing, or a thing
> Heroically lost, heroically found.
>
> No matter what disaster occurred
> She stood in desperate music wound,
> Wound, wound, and she made in her triumph
> Where the bales and the baskets lay
> No common intelligible sound
> But sang, 'O sea-starved, hungry sea.' (CP301)

In his other published poem on Margot, Yeats depicts her final freedom in insanity before the Spanish *Guardia* take her away to the clinic. He implores them to "Let her finish her dance" (CP294). The refrain of the poem: "*Ah, dancer, ah, sweet dancer!*" associates Margot with another system of images in Yeats's verse that has to do with the cosmic or metaphysical dance. His drawing of so abstract a myth and symbol in such detachment stirs the memory of Maud's statement to him: "You make beautiful poetry out of what you call your unhappiness and you are happy in that."

But Yeats's abstraction of poetic emotion from the real tragedy reached a deeper level of cold-bloodedness in that he had Margot herself read this second poem on the broadcast of April 22, 1937. The producer George Barnes remembers especially "the lilting way in which Yeats taught her to speak '*Ah, dancer, ah, sweet dancer.*'"[14]

—2—

Even before Yeats's brush with real madness in his relationship with Margot Ruddock, crazed figures had appeared in his poetry: Crazy Jane and Tom the Lunatic as early as 1930. Crazy Jane, originally Cracked Mary, is based on the old peasant women of Ireland that Yeats had known all his life and had always thought figures for the imagination:

> In Dublin I had often seen old women walking with erect heads and gaunt bodies, talking to themselves with loud voices, mad with drink and poverty . . . they belonged to romance. Da Vinci had drawn women who looked so, and so carried their bodies. (A155)

One of the earliest and most memorable of such women was his Uncle George Pollexfen's servant Mary Battle, who had the gift of second sight whereby she laid places at table for unexpected guests and dreamed in response to the magical evocations that Yeats and his uncle practiced after she had retired for the night (A258–60). She frequently saw the women of the Sidhe and once Queen Maeve, whom she described in homely detail: "'She had no stomach on her . . . she looked about thirty'" (A266).

Crazy Jane is untamed by the patriarchal culture. She is, therefore, a new voice in Yeats's work, unlike the Rose, who has no speech, and Sheba, who speaks the role set down for her in the masculine imagination. In her garden—under the shelter of a "blasted oak" at midnight—she debates the Bishop, the patriarchal culture's spokesman, about her unsanctified union with a highwayman, the culture's antihero. Their very argument is mad because the highwayman is dead, and both Jane and the Bishop are, by reason of her aged decay and his vow of celibacy, beyond the pale of sexual enjoyment. Nevertheless, they are both lustful, she openly envying the young in their procreative dance and he, under his garments of "holy black," twisted by his repression and desire. His arguments of *antithetical* lawfulness are lost on her because she lives in the *primary* world of absurdity and disorder. The evidence she sees proves to her that the same Heavens that yawn at nature's vast destructiveness labor over perfecting the whorl of a seashell. She rejects any reaching beyond the known physical for the unknown abstract: in her opinion, Europa "played the fool" when she left a human lover to let herself be carried away by a god.

The Bishop appeals to Jane to forget the "foul sty" of sexuality and to think now in her old age of a "heavenly mansion" for her soul, but she rejects the antithetical separation of fair and foul. "Fair and foul are near of kin," she insists, "And fair needs foul. . . . nothing can be sole or whole that has not been rent" (CP254-55). In her *primary* clear-sightedness she deals the coup de grace to all the idealization in courtly love by calling the Bishop's attention to what the *antithetical* lover finds the most offensive juxtaposition in all nature: " . . . Love has pitched his mansion in / The place of excrement."

Jane's knowledge of love differs from that of the archetypal Witch who imprisons men's wills under glamorous spells. She deals in the sophisticated economics of love. She is aware that sexual delight is a finite substance that must be wisely managed even against the urgency of desire:

I know, although when looks meet
I tremble to the bone,
The more I leave the door unlatched
The sooner love is gone.

A woman intent on the love of an *antithetical* man might have to don a mask "proud and stiff," but all this restrictive management that gives love temporal duration also kills its *primary* intensity, and herein is the paradox that she cannot easily accept:

'Love is all
Unsatisfied
That cannot take the whole
Body and soul'.

Faced with the choice, she takes intensity over duration and remains true to her primary self: "Take the sour / If you take me," she warns.

Further, she knows that love is of time and of the body, "a skein unwound between the dark and dawn." Although she believes that the return to God is a "leap into the light" lost to the human spirit at the moment of its physical conception, it is "a lonely ghost' that makes the return.

Jane's observations on the universe are played against an antithetical chant of "*Fol de rol, fol de rol,*" and when she interprets the murderous ferocity of the dance of the young lovers, the other voice changes to an agonized refrain, "*Love is like the lion's tooth.*" In view of Yeats's stated dislike of Jane and his concentration on memories of the painful hollowness of love in his youth, both the refrains can be taken to be the voice of the poet objecting to all that Jane is forcing him to see. If so, it seems to be a weak, even inarticulately "feminine" response to the *primary* baldness of Jane's thinking. It is, of course, the weakness and inarticulateness of a new beginning, a new evaluation. In his next book of verse, *A Full Moon in*

March (1935), Yeats can speak most clearly of his position and the change he has undergone. He would now rather be "anything else but a rhymer / Without a thing in his head / But rhymes for a beautiful lady. / He rhyming alone in bed" (CP 281), and he has learned to pray, "God guard me from those thoughts men think/ In the mind alone; / He that sings a lasting song / Thinks in a marrow-bone." He has arrived at wanting to think himself in the way he had once wanted a woman to think—with the body.

—3—

Harold Bloom calls *Words for Music Perhaps* (1932), in which Jane and Tom appear, "Yeats's Mad Songs."[15] From that volume on through *The Winding Stair* (1933), *A Full Moon in March* (1935), and into *Last Poems* (1939), images of madness multiply. Yeats recalls the madness of youth and concludes in age that

> Even Cicero
> And many-minded Homer were
> *Mad as the mist and snow.* (CP261)

He demands, "Why should not old men be mad?" (333) In terms of his own Phases of the Moon, he is long past his Fifteenth Phase of Unity. The intellectual is no longer embodied in the generative in these images: the feminine no longer reflects the masculine ideal. After his long struggle to bring the antinomies together, the goal so nearly realized in his marriage of Solomon and Sheba and in his re-creation of the Court of Urbino, Yeats approaches the Dark of the Moon in which the generative overwhelms the intellectual. His madness is the madness of the multiplicity of the generative world, against which the masculine principle turns desperate. It is as though he had turned from the art of Phidias to celebration of those "vague immensities" of the "many-headed foam" which Phidias was once celebrated as having overcome.

Like a man who has tired his eyes with pulling images together, Yeats relaxes the focus and revels in the contrasts between what the spiritual masculine has constructed and what the physical feminine is. The elements separate for him as do oil and water, or in Yeats's words, "Oil and Blood," In that poem, first published in 1929, the monument of the spiritually purified—based on the story of St. Teresa, a Virgin-bride among Christian mystics—differs from the remains of the blood-sodden:

> In tombs of gold and lapis lazuli
> Bodies of holy men and women exude
> Miraculous oil, odour of violet.

But under heavy loads of trampled clay
Lie bodies of the vampires full of blood;
Their shrouds are bloody and their lips are wet. (CP234)

Yeats also draws the difference between spirit and blood as polarities of theology in "Veronica's Napkin." The spiritual is couched in the old familiar images of his old high way of love: Berenice's hair is the drapery of the "Tent-pole of Eden," a figurative variation of the woman as tree in the garden. This "magnitude and glory" is a construct of the masculine principle made by "The Father and His angelic hierarchy," but there is also another construct: "Some found a different pole, and where it stood / A pattern on a napkin dipped in blood." The "different pole," being the Cross of Christ, marks the beginning of the new feminine religious millenium of Christianity.

Of this poem and its companion "Byzantium" (CP243), a masculine tirade against "all complexities of mire or blood," Yeats said that he warmed himself back into life after an illness in 1927, "looking for a theme that might befit my years" (CP457).

As he contemplates the two poles of comprehension, so he also yields again to multiplicity of speakers and personae. His early intellectual seekers Robartes, Aedh, Mongan, and Hanrahan had once come smoothly together in the Lover of the Rose, one man in devotion to one clear symbol. In his last poems it is as if the gyre had reversed itself to open again. Like the culture described in "The Second Coming," his center could no longer hold and the blood-dimmed tide was rushing in on the ceremony he had so carefully constructed from his fardel of legend and romance.

The character of Crazy Jane stands out as a key to Yeats's mental condition at this period of his life and work. He was, as are many creative writers, aware of a "real" existence of the figures he had created. "The Circus Animals' Desertion" (CP335) especially demonstrates this awareness. Crazy Jane, however, has a peculiar autonomy in that Yeats did not like her yet felt that she had a hold upon him. In the winter of 1931, he wrote to his wife that he wanted "to exorcise that slut, Crazy Jane, whose language has become unendurable."[16]

Jung could have warned Yeats of the dangers of becoming "anima possessed" or obsessed by the desire to realize his own qualities rising from the feminine principle by "projecting" them or reading them into the women who appealed to him by that mystery called sexual attraction. "Anima possession" is no mystery. It is merely devotion to a search in the wrong direction, becoming more and more intense as it more and more fails. In the terms of Plato's myth, with which Yeats was familiar, he was on a quest for his missing half. Such a search had created its perfect vehicle in the nineteenth-century understanding of courtly love exactly because of the most unrealistic aspect of that idea, physically unconsummated "pure love." The psyche that needs completion has little use for the physical union, as

Yeats had found in the impotence to which he succumbed whenever he came close to a woman who seemed to complete his soul, Olivia Shakespear being a case in point.

In following this path Yeats might better be called the classic courtly lover than the last courtly lover, for he stopped at every station on the way. Even after his realization of the hollowness of the pursuit of his completion in the person of Maud Gonne ("Adam's Curse," 1902), he was still ready fifteen years later to repeat the effort with her daughter Iseult. Seventeen years after that, years of experiencing the friendship and partnership of marriage to George Hyde-Lees, he made still another attempt to impose the ideal of his own making on Margot Ruddock.

But as recapitulation of earlier attempts at his quest, the Ruddock case differs in at least three important ways. First, it was decidedly shabbier, not only in its adulterous nature but in the attempts Yeats made to mold Margot's voice, appearance, and manner as if he were making do with a lesser clay. Second, his use of her was balder, his emotional detachment enabling him to abstract grist for his imagination from her real illness and very possibly providing the push that sent her over the edge of sanity. But third and most significant insofar as his work is concerned, the relationship departed from the pattern of courtly love in the abandonment of "pure love" for emphasis on the physical. His search for the resolution of antinomies in bed—of marriage or not—had become an obsession.

Again Yeats's experience finds enough parallel in Jung's psychoanalysis for the Jungian terms to elucidate it, this time positively. Jung's prescription for problems arising from unconscious pressures is a conscious, purposeful, creative exercise he called "active imagination," a process whereby the ego watches, as it were, as images from the unconscious are allowed to arise and function to their own ends.[17] The purpose of the exercise is self-understanding, or a moving toward such an understanding as the term *Auseinandersetsung* expresses.[18] It meant granting a figment of the imagination an autonomy such as Yeats granted to Crazy Jane, a figure whom he recognized as having risen from a period of sexual abstinence enforced by illness (L814). Through a series of seven poems, he allowed her to have her say whether he agreed with her or not. The way of active imagination is supposed to lead to health, but for Yeats it led first through the Valley of the Shadow. In Jung's analysis of the psyche, the shadow is composed of the dark possibilities of the ego that may come raging out into the light when the ego is frustrated in its conscious pursuits.[19] The dark side of Yeats's imagination had appeared early in his dreams of death for Maud as she rejected him. At the closing of his life the shadows of lunacy and of hatred appear. As he had with Crazy Jane, he allows the personae of these shadows, Tom the Lunatic and Ribh the Hermit, to present their arguments in their own series of poems.

—4—

Tom the Lunatic, as his name implies, is completely under the feminine, lunar influence. He has given up all the masculine glory of *antithetical* creation. As persona of Yeats, he constrasts with the earlier lover's mask of Solomon, who brought to his marriage bed intellectual comprehension of

> Whatever has been said, sighed, sung,
> Howled, miau-d, barked, brayed, belled, yelled, cried, crowed, (CP174–75)

as though this comprehension fitted him more than another man for the act of copulation. Tom knows instead that no intellectual analysis is necessary to find the resolution of antinomies, for the physical in its entirety is the expression of the intellect of God, and in this the generative world is eternal. For Tom this is a matter of faith rather than of reason:

> Whatever stands in field or flood,
> Bird, beast, fish or man,
> Mare or stallion, cock or hen,
> Stands in God's unchanging eye
> In all the vigour of its blood;
> In that faith I live or die. (264)

What sounds like a leap of faith to a solid resting place is, however, not so simple or so final. Yeats wrote to Edmund Dulac, to whom he dedicated *The Winding Stair*, that the poems subtitled *Words for Music Perhaps* were the result of "exultant weeks" in the spring of 1929 when his impression of life had been "of the uncontrollable energy and daring of the great creators," that, except for the "evasion and explanation" of journalists and critics (antithetical in their taming and ordering of the primary energies of the creators) would tear the world in pieces (CP457). In the retrospection of his work that begins in these poems, Yeats sees the energy manifest that has shaken his own soul. He uses that phrase in the verses on Tom asleep at Cruachan, the site of the court of the Celtic king Ailill and Queen Maeve, whose stormy relationship was itself a type of Yeats's experience with Maud Gonne in his youth.

At Cruachan was also located a cave understood to be a gateway into the body of the Earth herself, the Great Round embodying the mysteries of both love and death. Tom, asleep near this entrance, is destined to sing— "must sing"—of

> What most could shake his soul:
> 'The stallion Eternity
> Mounted the mare of Time,
> 'Gat the foal of the world.' (CP264)

The image must have been for Yeats like seeing into the *Thirteenth Cone* itself and watching the intercourse of the opposing principles.

"Old Tom Again" drives home the point that the "self-begotten," the naturally generated, will not fail no matter what *antithetical* construction "fantastic men" may place upon it. And, as if in exemplification, comes the last poem in the series, "The Delphic Oracle upon Plotinus," in which a new light shines—as from Apollo, the masculine principle itself—upon the true situation of that principle. Plotinus, who had held that art was a direct creation of the Idea in the mind of the artist, appears as a figure in a nightmare swimming for a shore that fades before his eyes because he is overwhelmed by the feminine image of the sea around him and within him: "Salt blood blocks his eyes." On shore he can recognize the giants of intellect—Plato, Minos, Pythagoras, "And all the choir of Love."

Ribh, the ninety-year-old hermit of *Supernatural Songs*, moves in the opposite direction from Tom. He has withdrawn into the antithetical life. He first appears lying upon the tomb of the lovers Baile and Aillin, where he is reading a book in the pitch darkness of midnight. The theme of *Supernatural Songs* is Ribh's explanation of the source of light by which he reads.

Yeats had published his version of the love story that ended in death in 1903. It appeared a year after "Adam's Curse" and within the period between 1891 and 1910 in which he seemed fascinated with death as the door to Unity of Being in love. Four poems especially illustrate his thinking: "A Dream of Death," written in late 1891 and sent to Maud as a warning against the rigors of her political involvement; "He Wishes His Beloved Were Dead" (CP70), "He Thinks of His Past Greatness" (CP70); and "His Dream" (CP87), written in 1910 shortly after Maud's offer to renew their spiritual marriage. In the essay "Certain Noble Plays of Japan" (1916), he wrote, "It is even possible that being is only possessed completely by the dead" (EI226). He was delighted with a tale Lady Gregory told him about two young ghosts who came to a priest to be married and by the story of Baile and Ailinn. In preface to his version, he states the argument:

> Baile and Ailinn were lovers, but Aengus, the Master of Love, wishing them to be happy in his own land among the dead, told to each a story of the other's death, so that their hearts were broken and they died. (CP393)

According to Denis de Rougemont, the yearning for death is an outcome of the philosophy of courtly love. The explanation of the love-and-death syndrome seems to be simply that perfect love should have—as Genesis states it—two people becoming one flesh, an idea that goes well enough in philosophy and religion and has even been assumed in law but in the physical world cannot be achieved. Human consciousness is individual. Intellects and sensory awareness may be shared but cannot be melded. As

Yeats says in *A Vision*, "from the first vague dawn of the ultimate *antithetical* revelation man, under the eyes of the Virgin, or upon the breast of his mistress, became but a fragment" (285). The fragmentation of self-awareness was a parting from the Virgin or mistress as from all that would forever be "other" to the individual consciousness. The greatest gift that the power of Love can give, therefore, is a change of form. For the Western mind that change seems to be most commonly death, although Yeats had also been intrigued by another story in which Aengus transformed human lovers to swans, a form of consciousness that, as far as we know, is not troubled by the fragmentation of self-awareness. From the grave of Baile and Ailinn spring a yew tree and an apple, further symbolism of the affinity of death and love, the yew being the source of both the archer's arrows and the poison for their tips and the apple being the symbolic fruit of consummation. [20]

As Ribh says of Baile and Ailinn, "death / Transfigured to pure substance what had once / Been bone and sinew; when such bodies join / There is no touching here, nor touching there, / Nor straining joy, but whole is joined to whole" (CP282). Yeats drew on his early reading of Swedenborg for the idea, saying that only in Swedenborg's belief do "the conscious and the subconscious become one—as in that marriage of the angels which he has described as a contact of the whole being" (A244). In the poem Yeats renders Swedenborg's description of whole contact in the image of pure light:

> For the intercourse of angels is a light
> Where for its moment both seem lost, consumed.

This is the light by which Ribh reads, but he can do so only because his life of asceticism has conditioned his eyes to antithetical sight. Starting from the opposite end of things from Tom the Lunatic in the primary world, Ribh comes to the intellectual conclusion that the primary generative world mirrors God whereas Tom had leapt to the faith that the generative, although continously birthing and dying, will remain forever in the will and design of God. Ribh, antithetical to the point of accepting the occult as Yeats had done, recites the creed Yeats had learned in his Hermetic studies that "things below" in the physical plane are "copies" of things above in the spiritual plane:

> Natural and supernatural with the self-same ring are wed.
> As man, as beast, as an ephemeral fly begets, Godhead begets Godhead. [21]

In ecstasy, Ribh speaks for Yeats across the years to Maud Gonne: "What matter that you understood no word!"[22] he shouts, but in a moment his ecstatic vision is blotted out: "Some shadow fell. My soul forgot / Those amorous cries that out of quiet come / And must the common round of day resume" (CP284).

Ribh realizes that the union his antithetical eye has seen is "There" (CP284) and not for the human condition:

> Why should I seek for love or study it?
> It is of God and passes human wit.

If the mind of man cannot grasp love, then Ribh will try the opposite antithetical mode:

> I study hatred with great diligence,
> For that's a passion in my own control,
> A sort of besom that can clear the soul.

At the time of writing *Words For Music Perhaps*, Yeats had written to Olivia Shakespear of a dream he had had, inspired, he thought, by something he had read in Blake: "'sexual love is founded upon spiritual hate'" (L758). He recounts to her how he had seen a ragged, excited crowd including a couple that he assumed were dancing:

> The man was swinging round his head a weight at the end of a rope . . . , and I knew that he did not know whether he would strike her dead or not, and both had their eyes fixed on each other, and both sang their love for one another.

Out of the dream came "Crazy Jane Grown Old Looks at the Dancers" (CP255), in which the action is made more mutual—hair-pulling on the man's part and feints with a knife on the woman's. Whether either really died or seemed to die is not specified; Crazy Jane only wishes that she still "had the limbs to try / Such a dance."

There is no such violence in the hatred of Ribh. His hatred is an intellectual choice to work where Christian love has failed "to bring the soul to God." He concludes that "At stroke of midnight"—the end of the Twenty-eighth Phase when again there is no human life for the "soul cannot endure / A bodily or mental furniture"—the soul, stripped of the "trash and tinsel" of all human thought about consummation of love, can become the bride of God at last. But even before the soul goes to face God, such purification enables it to live alone, freed from the terror and deception of love that fails Heavenly purity. Hatred sheds its own light that shows

> How soul may walk when all such things are past,
> How soul could walk before such things began.

Behind the high talk of Yeats's philosophical hermit lurks the shadow of the middle-class man—whom De Rougement treats at length—who is disillusioned on finding that a woman is no more Beauty than he is Strength and who is supported and justified in his disillusionment by a culture devoted to courtly love. Hatred does not solve the antinomies for Ribh as it does not solve the bitterness of the middle-class man. The soul purified by hatred is not whole-in-itself. It is more than ever, in Yeats's words, the image of the purified Virgin-bride waiting upon her Heavenly Bridegroom for her fufillment:

> What can she take until her Master give!
> Where can she look until He make the show!
> What can she know until He bid her know!
> How can she live till in her blood He live! (CP285)

Although Ribh and Tom the Lunatic together express Yeats's own multiple personality as he approached his seventieth year, the poet gives more space to Ribh than to Tom. He seems to make his greatest effort through the Hermit to find a new myth and symbol for wholeness. He argues well that hate may in its way be as purifying as love but like the medieval Flagellants (CP286), who turned their hate upon their own bodies, he again arrives, as these lines tell, at the old symbol of the purified feminine united receptively to the powerful procreative masculine.

—5—

Ribh disappears after the fifth of the twelve *Supernatural Songs*, but three more of the poems contain Yeats's most mystical ponderings in terms of the feminine and the masculine. Yeats told Olivia Shakespear, with whom he seems to have had the greatest intellectual camaraderie of all the women he knew, that "He and She" (CP285) was a poem about the soul that expresses his "centric myth" (L828–29). The lines seem to describe a chase between the sun and the moon reminiscent of mythological tales of romantic conjunctions of the planets. The moon is fated, presumably by the fact of orbit, to sidle up to the sun but then to flee because "His light had struck me blind / Dared I stop." On the most obvious level, it is true that the moon is struck blind or at least dark when it appears in the sunlit sky. On an allusive level, the moon's fear is that of Psyche, Semele, and other wives of deities who are forbidden sight of their husbands on pain of their own destruction. On the mythic level, the speaking moon is only a simile for another "she" who must also sidle up to the masculine power and flee to avoid blindness, becoming brighter the further she flies. A disagreement over a key word in the poem makes the myth even more elusive: the Definitive Edition, here referred to as

CP, says the "scared moon," which agrees with fear of blindness, but the Variorum says "sacred moon," (P. 559) as does the *Collected Poems* of London, 1961. In either reading, the feminine element moves eratically by sidling, tripping, and flying, partly under duress, partly from fear of being overwhelmed, and partly in a kind of delight. One thing is clear: that the poem belongs to a definite category of Yeats's work marked by his special imaginative effort to investigate what manner of mind is in woman.

In the cycle "A Woman Young and Old," written before 1928 (CP456), he begins with woman's mind in childhood, where he finds it already thinking outside the boundaries of male judgment ("Father and Child," 266). Yeats's letters make frequent reference to his daughter's maturing into the ways of womanhood. He was watching her for signs of the feminine mystique, which he thought included intuitive knowledge from the *Spiritus Mundi*—his term that has been compared to Jung's "collective unconscious":

> When I watch my child, who is not yet three years old, I can see so many signs of knowledge from beyond her own mind; why else should she be so excited when a little boy passes outside the window . . . and why, above all, as she lay against her mother's side, and felt the unborn child moving within, did she murmur, "Baby, baby"? (A271–72)

When Anne was about ten years old, Yeats worried over her "desire to debauch her intellect with various forms of infantile literature presented by servants etc" (L743), but later comments on her schooling indicate that he was serious when in "A Prayer for My Daughter" he had said, "In courtesy I'd have her chiefly learned" (CP186). In a letter of 1934, he wrote,

> My daughter is fifteen and has just discovered Shakespeare and at her own suggestion is writing an essay upon Hamlet. Her sole education is languages, the Academy Art school and my conversation. My son aged 12½ toils through the ordinary curriculum and will go to St. Columba's in a year or so and then to College. (L821)

One of his essays reveals why he was not eager to send Anne away for a boarding-school education:

> I have just been talking to a girl with a shrill monotonous voice and an abrupt way of moving. She is fresh from school, where they have taught her history and geography whereby 'a soul can be discerned,' but what is the value of an education, or even in the long run of a science, that does not begin with the personality, the habitual self, and illustrate all by that? Somebody should have taught her to speak for the most part on whatever note of her voice is most musical, and soften those harsh notes by speaking, not singing, to some stringed instrument, taking note after note and, as it were, caressing her words a little as if she loved the sound of them, and have taught her after this some beautiful pantomimic dance, till it had grown a habit to live for eye and ear. (EI269–70)

In "Before the World Was Made" and "A First Confession," he imagines the woman aware of embodying an eternal essence that counters the invitation of her intellect which Yeats has her recognize as a superior quality:

I long for truth, and yet
I cannot stay from that
My better self disowns,
For a man's attention
Brings such satisfaction
To the craving in my bones. (267)

Her images of sexual union are of the body in cancellation of the mind. While her Yeatsian intellect mulls the concept of the "crime of being born,' she urges sexual enjoyment as an escape from thinking:

But where the crime's committed
The crime can be forgot.

When she says "heart," she means the throbbing organ, not the masculine abstraction of sentiment:

If questioned on
My utmost pleasure with a man
By some new-married bride, I take
That stillness for a theme
Where his heart my heart did seem
And both adrift on the miraculous stream
Where—wrote a learned astrologer—
The Zodiac is changed into a sphere. (268)

The idea of the new bride questioning the experienced woman on the issue of sexual satisfaction evokes all the medieval scenes of the young woman shadowed by the older, wiser, and more cynical one—Ovid's beloved and Dipsas, the Rose and La Vieille, Juliet and her Nurse. The woman is able to give answer; she has experienced satisfaction, but it is physical; the antithetical abstraction of the Zodiac changed into a sphere is not her experience, but something she has heard a man say. Yeats's reference to himself as "a learned astrologer" is coy, and, indeed, the rest of the cycle becomes self-indulgent as the woman of his own making responds flatteringly to his ideas.

In "A Last Confession" the woman's concentration on the body is her protection from suffering. It is her reaction of hatred in which she denies feeling, as Ribh denies the physical body and transfers all his desire to the spiritual one:

> Flinging from his arms I laughed
> To think his passion such
> He fancied that I gave a soul
> Did but our bodies touch,
> And laughed upon his breast to think
> Beast gave beast as much. (270)

Such an attitude on the part of woman is unspeakable in the culture that embraces courtly love. It may, of course, be allowed in man but only where it is the woman's fault or where it waits to be changed by the transforming love of a purified woman. But Yeats's female persona knows that, purified to the soul, she would recognize her master in the male and risk the same misery that the culture of courtly love assumes the faithful man suffers at the hands of the unworthy woman:

> But when this soul, its body off,
> Naked to naked goes,
> He it has found shall find therein
> What none other knows,
>
> And give his own and take his own
> And rule in his own right;
> And though it loved in misery
> Close and cling so tight,
> There's not a bird of day that dare
> Extinguish that delight. (271)

This poem, like "Ribh in Ecstasy," also recalls one of Yeats's early lyrics. In "Down by the Salley Gardens" (CP20), published in 1889, when Yeats's passion was yet totally imaginative, he had feared a self-preserving lightness in woman's attitude toward love. The girl in that poem tells him to take love easy because it is only natural, "as leaves grow on the tree."

Another segment of the series, entitled "Her Triumph," harkens back to courtly love through the myth of the rescue of the maiden from the dragon. Yeats had used it previously in "Michael Robartes and the Dancer" (1921), a debate between man and woman like the love *debat* of medieval poems. In that poem, Yeats's figure *He* sings a melodious argument to convince *She* that perfecting her body rather than developing her mind is her true course of blessedness. Women can live in a blessed state, he says, and lead men to the like

> . . . if they
> Will banish every thought, unless
> The lineaments that please their view
> When the long looking-glass is full,
> Even from the foot-sole think it too. (CP174)

He has explained the myth of Perseus or St. George as the man's effort to free the Lady he loves from the terrors of abstract opinion:

> ... it's plain
> The half-dead dragon was her thought,
> That every morning rose again
> And dug its claws and shrieked and fought.

If the dragon were dead, then "She would have time to turn her eyes / ... upon the glass / And on the instant, would grow wise."

In this earlier poem it is the will of the lover, not the primary essence within herself, that loosens the women's grasp on her own intellectual potential. The very flatness of her response, "May I not put myself to college?"—asking to know the limit to which she might develop her mind without risking the appeal of her body—indicates her failing under the pressure of his ardent courtship. His reply soars in masculine levity and compliment:

> ... what mere book can grant a knowledge
> With an impassioned gravity
> Appropriate to that beating breast,
> That vigorous thigh, that dreaming eye?
> And may the Devil take the rest.

When she says that she has been warned, as she would have been in the Christian patriarchy, that there is great danger in the body, he counters with sacramental argument. The perfecting of the body for which he pleads would be also a purifying of it as for sacrifice:

> Did God in portioning wine and bread
> Give man His thought or His mere body?

She answers that her "wretched dragon is perplexed." Yeats gives her the last word in the debate, but it is a statement that indicates how far she has been led astray by modern education: "They say such different things at school."

In "A Woman Young and Old" the slaying of the dragon is again accomplished by the man—

> I did the dragon's will until you came
> Because I had fancied love a casual
> Improvisation, or a settled game
> That followed if I let the kerchief fall. ...
> And then you stood among the dragon-rings.
> I mocked, being crazy, but you mastered it
> And broke the chain and set my ankles free. (267)

But the triumph now is the woman's. Instead of entering into the light of his intellect, the woman and the man who slew her dragon find themselves surrounded by the symbols of the unconscious and the irrational:

> And now we stare astonished at the sea,
> And a miraculous strange bird shrieks at us.

"Her Vision in the Wood" (269–70) is the darkest poem in the cycle, going even more deeply into the unconscious for its revelation. The speaker, a woman "Too old for a man's love," stands in a dark wood at midnight, tearing her veins so that the blood might cover whatever part of her body "could recall the lip of lover." This covering or reveiling of the sexual parts symbolizes a restoration of virginity, and the association of the blood with wine implies sacramental cleansing. The miracle of restoration occurs as the wine-dark blood changes to red and, to the accompaniment of torches and deafening music that shakes the leaves, a group of stately women appears. "With loosened hair or foreheads grief-distraught," they carry a dying man on a litter. Like Adonis he has been wounded by a beast. Caught up in the women's frenzy, the speaker sings her "malediction" with the rest against "That thing all blood and mire, that beast-torn wreck." Suddenly the dying man catches the eye of the speaker, and she recognizes him, not intellectually as a "fabulous symbol," but internally as her "heart's victim and its torturer."

The poem can be compared to Yeats's early verse play "the Seeker" (VPy1259–62) as the picture on the reverse of a coin. In the play the male figure, aged and unsatisfied, follows the summons of a sweet voice into a dark wood where a shadowy Figure stands in a ruined house. He has wandered like Alastor for over sixty years and in the course of his devotion has become more spirit than flesh. With his last energy he kneels before the Figure and begs the kiss of revelation, but as he touches her hem, the Figure is lighted to reveal

> A bearded witch, her sluggish head low bent
> On her broad breast! Beneath her withered brows
> Shine dull unmoving eyes.

The Figure raises a mirror in which he sees his own face, and he falls to die with the sweet voice still whispering to him: "What, lover, die before our lips have met?"

The Knight's revelation is an alienation. He learns that the thing which he has pursued, a thing external to himself, is an illusion, but the revelation does him no benefit because the thing remains external and remains an illusion even as he dies. The revelation in "Her Vision in the Wood" is final self-knowledge. The woman sees that she is part of the mythical pattern; she sees herself archetypically. The protecting ego that Esther Harding says prevents man or woman from experiencing his or her own sex as demonic dissolves when the speaker of "Her Vision" involuntarily joins her voice to those of the mythical female horde. Then she realizes that she has played out in her individual life the pattern of the Mother goddess and the slain god. In both poems the male is the victim, and the female is not rationally in control of her actions. The Figure in "The Seeker" confesses, "I know not what I am," and the speaker of the later poem is driven by unconscious forces in tearing her own veins. The male figures also die, but the female speaker only falls senseless; still following the myth into which she is locked, she will make her cyclical return. But her experience of self-revelation has made her whole-in-herself, and Yeats has repeated the depiction of female wholeness that he gave in *The Countess Cathleen* and that he admitted to be a tantalizing element in his attraction to Maud Gonne.

—6—

Yeats pursued the images of the Mother goddess and the slain god in two plays, *The King of the Great Clock Tower*, finished in October 1934, and *A Full Moon in March*, published November 22, 1935. In these plays the slain god—or slain male principle as in "The Seeker" and "Her Vision in the Wood"—becomes at last the victor even in death. The great Yeatsian melange of the traditional, the philosophical, and the occult in these plays has been exhaustively studied by Harold Bloom, Helen Vendler,[23] and F. A. C. Wilson.[24] The plays tell basically the same story from Celtic myth, that of the strolling bard Aodh and the Irish queen Dectira. Yeats included it in *The Secret Rose* of 1897 but omitted it from later editions. The name of Aodh or Aedh also occurs as one of Yeats's early personae of seekers and lovers. It refers to fire as it flames up in sacrifice of "the myrrh and frankincense that the imagination offers continually before all that it loves" (WAR74). In his adolescence Yeats had found a scene of the offering of myrrh and frankincense to idealized woman in Morris's tale of Pygmalion.

Aodh falls in love with the queen while watching her bind up her hair, a scene to which he is privileged as bard admitted to the queen's chambers. Yeats made repeated use of "folded" or bound hair as companion symbol to the quietened feet in *The Wind Among the Reeds*. The folding of the hair symbolizes the pacifying and the ordering of the fierce powers of the feminine as achieved by the sacrifice of self-castration in "The Cap and Bells." Aodh's reaction to the queen's gesture provides a poetic parallel to Yeats's father's remark that hung in the poet's memory: "A man does not love a woman because he thinks her clever . . . but because he likes the way she has of scratching her head" (M144).

Just as Aodh is preparing to sing to the queen, he is called away to meet an invasion of her enemies. As he leaves he swears that he will complete his song to her no matter what his fate in battle. He is killed, but the next morning when the queen finds his severed head hanging from a bush, it is singing. The lyric Yeats wrote for the head compares the effortless art of the body of the woman with the labor of the poet, a recapitulation of the idea of "Adam's Curse" (CP61), omitting the earlier parallel that women, too, must "labor to be beautiful," for this queen is too primary for that self-awareness.

In *The King of the Great Clock Tower* the proper names are dropped; Dectira becomes simply the Queen and Aodh, the Stroller. A King is added, and Wilson interprets the trio as Cybele, Attis-Dionysus, and Zeus in line with Yeats's own statement that the play is about the Mother goddess and the slain god (FMMv–vi).[25] The Stroller speaks and behaves as one fated or under the ancient Celtic *geasa* or sacred duty. The aspect of governance by an unself-determined fate gives the Stroller a primary feminine quality that is a departure from other Yeatsian male figures. He arrives at court saying that the Queen will dance for him. Using the same meaning of the verb that Yeats had given Crazy Jane, the Stroller announces that he has come to have intercourse with the Queen. Afterwards, he says, he will sing to her out of gratitude for the dance. The King, displaying all the masculine characteristics of articulateness, objectivity, logic, and consciousness of property, orders the Stroller beheaded. But the Stroller insists, counting off the items on his fingers:

> . . . this must happen; first the Queen
> Will dance before me, second I shall sing. (CPy637)

The Queen's passivity is expressed in her utter silence. "Dumb as an image made of wood or metal," she sits upon her throne, listening as the King tells her how he raised her to that eminence and how that fact gives him the right to demand an accounting from her. An attendant sings for her verses that suggest that the Stroller's decapitation will accomplish her impregnation. The first stanza recalls a phrase from Yeats's earlier poem about miraculous conception, "Leda and the Swan" (1923) and the violence of the dancers that Crazy Jane envies:

> He longs to kill
> My body, until
> That sudden shudder
> And limbs lie still. (638)

What the Stroller and Crazy Jane call the "dance" the enthroned woman calls death. The second stanza suggests Blake's poem, "The Sick Rose,"[26] but substitutes "caterpillar" for "invisible worm":

O, what may come
Into my womb,
What caterpillar
My beauty consume?

The song introduces a new dimension to the cold chastity of the Virgin. Her virginity no longer renews itself with the new moon; the Rose is no longer immutable but can sicken and die in time. The idea of virginity moves away from that of the sacred prostitute, the *hierdule*, to that of the popular nineteenth-century understanding of virginity and its place in courtly love as a treasure to be guarded. A song at the opening of the play speaks of a woman clasping "an apple tight for all the clamour of a famished man." It was this understanding that prompted James Joyce's characterization of courtly love as a "refrigerating apparatus."

When Yeats revised the play under the title *A Full Moon in March*, he greatly emphasized the issue of virginity. He dropped the King as a superfluous character and lowered the Stroller to a Swineherd, a figure suggesting more of the foulness of the flesh in contrast with the Queen's "immaculate" virginity. The Swineherd is no Narcissus. He confesses that when he looks at his reflection in the mirror of a stream,

... the face
That trembles upon the surface makes me think
My origin more foul than rag or flesh. (CPy623)

Every detail of the play accents the difference between the *primary* and *antithetical* worlds. The Attendants, musicians who serve as chorus, are designated soprano and bass. At the opening they suggest "the dung of swine" as a good subject for a song. Opposed to the organic dung is the antithetical crown of gold. The Queen, now without consort, and the Swineherd, who would be king, are irrationally drawn to each other. The Queen, like the demanding Lady of courtly love, grants him her favor to hear his song because of the "perils" he has passed through for her sake. She warns him of her cruelty to those whose songs do not please:

Men hold
That woman's beauty is a kindly thing,
But they that call me cruel speak the truth,
Cruel as the winter of virginity.

But he replies,

I shall embrace body and cruelty
Desiring both as though I had made both.

He speaks the psychological and sociological truth. By his imagination he has created of her body the ultimate emblem of his desire. By his assertion of boundaries he has declared this emblem his individual property and demanded that she guard it for his single possession. Yeats had made his statement of the courtly pretenses and their resultant behavior between men and women in "The Hero, the Girl, and the Fool" (1922). The Girl speaks her rage at her image in the mirror that she has been taught to present to the man as her real self, knowing it to be deception:

> And when I wake towards morn I dread myself,
> For the heart cries that what deception wins
> Cruelty must keep; therefore be warned and go
> If you have seen that image and not the woman. (CP216)

Like a lady in a Medieval court of love speaking to a competing troubadour, the Queen asks the Swineherd what "novel simile," what "wild hyperbole" praising her beauty he has prepared. He offers neither but instead puts forward exactly what he can give:

> A song—the night of love,
> An ignorant forest and the dung of swine. (CPy625)

This not being the courtly answer, which should promise the *antithetical* golden crown, the Queen is angered. She speaks as if appealing to a court for judgment against the man and justification of herself because

> . . . he came hither not to sing but to heap
> Complexities of insult upon my head.

Yeats gives the angry Queen his term "complexities," hitherto used to describe the teeming generative world—"complexities of mire or blood," "complexities of fury" ("Byzantium," CP243–44)—from the masculine viewpoint. With her complaint the ritual of courtly love becomes not a gratuitous antithetical construct but a need on the part of the feminine principle to grant the woman at least the appearance of self-determination through response to the lover. The Queen's complaint seems to be that the Swineherd is less the man for his direct, or in contemporary usage "macho," approach. Manliness to her requires evidence of antithetical imagination.

Ignoring the charge of insult, the Swineherd speaks only to make his meaning even clearer. He will bring the Queen down from her antithetical throne to be what the primary world depends on her being, a mother. As a woman she will experience what Crazy Jane knows—that "Love's mansion" is an antithetical construction built on the cite of primary excrement. As a symbol she will be regressed to the sow—"She shall bring forth her farrow in the dung"—that along with the cow and the mare symbolized the Great Mother to primitive Celts. Having forced her to see herself through primary eyes, the Swineherd is willing to shift back into the antithetical mode for the love song she wants. He will honor the ritual of the courtly approach although he knows it is meaningless: "But first my song—what nonsense shall I sing?" If Yeats had given the Swineherd a name so that he would be an individual rather than a symbolic figure, he would fall into that category of disillusioned lovers in literature, men like Rhett Butler, who play out the ritual for the sake of the culture even after they have seen that their particular women are "unworthy" of it. Such figures never fail to engage the sympathy of the traditional culture.

Her anger unassuaged, the Queen sends for her headsman, but the threat does not deter the Swineherd, who taunts her with a story similar to tales of miraculous conceptions in Celtic myth of a woman who bathes in the blood of a severed head only to find that a drop has entered her womb and impregnated her. In revulsion the Queen orders the headsman to take the Swineherd away. While the chorus of Attendants close an inner curtain to shut the Queen from sight, they sing a song comparing the victorious ecstasies of the Empress Theodora and of Helen of Troy with the supreme ecstasy that Dectira experienced:

> Girls that have governed cities,
> Or burned great cities down, . . .
> O they had their fling,
> But never stood before a stake
> And heard the dead lips sing. (627)

Wilson, interpreting the play from the mythical and masculine points of view, explains that the Mother goddess castrates Attis-Dionysus to save him from falling further away from the divine into the material world. He cites *The Works of the Emperor Julian,* with which Yeats was familiar in Thomas Taylor's translation:

> After that [i.e. the castration], the Hilaria must by all means follow. For what could be more blessed, what more joyful, than a soul which has escaped from limitlessness and generation and inward storm, and has been translated up to the very Gods?

Wilson's interpretation, and Julian's, find an unhappy parallel in the dark days when Christianity also turned antithetical and the abstract soul of the heretic could be cleansed by the fire that burned his body at the stake of the *auto-da-fe.*

But no Hilaria is found in the release of Yeats's Swineherd from the generative world, for generation was his purpose. The ecstasy is the Queen's, and Wilson does remark that "as with several of the women in Yeats's gallery, ecstasy and cruelty are associated in Dectira's mind." He suggests both Blake's "The Mental Traveller" and certain lines from *The Four Zoas* as formative of that association in Yeats's mind:

> The joy of woman is the death even of her most beloved
> Who dies for love of her
> In torments of fierce jealousy and pangs of adoration.
>
> (II, 349–51)

When the Attendants open the inner curtain, the Queen is discovered standing in place as before, but her symbolic virginal veil lies discarded at her side and in red-gloved hands she holds the severed head of the Swineherd high above her own. The image of the priestess or of the Mother goddess holding up hands stained with the blood of sacrifice and the idea of using red dye, "raddle," to represent the bloody potentiality in archetypal woman had occurred to Yeats much earlier. In "Cuchulain's Fight with the Sea" (CP33), the hero's wife Emer is "raddling raiment in her dun" when a swineherd brings the news that Cuchulain is bringing a beautiful younger woman home with him. Emer listens posed as the bloody priestess:

> Then Emer cast the web upon the floor,
> And raising arms all raddled with the dye,
> Parted her lips with a loud sudden cry.

Her revenge upon her husband was to trick him into killing his only son. The raddle appears again in the closing song of *A Full Moon in March.*

The Queen sings a song of contrition to the head of the Swineherd, calling it now her "Child and darling" and explaining that any wrong she has done came not from her whole being but from her "virgin cruelty." She explains the psychology of woman in love, showing that passion and cruelty do indeed grow in parallel proportions:

> Great my love before you came,
> Greater when I loved in shame,
> Greatest when there broke from me
> Storm of virgin cruelty. (628)

Her contrition is real. She is now truly a different being, having moved into her second lunar phase, that of the Good Mother, but still being the feminine principle incarnate, she has no more power of choice over her motherly tenderness than she had over her virgin cruelty. The death of the Swineherd has not changed or "redeemed" her essential nature.

Then she, whom the Swineherd would have brought down to be his equal among the swine, performs her Mother goddess's mystery of transformation, as Neumann calls it, by placing the Swineherd's head upon the throne. As the Swineherd has acted generatively, she now acts antithetically, making a king of a severed head. The transformed head begins to sing.

Yeats's lyric for the head brings together several of his poetic and personal themes. The personae of the song are the nursery figures Jack and Jill, but in this tale Jill has murdered Jack and has hung his heart "beyond the hill, / A-twinkle in the sky," a transformation like those of mythic heroes raised to become starry constellations. The allusion is to the tale of Dionysus and Athena in which the goddess tears the god's heart from his dead body after his death in order to save it to assure his resurrection, and Yeats's application of the myth in "Two Songs from a Play" (CP210) becomes the transforming act of the feminine principle that turns the end of one Great Year into the beginning of another. Yeats's "centric myth" of the flying moon ("He and She," CP285) is present as the moon, shining brightly, "Ran up the hill, and round the hill, / Round the hill and back" following Jill. Finally, the hollowness of love from "Adam's Curse," is remembered: "Jack had a hollow heart, for Jill / Had hung his heart on high."

After the song, the Queen dances in adoration before the head, suggesting a renewal of her virginal self in that her movements are once more "alluring and refusing." The dance recalls the scene in Wilde's *Salomé* and the only one of Beardsley's drawings that Yeats had considered beautiful. Yeats's explicit stage directions—including the female counterpart of "the shudder in the loins"—achieve the eroticism that failed in "Solomon and the Witch":

> *She takes the head up and dances with it to drum-taps, which grow quicker and quicker. As the drum-taps approach their climax, she presses her lips to the lips of the head. The drum-taps cease. She sinks slowly down, holding the head to her breast.*

While the Attendants again close the inner curtain, they sing what Curtis Bradford calls "Yeats's final word on the function of sexual love in the search for Unity of Being":[27]

> Why must those holy, haughty feet descend
> From emblematic niches, and what hand
> Ran that delicate raddle through their white?
> My heart is broken, yet must understand,
> What do they seek for? Why must they descend?
>
> For desecration and the lover's night.

In the stanza of the song Yeats implies a procession of women carrying pitchers, and the singers invite the audience to "look with understanding eyes," for "tight / Therein all time's completed treasure is." Then they repeat their question and answer:

What do they lack? O cry it out again.
Their desecration and the lover's night.

These women with the pitchers are the Danaids, perpetual prisoners in
Hades along with Tantalus, Sisyphus, and Ixion, who labor to fill a
bottomless barrel with their pitchers for their refusal to grant their husbands
their conjugal rights on their wedding night.

Writing *The King of the Great Clock Tower* and *A Full Moon in March*
was a purgation for Yeats, following as they did the Steinach operation and
accompanying his involvement with Margot Ruddock. According to
Richard Ellmann, Yeats began the first one to test whether he was too old at
sixty-nine to write poetry.[28] Ezra Pound's evaluation of an early version as
"Putrid!" hurt him. Of the final version he wrote to Edmund Dulac, his
confidant in matters concerning Margot, that it was "theatrically coherent,
spiritually incoherent" (L830). In the same letter he says of *A Full Moon in
March*:

> I have been working at something opposed to the clear, bright air of your genius. I do not
> understand why this blood symbolism laid hold upon me but I must work it out.

He told Dorothy Wellesley that the play represented a "fragment of the past
that I had to get rid of" (L843). With its completion he had finally succeeded
in asking the question "Why must she descend?" that is implicit in his
question of the 1890s: "How could life be ritual if woman had not her
symbolic place?" For answers he had struggled to the realization that she
must descend from the symbolic place, the emblematic niche, so that the
union that is *antithetical* in ritual can become *primary*—as it must or there
will be no new beginnings and life will end, taking all ritual and order with it.

In his recapitulation of the problem, Yeats had arrived at a full change
of mind similar to the change expressed in "Adam's Curse" that ended his
personal quest on "the old high way of love." But his personality seems to
have consistently required one more step—purgation through comedy of the
struggle he had depicted in blood and tragedy. His taste seems to have been
one with that of the playwrights when the theatre dealt with high tragedy.
After the blinding of Oedipus or the death of Lear, he wanted a satyric turn
to balance his wits. Immediately after finishing *A Full Moon in March*, he
plunged with vigor into writing *The Herne's Egg*, which he called somewhat
paradoxically "as wild a play as *Player Queen*, as amusing but more tragedy
and philosophical depth" (L843). He seems to have enjoyed the process of
writing it, mentioning it often in his letters, expecting it to give impetus to
further lyrics, and expressing detached amusement at its episodes.

The tragedy and philosophic depth he speaks of come at least in part
from the two people who had the greatest influence on him at the time of
writing—Margot Ruddock and Shri Purohit Swami. On Christmas Day

1935 he wrote to Margot from Majorca, where he was working with the Swami on a translation of *The Upanishads* and writing *The Herne's Egg*:

> I wish I could have seen more of your acting, it would have helped me to write the strange play I am now writing. My heroine, a holy woman, is raped by seven men and next day calls upon the heavens to testify that she has never lain in any arms but those of her god. Heaven thunders three times, and the men who have raped her fall upon their knees. This is but one episode in a wild fantastic humorous, half-earnest play, my first full-length play.[29]

The Herne's Egg has been most fully treated by F. A. C. Wilson in *Yeats and Tradition*, pages 95–136. Most critics ignore it; others take off gleefully from Yeats's reference to the play as humorous: Curtis Bradford says that it is concerned "hilariously but seriously with the problem of how to get the bird out of a woman."[30] Harold Bloom calls it a "squalid play," a "deliberate outrage," and a "mockery of human foulness in envisioning the divine."[31] Helen Vendler is interested in the relation of the play to the system of *A Vision* and, therefore, interested in the "holy woman" more as an allegorical figure than as a reflection of sexual attitudes.[32]

Only Margot Ruddock, on whom the "holy woman" seems partly based, sees her as a woman and understands that she could be almost any woman:

> One could make her anything one chose, either a rather timid secretive woman unaware of her own voluptuousness, or else a cold, blade-cold woman with no actual voluptuousness but fierceness—or else one might play her completely oneself and let them guess *which* one really was.[33]

Margot's instincts led her to moon imagery in planning clothes for the role:

> . . . if I had beautiful feet no shoes. As I have *not* beautiful feet, sandals, silver sandals perhaps and a silver ribbon round my head!

The Herne's Egg has none of the atmosphere or accoutrements that Yeats used to varying effects in *The Countess Cathleen, The Player Queen,* and *A Full Moon in March.* Like *Cathleen ni Houlihan* and the plays of the Cuchulain cycle, it is set in an ancient Celtic background in which the Mother goddess is so close to the roots of her power that the male characters do not pay court to her. They are rather at her beck and call as they were for such mythical figures as Queen Maeve. The final scene of *The Herne's Egg,* in which the holy woman orders her donkey driver to copulate with her on the instant, ridicules all the pretense of courtliness and shows it to be one culture's veneer for a deep-lying, universal and metaphysical struggle. The play does, however, complete Yeats's recapitulation of his quest for the old high way of love with a critique far too acerbic for cultural digestion. This was made clear in the Abbey Theatre's refusal to produce the play in 1936 and in Yeats's comments to Dorothy Wellesley on their decision:

> I am greatly relieved. I am no longer fit for riots, and I thought a bad riot almost certain. (L871)

—7—

In the spring of 1935, as his passionate early interest in Margot Ruddock began to abate, Yeats was busy reading contemporary poetry to make selections for *The Oxford Book of Modern Verse*. He was attracted to the work of Dorothy Wellesley, wife of the heir to the Duke of Wellington, who acceded to the title in 1943. Vita Sackville-West, a life-long friend, describes Lady Wellesley:

> Slight of build, almost fragile, with blazing blue eyes, fair hair, transparently white skin, she was a natural rebel, rejecting all conventions and accepted ideas, loving to proclaim herself an agnostic, a fiery spirit with a passionate love for beauty in all forms.[34]

Yeats asked his friend Lady Ottoline Morrell to arrange an introduction, and so began his recapitulation of the courtly life he had known with Lady Gregory. The courtly relationship was not exactly repeated because his new Duchess, born in 1889, was some years younger than he and actively concerned in the affairs of two adolescent children. But Yeats did again realize the benefits of noble patronage—the great house in the country, the car and chauffeur, the household routine geared to his needs, the guests invited to his pleasure. The new Duchess held a personal attraction for him that the older one had not, and perhaps for this reason Yeats did not discuss Margot Ruddock with her. On May 22, 1936, the day on which he wrote to Olivia Shakespear a full account of Margot's breakdown in Barcelona, he wrote to Lady Wellesley much news of poetry and publication, quoted Castiglione to her, and said of the events in Barcelona, of which Lady Wellesley would have known through the newspapers, only that

> After this wild week—not without its fineness—I long for your intellect and sanity. Hitherto I have never found these anywhere but at Coole. (L875)

Lady Wellesley seems to have been at this time somewhat more conservative than she appears in Sackville-West's description. McHugh says that she told Yeats she did not care for his poem "Sweet Dancer." Nor did she care for another aspect of Yeats' thinking, as she recorded in the notes she made during his visits to Penns in the Rocks in July, September, and October 1938:

Sex, Philosophy, and the Occult preoccupy him. He strangely intermingles the three. The old masters, the dead accepted poets about which I much desire his opinion, appear to weary him. He seems to have passed through these, and out beyond; this is much to my loss.[35]

Despite these differences their friendship deepened. Lady Wellesley was with the Yeatses at Cap Martin during the last month of the poet's life, and she was present at his burial at Roquebrune on January 29, 1939. In her tribute to him she writes that

Yeats will live not only as one of the finest lyrical writers of the English tongue, but, on account of his later work, with the greatest of all the dead poets.[36]

Then with the directness that characterized her thinking and speech, she adds, "Not however with the great dramatists of the world."

Her directness may have been—along with her slight boyish figure that had been the stylish "norm" of the twenties—another "masculine" characteristic that caused Yeats to say that the woman in him responded to her (L868). He met that directness when, as he was doing at the same time for Margot, he helped Lady Wellesley select and revise certain of her poems for a volume to which he provided the Introduction.[37] He found his revisions meeting counter-suggestions, an exchange he would have found abhorrent in the 1880s and 90s. Dorothy Wellesley was particularly intent that any work published under her name should indeed be her own work:

Have you decided which of my poems you want for the Oxford book? If any of them are among those which were revised for the Selection from D. W. I should like very much to have a chance of considering those revisions again before they go to press.[38]

These indications of her mind and of her professional attitude toward her writing elucidate the last stanza of Yeats's tribute to her in his *Last Poems.* He placed it following "Beautiful Lofty Things" and "A Crazed Girl," thereby making her part of the lofty list. He asks, "What climbs the stair?" referring to the study she had arranged for herself in isolation high in the attic of Penns in the Rocks. Then he answers:

Nothing that common women ponder on
If you are worth my hope! Neither Content
Nor satisfied Conscience, but that great family
Some ancient famous authors misrepresent,
The Proud Furies each with her torch on high. (CP301–302)

There is little in these lines to indicate the rooted tree, the singing bird, or the enclosed garden. Indeed the stair and the picture of the poet working at the top of the house relate to his own descriptions of himself at the top of his winding stair. To place a woman in this setting of antithetical symbolism parallels the exchange in Yeats's giving the generative compulsion to the Swineherd in *A Full Moon in March*. The denigration of the passive female virtues of Content and satisfied Conscience in his "hope" for Dorothy Wellesley, his daughter in poetic tutelege, makes it clear that the mind of the poet had changed in regard to the mind of a woman, even one whom he could still place into a symbolic cultural role.

This change in the mind of the poet is delineated in the adaptation he made of an idea for a ballad that he took from Dorothy Wellesley. She had begun it under the title "The Squire, the Dame, and the Serving Maid." This is how the verses read when Yeats returned it to her on July 2, 1936, with his first revision and the comment, "You have a masterpiece":[39]

I

She sent her maid unto the man
    That would her leman be
'O Psyche mimic me at love
    With him I will not lie
'Tis sweetly done, 'tis easy done
    So child make love for me'.

II

'Why will you never meet the dawn,
    Nor light the torch my child?'
Said lover to the serving maid
    'Lie down, lie down you are wild,
O you are wild for love of me
    And I with love as wild'.

III

The black death came or another death
    And took the lady and lord,
The serving maid, the sewing maid
    Sat down to hem the shroud.
'O all goes well, O all goes well
    And I can sing it aloud'.

IV

She that did what she was bid
    Sang to the feather stitch,
'What of the man and the lady
    No matter which is which,
All goes well with a man in the dark
    And well with the feather stitch'.

The poems that Yeats ultimately drew from Lady Wellesley's idea appear in *Last Poems* as the ballad "The Three Bushes" and the six accompanying songs sung by the characters of the ballad (CP294–99). They are the last of his works in the courtly mode and the songs can be read as Yeats's final statement on the dichotomy of male and female assumed and preserved by the ritual of courtly love.

Yeats first changed Dorothy Wellesley's characters into three that occupy even more emblematic niches than she had given them. The Dame, who was merely a woman of some property but no high-born pretensions, is elevated to the Lady, with all the implications of Intellectual Beauty and spiritual transformational powers that traditionally serve to disembody her into an antithetical image. The Squire, whose original designation brings back Chaucer's "lusty bacheler," appears more idealistic as the Lover, as well as recalling the persona of Yeats's early romantic poems written at the height of his infatuation with Maud Gonne. The Serving-Maid/Sewing-Maid, no longer called Psyche, acquires earthy overtones as the Chambermaid—*chamber* meaning bedroom and *chamber* meaning a vessel and hence a female symbol like the pitchers carried at the end of *A Full Moon in March*, most specifically that vessel made to serve the organs of excretion that neighbor "Love's mansion." Her title of "maid" with its double reference to virginity and to her servile status illustrates that the idealism of courtly love was supported by the idea of property, both the property that the high-born Lady owned and that set her apart from other women and the property that she became through her Lover's proprietorship and that also set her apart for him. The Chambermaid's virginity is of the common herd, virginity that exists to be of service.[40] The courtly mode seems to have reasserted itself as Yeats worked through his revisions of the poem. He has the Lover first saying, "My darling poppet came"; then "Because my lady came." And the Lady's fear is changed from simply "If he stopped loving me" to include "If I lost my chastity."[41]

The ballad begins with the Lady's fears that her Lover will lose interest in her unless she allows their love to be consummated, for "None can rely upon / A love that lacks its proper food." The phrase recalls all that Yeats suffered in his spiritual marriage to Maud.[42] The Lover, like Yeats, is a poet whose songs spring from his love for the Lady, and she, aware of her function as his inspiration, fears that if she allows his love to die of malnutrition, he will no longer be able to sing. "I should be blamed, young man," she says in a departure from the attitude of Maud, who thought the world should thank her for giving Yeats the denial that he could turn into poetry and agreeing to the implication of blame Yeats made in "Reconciliation" (CP89). But the Lady, knowing that she owes, her position to her treasure of chastity—as the Enchantress of *The Island of Statues* owed her power to the sanctity of the goblin flower in its cleft rock—faces a dilemma:

I know that I must drop down dead
If he stopped loving me,
Yet what could I but drop down dead
If I lost my chastity?

She solves the problem by sending her Chambermaid to her lover at midnight, the time of the sphere and of the resolution of the antinomies of the body and soul in *A Vision*. In the dark, in the absence of antithetical light, the Lover cannot tell one woman from another. It proves true as the Lady wonders—and as Crazy Jane knows—that "maybe we are all the same / That strip the body bare." Although relieved that her problem is solved, the Lady feels that her life is incomplete; she sighs to see the Chambermaid look half asleep all day. This detail introduces a critique of courtly love from the woman's point of view, which Yeats had come recently to comprehend, and it moves the lady one step away from being "myth and symbol" and toward being a true character. It also provides the theme of the Lady's songs that follow the ballad.

The ruse succeeds for a year, or more precisely, for a year and a day, ending on its anniversary. The exact measure of time is significant in that the old romantic formula "a year and a day" for the lover's quest is the full lunar year that completes the thirteenth moon.[43] It is the duration of the "glamour," or magic spell of love in which the lover is supremely happy, thinking that he possesses all. Yeats's Lover, in high spirits, sings to his friends a song that might well describe *The Herne's Egg*, on which Yeats was at work at the same time he was planning "The Three Bushes":

A laughing, crying, sacred song,
A leching song . . .

But the Lover is, of course, being duped because his Lady is not there in his bed at all. Duplicity is not her intention but rather the failure of Yeats's last attempt to manipulate the myth of courtly love to the end that physical union could indeed become the earthly copy of "things above" where "Godhead on Godhead in sexual spasm begot / Godhead." He can give his lady the intellect but not the body that would make her a real woman.

The failure is signaled by the death of the Lover, whose horse, racing to the midnight rendezvous, steps into a rabbit hole and throws him. When the Lover dies, the Lady, who "saw it all," also dies. Rabbits occur in Yeats's work as symbols of the mortality of the body. Hearing the cry of a rabbit he had shot as a boy changed Yeats from a hunter to a fisherman for life. He uses the cry of a stricken rabbit to end his poem "The Man and the Echo" (CP337–39). The poem is a meditation on the power of the word that is frequently interrupted by an Echo reminding the Man that death will end intellectual problems for him. The Man is not deterred by the Echo from his intellect, but when he hears the wordless cry of the rabbit that a hawk has struck, his intellectual pursuit becomes "but a dream" in the presence of mortality. The Lover's experience is similar to the Man's. When his sexual drive, in its archetypal symbol the horse, trips over the fact of mortality, he loses his illusion of intellectual union in love-making. The illusion gone, his idealization of himself as Lover is dead, and his idealization of woman as courtly Lady is also dead. The Lady, however, does not die simply because she is his illusion; she dies because she sees the failure of the illusion. Having become here an autonomous figure, she cancels her role when she sees that it has lost its validity.

The Chambermaid lives on to bury the Lady and the Lover and to plant the traditional roses on their grave. This image of buried lovers recalls Yeats's fascination with the idea of lovers united in death from his earliest throes of romanticism to his recounting the story of Merlin and Vivienne in *A Vision* (V286). With the disruptive presence of the body removed, the antithetical image works well. It has light to shed, as it does for Ribh the Hermit and others like him whose eyes have been conditioned to receive it. It seems the only satisfactory ending to the metaphor of courtly love, buried in tradition and translated into the intertwined Roses of Intellectual Beauty.

But Yeats has not truly buried the body so long as the Chambermaid is alive. For this purpose he introduced a fourth persona into the ballad, a priest who hears the Chambermaid's last confession, grants her wish to be buried with the Lady and the Lover, and records the events of the story. The third bush, which the priest plants on the grave, achieves symbolically the union of mind and body that the act of copulation could not.

This fourth persona appears in a subscription to the title by which "The Three Bushes" is purported to be "An incident from the 'Historia mei Temporis' of the Abbé Michel de Bourdeille," an accreditation in keeping with Yeats's practice of presenting his mystical writings as translations from obscure sources. He had supplied a fictitious origin for the first edition of *A Vision* in 1927; not until 1938 did he begin with the truthful and much more intriguing account of his wife's automatic script.

His choice of a celibate man as his own mask at the end of what had become a very active sexual life seems ironical, but the purpose of celibacy, it must be remembered, is not mere sexual abstinence but consecration of sexual energies to what the celibate deems a higher creativeness than the physical. It is not Yeats the man who is celibate but Yeats the poet. Even so, he suggests celibacy sardonically: the abbot's title is drawn from a place name whose French root *bourde* can mean a "blunder" or a "mockery" and whose ending relates it to the more familiar Italian *bordello*. The persona is therefore a celibate man living in a brothel. It symbolizes Yeats the poet whose intellect, consecrated to art, insists on worshipping the Virgin while it lives in the body, the very seat of sensuality. It is Yeats's way of saying in the metaphor of sex what he had said in the metaphor of art in the Byzantium poems. The celibate man does not deny the Chambermaid her role. When he hears her confession, he "understood her case," and performs his priestly act of transformation so that the body is absorbed into the mind. The midnight of the sphere is achieved at last, and "now none living can, / When they have plucked a rose there, / Know where its roots began."

All the stanzas of the ballad end with the refrain, "*O my dear, O my dear,*" which appears as a personal expression of yearning in Yeats's letters to Dorothy Wellesley.[44] It usually occurs when he is thinking of his age. Yeats, who liked his revision of the poem, tells Edmund Dulac how the poem sung to Dulac's music affected members of the Irish Academy:

> I never saw an audience more moved, a good many joined in the chorus but softly and with evident feeling. (L890).

In spite of its success and his fondness for it, Yeats did not try to include the ballad on any of his BBC broadcasts because of its length and because he thought it "would probably be barred out on moral grounds" (L890). If he had managed to get the ballad itself approved by the radio censors, he surely would have failed with the songs that are more explicit and in the case of the Chambermaid realistically vulgar. Dorothy Wellesley, who found no fault with Yeats's changes in the poem once he began writing in his own name, objected to the Chambermaid's terms. It is in the songs, however, that the morality of the whole piece lies.

The Lady sings first, and her three songs follow a progression of intellectual comprehension. In the first song, she comprehends her own paradoxical position:

> I am in love
> And that is my shame.

Suddenly aware of an aspect of herself that she has been trained to deny, she finds it alien to her soul and degrading:

> What hurts the soul
> My soul adores
> No better than beast
> Upon all fours.

In the second song, addressing the Chambermaid as if her "bestial" self, the Lady defines their dual function for the man:

> He shall love my soul as though
> Body were not at all,

He shall love your body
Untroubled by the soul.

What the Lady comprehends in the last two lines is the gist of Freud's essay "On the Universal Tendency to Debasement in the Sphere of Love":

> ... we cannot escape the conclusion that the behavior in love of men in the civilized world to-day bears the stamp altogether of psychical impotence. There are only a very few educated people in whom the two currents of affection and sensuality have become properly fused; the man almost always feels his respect for the woman acting as a restriction on his sexual activity, and only develops full potency when he is with a debased sexual object.[45]

Yeats's own early experiences with impotence, which he called "nervous inhibition," illustrate Freud's contention, but the direction of Yeats's yearning throughout his work places him intellectually at least among the "very few" of whom Freud speaks.

By the end of her second song, the Lady is intent on learning to accept the duality of love:

Soul must learn a love that is
Proper to my breast,
Limbs a love in common
With every noble beast.

This song differs from all the others by having its own refrain. It is the prayer called the *Kyrie* that begins the Celebration of the Mass: "*The Lord have mercy upon us.*" Its appearance indicates that a sacrifice is about to be made or a sacrament partaken. With his dethronements, decapitations, and desecrations, Yeats had already been very clear on the nature of sacrifice in love. But the Lady's third song shows a path more to sacrament than to sacrifice. Sacrament, the apprehension of the divine in the human act, is the level of understanding at which the antinomies are solved.

The Lady arrives at the sacramental solution through no creed but through her own yearning for wholeness and through the power of her own creative intellect. In the third song she proposes a contract "in honour" with the Chambermaid, her physical self, to the end that she will realize that her spiritual kisses are given with physical lips and the Chambermaid will know that bodily union conveys both physical and spiritual generation:

That I may hear if we should kiss
A contrapuntal serpent hiss,
You, should hand explore a thigh,
All the labouring heavens sigh.

If she can realize physical love as sacramental, the Lady will have overcome "the perpetual virginity of the soul" that Yeats said was the tragedy of sexual intercourse.[46]

Beyond that, she will have achieved Unity of Being based on the unifying image of her whole self, no longer a shameful intuition of the unconscious deplored by the patriarchal culture, but a clear and welcome image of her own intellect. Her relations with her Lover will no longer be shameful, desecrating; therefore, she will no longer need to destroy him. There will be no more castration or madness. With the woman whole-in-herself and in control of herself, the Witch will no longer need to avenge the rape of the Virgin. Having rejected these masculine abstractions and divisions of her self, the woman can also reject the imitation of masculine thinking into which she has fallen. She will no longer need to re-create the man into a god as does the deluded priestess of *The Herne's Egg*. She is ready to take her place in the new phase of love that Yeats prophesied—"the love of some living person, and not an image of the mind."

The Lover's song, however, reveals that no such solution is at hand for him. His restless intellect stands between him and his own wholeness. The Lover sees that everything in nature has its designated goal and satisfaction except his own thought. When the oblivion of sleep or death comes to nature, it overtakes his mind still unsatisfied:

> Bird sighs for the air,
> Thought for I know not where,
> For the womb the seed sighs,
> Now sinks the same rest
> On mind, on nest,
> On straining thighs.

The Chambermaid concludes the songs with her statement of the Lover's reduction by his sexual experience with body alone, "Untroubled by the soul":

> From pleasure of the bed,
> Dull as a worm,
> His rod and its butting head
> Limp as a worm,
> His spirit that has fled
> Blind as a worm.

Between them, the female speaker of Yeats's cycle "A Woman Young and Old" and his Lady of "The Three Bushes" demonstrate more intuitive and analytical powers to a more healthy and hopeful end than do any of Yeats's restless, yearning, intellectual male figures. Michael Robartes, Owen Aherne, Red Hanrahan all end in disillusionment or obscurity. Others become images in ritual castrations. Even great Solomon finds himself going

```
. . . round and round
In the narrow theme of love
Like an old horse in a pound. (CP136)
```

They remain, like the Lover, blind-spirited. No one of them is brought face to face with "that fierce Virgin," as the Woman faces the dying man in "Her Vision in the Wood," and made to recognize her as "no fabulous image," but his mind's victim and its torturer.

—8—

Yeats ends his mythopoesis of courtly love far from being the patriarchal chauvinist who wants to enclose a bird-brained woman behind garden walls, praising her the more for the more of her mind that she gives up. He ends instead by praising her for using her mind, analytically and intuitively. The intuitive glimpse of Maud's completeness that he had in his dream of the lump of meerschaum (M63) never left him. In the half of his life remaining after that dream he worked at the problem in his imagination. As with other pursuers of myth—Faust and Oedipus are two that Slochower names and that Yeats knew well—his course took him for a time into a feminine under-world. There, seeing through the eyes of his female personae, he compre-hended that a woman cannot have Unity of Being without her own intellect and that a man cannot have Unity of Being without recognizing the feminine principle at work in himself.

In regard to the need for an image to serve Unity of Culture in a future that would have forgotten all about courtly love, Yeats was left with only a question. In its most famous form it is found at the close of "The Second Coming':

```
And what rough beast, its hour come round at last,
Slouches towards Bethlehem to be born?
```

But Yeats seems to have been entertaining the same idea in one of the "Supernatural Songs." "What Magic Drum?" (CP285) is a strange poem that seems an experiment in understanding what "Primordial Motherhood" would feel like to a male being. In a garden where the solar light is "obliter-ated" by the trees, a male of some species represses his natural force—"all but stops his breathing"—for fear that "the child no longer rest, / Drinking joy as it were milk upon his breast." The parent is licking his young: "Down limb and breast or down that glimmering belly move his mouth and sinewy tongue."

In superstition of the Middle Ages, such licking of the newborn was taken to be literally "licking them into shape." In Yeats's system of the Great Years and their phases, the new revelation from the feminine principle was always rough, distressing to the antithetical culture it was replacing and, in the passage of time, destined to be refined and reshaped by the masculine principle. When Yeats asks at the close of this poem, "What beast has licked its young?" could he possibly be understood as suggesting a union of natures or principles on the order of the Greek androgynous statues of which he had written to Dorothy Wellesley—"woman in man, never the man in woman" (L875)—a union that would not violate the femininity of the Lady of the old culture but complement the masculinity of the new male and allow the feminine, through him, to be formative of the coming culture?

The question defies answer because Yeats himself, contemplating the nature of the revelation imminent in Phase 1 of the post-Christian Great Year, found that the symbol eluded him. He prophesied that the new age would be antithetical, begotten of the East—specified as Asia Minor, the site of his Byzantium—upon the Body of the Western culture and that it would resemble its Mother (V203). It would therefore reverse the Christian era begotten of the West upon the heritage of the East, the remains of the classical Greek culture, but the reversal would not be simple or direct because of the unpredictable intervention of the Thirteenth Cone. Beyond that, it would, like all First Phases to those who watched them approach, have "no description except complete plasticity" (V183).

A Vision closes with Yeats's description of himself as a man absorbed in the critique of the art he has lived and created: "Day after day I have sat in my chair turning a symbol over in my mind, exploring all its details, defining and again defining its elements, testing my convictions . . . attempting to substitute particulars for an abstraction like that of algebra. . . . But nothing comes—though this moment was to reward me for all my toil" (V301). Thus the poet at the end of his quest, an aged man still fevered by the sexual drive that had been so late in its satisfaction and facing the oblivion of his own antithetical creation which could give him neither personal assurance nor a clear vision of the cultural future. Where was his discovery of "supra-historical or symbolic reality"? What "heavenly gain" had he realized from his quests and recapitulation?

He had traced his old high way of love—"that sweet extremity of pride" he calls it in the Epilogue of *A Vision*—to castration and death in the *primary* world but to symbolic resolution of antinomies in his *antithetical* art. In the doing he had discovered the symbolic reality of the feminine within himself and had given the principles of new interpretation as the supra-historical symbols of mankind's binary psyche in the art of *A Vision*. Finally, his "heavenly gain" is also in his art, for what greater gift can Heaven give the poet than inspiration—as Maud Gonne had seen so many years before: "You make beautiful poetry out of what you call your unhappiness and you are happy in that."

Notes

Introduction

1. Curtis Bradford, "Yeats and Maud Gonne," *Texas Studies in Literature and Language*, 3:4 (Winter 1962), 452.

2. Harry Slochower, *Mythopoesis: Mythic Patterns in the Literary Classics* (Detroit: Wayne State University Press, 1970), p. 34.

3. Ibid., p. 107.

4. "The Concept of Courtly Love as an Impediment to the Understanding of Medieval Texts," *The Meaning of Courtly Love*, ed. F. X. Newman (Albany: State University of New York Press, 1968), p. 17.

5. I am aware of following the now discountenanced convention of using Yeats's surname when referring to him as an adult while using Maud Gonne's first name for all reference to her. The use of first name for women is patronizing, as linguists like Robin Lakoff have pointed out; nevertheless, I will follow the convention both to avoid the distraction of innovation and to maintain the linguistic difference between the sexes that was employed in the generation that produced Yeats and Maud.

    Lakoff discusses the problems of female reference by first name, last name alone, last name with title, and both names in *Language and Women's Place* (New York: Harper and Row, 1975), pp. 36–42. The use of both names of a woman, she says, gives her a neutral position; it is the only way to recognize her as an adult and an equal. "Maud" is patronizing; "Miss Gonne" makes her an outsider; "Maud Gonne" is the neutral solution. Yeats used the neutral formula almost exclusively both in correspondence with mutual friends and in memoirs. He used "Miss Gonne" with strangers. He almost never called her simply "Maud." In poetic reference she is either "His Beloved" to his role as Lover or "you" or "one" without antecedent. He uses her full name once, in "Beautiful Lofty Things."

    In his own turn, Yeats was subjected to a variety of styles. Maud always called him "Willie," which he disliked. His wife called him "W. B." His teenaged first love called him in the pastoral manner "Clarin"; in his last affair Margot Ruddock followed the example of his male friends and called him "Yeats," which he preferred.

6. Slochower, p. 107.

7. Yeats gave this date to astrologers he commissioned to read Maud's horoscope. Denis Donoghue gives her birthdate as December 20, 1865 (M40n).

8. Elizabeth Coxhead, *Daughters of Erin* (London: Secker and Warburg, 1965), "Maud Gonne," pp. 17–77.

9. Sean O'Casey, *Inishfallen, Fare Thee Well* (London: Macmillan; copyright 1949 by Sean O'Casey, renewed 1977 by Eileen O'Casey, Breon O'Casey and Shivaun O'Casey), pp. 152–53. Cited in M132n.

10. Maud Gonne MacBride, *A Servant of the Queen* (London: Victor Gollancz, 1938), pp. 11, 15–16.

11. MacBride, *A Servant of the Queen*, p. 177.

12. Ibid., p. 27.

13. Ibid., p. 212.

14. Ibid., p. 176.

15. Ibid., p. 62.

16. Ibid., p. 67.

17. Ibid., p. 79.

18. W. T. Stead, *Review of Reviews,* American edition, 5, No. 25 (February 1892), 6–7. Yeats, who had probably read the article in the earlier British edition, answered it in "Clovis Huges on Ireland," *United Ireland* (January 30, 1892), reprinted in *Uncollected Prose by W. B. Yeats,* ed. John P. Frayne (New York: Columbia University Press, 1970), I, 218–21. Maud liked the article enough to quote it at length in her autobiography (MacBride, p. 84).

19. Thomas Whitaker, *Swan and Shadow: Yeats's Dialogue with History* (Chapel Hill: University of North Carolina Press, 1964) and Bloom, *Yeats* (New York: Oxford University Press, 1970), chapters 14–15 and Conclusion.

20. MacBride, pp. 329–30.

21. A. Norman Jeffares, *A Commentary on the Collected Poems of W. B. Yeats* (Stanford: Stanford University Press, 1968), p. 31.

22. C. S. Lewis, *The Allegory of Love* (New York: Oxford University Press, 1958), p. 1.

23. Bradford, "Yeats and Maud Gonne," p. 464.

24. *Letters to W. B. Yeats,* ed. Richard J. Finneran, George Mills Harper, William M. Murphy (New York: Columbia University Press, 1977), p. 200.

25. *Letters to Yeats,* p. 202.

26. "The Philosophy of Shelley's Poetry" (1900), "The Happiest of the Poets" (1902), and "Edmund Spenser" (October 1902) in EI.

27. Quotations from the Maud Gonne Notebook are by courtesy of Professor George Mills Harper.

28. "Yeats and Ireland," *Essays in Tribute,* ed. Stephen Gwynn (1940; rpt. Port Washington, New York: Kennikat Press, 1965), pp. 17–19.

29. "Yeats and Ireland," pp. 31–32.

30. Bradford, "Yeats and Maud Gonne," p. 472.

31. Olivia Shakespear, "Beauty's Hour," *The Savoy* (September 1896), p. 18.

32. Shakespear, "Beauty's Hour." *The Savoy* (August 1896), p. 24.

Chapter 1

1. Gaston Paris, "Etudes sur les romans de la Table Ronde, Lancelot du Lac, II, *Le Conte de la Charrette*," *Romania*, XII (1883), 459–534.

2. Lewis, p. 11.

3. Irving J. Crain, M. D., "The Origin of Love," *Diseases of the Nervous System*, 30 (1969), 774–76.

4. Lewis, p. 9.

5. *The Art of Courtly Love*, trans. John Jay Parry (1941; rpt. New York: W. W. Norton, 1969), p. 3; quoting Robert Boussuat, *Drouart la Vache, traducteur d'Andre la Chapelain* (Paris: Champion, 1926), p. 31.

6. D. W. Robertson, Jr., "The Subject of *De Amore* of Andreas Capellanus," *Modern Philology* 50 (1952–53), 145–61.

7. D. W. Robertson, Jr., *A Preface to Chaucer* (Princeton: Princeton University Press, 1962) pp. 444–46.

8. John F. Benton, "Clio and Venus: An Historical View of Medieval Love," *The Meaning of Courtly Love*, ed. F. X. Newman (Albany: State University of New York Press, 1968), p. 37.

9. *The Art of Courtly Love*, p. 122.

10. Benton, "Clio and Venus," *The Meaning of Courtly Love*, p. 32.

11. James Joyce, *A Portrait of the Artist as a Young Man* (1916; rpt. New York: Viking, 1974), p. 252.

12. Stead, p. 7.

13. Denis de Rougemont, *Love in the Western World*, trans. Montgomery Belgion (New York: Pantheon, 1956), pp. 63–74.

14. Erich Neumann, *The Great Mother*, trans. Ralph Manheim, Bollingen Series XLVII (Princeton: Princeton University Press, 1963), *Schema* III.

15. J. J. Bachofen, *Myth, Religion, and Mother Right*, trans. Ralph Manheim, Bollingen Series LXXXIV (Princeton: Princeton University Press, 1967), p. 77.

16. D. W. Robertson, Jr., letter of March 17, 1976.

17. For more on the male reaction, see Louis B. Salomen, *The Devil Take Her: A Study of the Rebellious Lover in English Poetry* (Philadelphia: University of Pennsylvania Press, 1931).

18. Anna Bonus Kingsford and Edward Maitland, *The Perfect Way; or, The Finding of Christ*, revised and enlarged edition (London: Field and Tuer, 1887), p. iii.

19. Otto Weininger, *Geschlecht und Charackter* (Wien and Leipsig, 1904), p. 10; translated by Lisa Appignanesi, *Femininity and the Creative Imagination* (London: Vision Press, 1973), p. 5.

20. Ann Belford Ulanov, *The Feminine in Jungian Psychology and in Christian Theology*, (Evanston: Northwestern University Press, 1971), p. 42.

21. Erich Neumann, "On the Moon and Matriarchal Consciousness," *Dynamic Aspects of the*

Psyche, trans. Hildegard Nagel (New York: The Analytical Psychology Club, 1956), p. 51; cited in Ulanov, p. 169.

22. Bachofen, p. 185.

23. Neumann, *The Great Mother*, p. 98.

24. Bachofen, p. 177.

25. Ibid., p. 93.

26. Ibid., pp. 143–44.

27. Ibid., pp. 83–84.

28. Robertson, *A Preface to Chaucer*, pp. 394, 476.

29. Mary Daly, *Beyond God the Father* (Boston: Beacon Press), 1973.

30. A. E. Waite, *The Real History of the Rosicrucians* (London: George Redway, 1887), p. 13, 13n.

31. See Frederick Goldin, *The Mirror of Narcissus in the Courtly Love Lyric* (Ithaca: Cornell University Press, 1967).

32. Trans. Harry W. Robbins (New York: E. P. Dutton, 1962), p. 11.

33. Neumann, *The Great Mother*, p. 222.

34. Virginia Woolf, *A Room of One's Own* (New York: Harcourt Brace, 1929), p. 60.

35. *No More Masks! An Anthology of Poems by Women*, ed. Florence Howe and Ellen Bass (Garden City, NY: Anchor Press, 1973), p. 129.

36. *The Art of Courtly Love*, p. 77.

37. *Enneads*, trans. Stephen MacKenna (London: 1969), v. viii. I.

38. Yeats's Theosophy, like so much else in his thought, was an amalgam. He had read A. P. Sinnett's *Esoteric Buddhism* in 1885; he had read Boehme following Swedenborg in the late 1880s; he had joined Madame Blavatsky's Theosophical Society in London, where he was struck especially by her statement: "It is necessary to crush the animal nature. . . . Initiation is granted only to those who are entirely chaste" (A177).

39. Jacob Boehme, *Six Theosophic Points*, trans. Nicholas Berdyaev (Ann Arbor: University of Michigan Press, 1970), p. 6.

40. Boehme, pp. 8–9.

41. Boehme, pp. 70–71.

42. Boehme, p. 66.

43. Boehme, p. 69.

44. Stanley Stewart, *The Enclosed Garden: The Tradition and the Image in Seventeenth-Century Poetry* (Madison: University of Wisconsin Press, 1966).

45. Stewart, Fig. 12.

46. Neumann, *The Great Mother*, p. 277.

47. W. B. Yeats, *Uncollected Prose*, I, ed. John P. Frayne (New York: Columbia University Press, 1970), p. 116.

Chapter 2

1. Quoted by Richard Ellmann in *Yeats: The Man and the Masks* (New York: E. P. Dutton, 1948), p. 101.

2. Yeats says that Maud lived "surrounded by dogs and birds" and that she had a patience beyond his reach in handling birds and beasts. She liked to travel with her monkey on her shoulder, hidden by her veil. This affinity was an attribute like her height and queenly carriage that made her especially fitted for the play of Yeats's imagination. Donegal peasants identified her with the Sidhe because she came to them riding on "a white horse surrounded by birds to bring victory" (MacBride, p. 134). For the archetypal significance of this affinity with animals, see Neumann's chapter, "The Lady of the Beasts" in *The Great Mother*, pp. 268–80.

3. Joseph Hone, *W. B. Yeats, 1865–1939* (1943; rpt. Harmondsworth, Middlesex: Penguin Books, 1971), p. 17.

4. The volume called *Memoirs*, transcribed and edited by Denis Donoghue (1972), consists of the first draft of an autobiography begun in 1915 and a Journal begun in December 1908 and continued irregularly until October 1930. Yeats explained to his father that the first draft, which brings his account from 1887 to 1898, was meant "for my own eye alone" (L603), and to Florence Farr he wrote of the Journal:

     I have a large MS book in which I write stray notes on all kinds of things. . . . They will amuse you very much. They are quite frank and the part that cannot be printed while I am alive is the amusing part. (L526)

5. Lady Gregory, *Seventy Years, 1852–1922: Being the Autobiography of Lady Gregory* (Gerrards Cross, Bucks.: Colin Smythe, 1974), p. 350.

6. Helene Deutsch, *The Psychology of Women* (New York: Grune and Stratton, 1944), I, 190.

7. Richard Finneran thinks that another early woman friend Mary Cronan, to whom the first letter in Wade's collection is addressed in 1884 (L30), is the basis of Mary Carton in Yeats's early novel *John Sherman*. The character is a friend, however, not a lover. In the novel Yeats makes much the same differentiation that he later gave to Lady Gregory:

     They were such good friends they had never fallen in love with each other. Perfect love and perfect friendship are indeed incompatible; for the one is a battlefield where shadows are beside the combatants, and the other a placid country where Consultation has her dwelling. (*Dhoya and John Sherman*, ed. Richard Finneran [Detroit: Wayne State University Press, 1969], pp. 54–55.)

8. "A Dream of Death" is the only work by Yeats besides "Adam's Curse" that Maud quotes in her autobiography. She was at St. Raphael in southern France when she received it:

     I was getting steadily better and was greatly amused when Willie Yeats sent me a poem, my epitaph he had written with much feeling. (MacBride, p. 147)

   Millevoye had joined her at St. Raphael that winter and Maud writes happily of their time together. Knowing this, one feels sad for Yeats at the line about her being "Near no accustomed hand."

9. See *Florence Farr, Bernard Shaw, and W. B. Yeats*, ed. Clifford Bax (Dublin: Cuala Press, 1941), and for their sometimes stormy relationship in the Hermetic Order, see George Mills Harper, *Yeats's Golden Dawn* (New York: Macmillan, 1975).

10. The girl Costello loves has no personality beyond her faithfulness to him. She epitomizes the mesmerized, passive woman: "The girl lifted her eyes and gazed at Costello, and in that

gaze was the trust of the humble in the proud, the gentle in the violent, which has been the tragedy of woman from the beginning" (102–03). In the revision of the story that appears in *Mythologies*, the girl's attitude remains unchanged but the warning against tragedy has been removed. The comparison between Oona and the Girl of "The Hero, the Girl and the Fool" (CP216) provides a stark revelation of Yeats's change of mind with maturity.

11. George Yeats, *Florence Farr, Bernard Shaw and W. B. Yeats,* ed. Clifford Bax (Dublin: Cuala Press, 1941), Foreword.

12. George Bornstein, *Yeats and Shelley* (Chicago: University of Chicago Press, 1970), pp. 84–84.

13. F. A. C. Wilson, *W. B. Yeats and Tradition* (New York: Macmillan, 1958), pp. 21ff.

14. Bradford, "Yeats and Maud Gonne", p. 455.

15. Theodore H. Gaster, *Myth, Legend, and Custom in the Old Testament* (New York: Harper and Row, 1969), I, 79. Gaster is commenting on the mysterious passage in Genesis 6: 1–4, and cites E. Crawley, *The Mystic Rose* (1927), a Rosicrucian work.

16. *The Notebooks of Leonardo da Vinci*, trans. Edward McCurdy (London: Cape, 1938), I, 80–81; cited in Yeats, M88n3.

17. In his youth Yeats had been drawn to the island of Innisfree by a legend telling how a girl sent her lover to the island to bring back a fruit that was food of the gods. The lover slew the dragon guarding the tree but made the mistake of tasting the fruit. When he returned to the girl, she saw that he was dying, and in remorse, also ate of it to die with him (A47).

18. Hone, p. 60.

19. J. Ernest Renan, *The Poetry of the Celtic Races*, trans. W. G. Hutchinson (London: 1896), p. 8; cited in *Frank Pearce Strum: His Life, Letters, and Collected Work*, ed. Richard Taylor (Urbana: University of Illinois Press, 1969), p. 14.

20. After their first meeting, Yeats was invited to dine with Maud on all but one of the nine nights she stayed in London (M40). Thereafter, he saw her chiefly on the move. A skimming of his letters in the Wade collection gives the impression of a man trying to keep track of an irregular comet.

    On October 23, 1889, he writes to Katharine Tynan to find out more about the death of Ellen O'Leary, sister of the Fenian leader:

> . . . on Monday I heard by chance that Miss Gonne was in London and rushed off at once and saw her for about five minutes or less. She was just starting for Paris. She knew no more than that Miss O'Leary died at Cork some few days ago. (L139)

In April 1891 he asks O'Leary if Miss Gonne has returned to Dublin (L168).

    Even after the meeting of July 1891, in which his love turned to pity—that meeting itself occurring only because he had "heard" that Maud was in Dublin—he had difficulty keeping up with her and took courage from very small evidence as indicated in confessions to AE on November 15, 1891, while Maud was visiting in London:

> I have seen Miss Gonne several times and have I think found an ally in the cousin with whom she is staying. An accidental word of the cousin showed me they had been discussing me together and reading my poems in the vellum book [a MS book into which Yeats had copied love poems for her], and yesterday the cousin gave me a hint to go to Paris next Spring when Miss Gonne did—so you see I am pretty cheerful for the time until the next regiment of black devils come. Tomorrow Miss Gonne is to be initiated into [the] G[olden] D[awn]—the next day she goes to Paris but I shall see her

on her way through London a couple of weeks later. She promises to work at the Young Ireland League for me this winter. [Instead, she was to spend that winter in St. Raphael and Yeats would send her "A Dream of Death."] Go and see her when she gets to Dublin and keep her from forgetting me and occultism. (L182–83)

On November 25, Yeats wrote to O'Leary asking a loan of one pound because

Miss Gonne will be in Dublin in 10 days or less. She returns to London from Paris in two or three days. . . . I do not want to be without the price of cabs etc while she is here & have promised to take her to one or two plays. (L185)

O'Leary obviously chided Yeats for borrowing money to spend on Maud, for Yeats writes in December,

You misunderstood me about the cabs. She does not let me pay the whole fare but stipulated a good while ago that she should pay her own share. (L186)

But there is no need for cab fare; she is still in Paris, has written that she will come soon; he has heard nothing more definite. In the same month he writes to Katharine that he is in a "fit of depression" and has not written to her because of his "black moods" (187).

And so throughout.

21. Thomas Aquinas, *Summa Theologica*, Question 66, Article 2, cited in MacBride, p. 228.

22. Bradford, "Yeats and Maud Gonne," p. 468.

23. Neumann, *The Great Mother*, p. 332.

24. Yeats's "pure love" for Maud was the subject of comment by his friends. The mystically inclined AE seemed to approve of the relationship, if not of its object, but earthy George Moore deplored it: "A detestable phrase, AE! for it implies that every gratified love must be impure. . . . Love that has not been born again in the flesh crumbles like peat ash." (Monk Gibbon, *The Masterpiece and the Man* [London: Rupert Hart-Davis, 1959], p. 65.)

25. Harold Bloom, *Yeats* (New York: Oxford University Press, 1970), pp. 128ff.

26. Bradford, "Yeats and Maud Gonne," p. 458.

27. Esther Harding, *Woman's Mysteries, Ancient and Modern: A Psychological Interpretation of the Feminine Principle as Portrayed in Myth, Story and Dreams* (London: Longmans, Green, 1935), p. 142.

28. A. Norman Jeffares, *W. B. Yeats: Man and Poet* (New York: Barnes and Noble, 1961), pp. 102–03.

29. This passage illustrates the free hand with which Yeats grouped his images and the hearsay evidence on which he was often forced to rely because his tremendous range of reading lacked the discipline of formal education and because he did not have the languages that would have enabled him to read primary materials. Monk Gibbon's criticism of Yeats on this score is stringent:

In literature his influence has been in some degree detrimental. Because his use of symbolic idiom was so effective, a whole generation presently grew up who imagined that poetry could discard not only logic but all formal thought, and subsist like a rootless plant on a jumble of exotic images and curious adjacencies. Apollo requires more than that of his votaries. One must never forget that he is also the god of light. (*The Masterpiece and the Man*, p. 212)

It can be argued in view of this criticism that archetypal analysis is therefore the most reliable in Yeats's case since it would set out to find the pattern in his "curious adjacencies." It can also be argued that Yeats's apparently indiscriminant eclecticism is evidence of a feminine mind at work, a mind more inspired by Dionysus than disciplined by Apollo. Mary Daly gives one example of a feminist scholar impatient with the boundaries that strictly masculine tradition has imposed on scholarship:

> One of the false gods of theologians, philosophers, and other academics is called Method. It commonly happens that the choice of a problem is determined by method, instead of method being determined by the problem. . . . The tyranny of methodolatry hinders new discoveries. It prevents us from raising questions never asked before and from being illumined by ideas that do not fit into pre-established boxes and forms. . . . Under patriarchy, Method has wiped out women's questions so totally that even women have not been able to hear and formulate our own questions to meet our own experiences. (*Beyond God the Father*, pp. 11–12)

30. George Mills Harper, *Yeats's Golden Dawn* (London: Macmillan, 1974), 114–16.

31. Ellmann, *Yeats: The Man and the Masks*, p. 123.

32. Letter of April 19, 1975.

33. The Maud Gonne Notebook.

34. Yeats does not give full credit here. Ezra Pound advised him to try the play as a comedy (Ellmann, p. 212). Pound and Yeats were mutually influential friends. They shared bachelor quarters at Stone Cottage near Ashdown Forest in England during the winter of 1913–14, and in April 1914 Pound married Olivia Shakespear's daughter Dorothy. Three years later Pound was Yeats's best man.

35. Hone, p. 306.

36. "George Yeats: Poet's Wife," *Sewanee Review*, 77:3 (July–September 1969), 386.

37. The authenticity of George Yeats's "automatic writing" has never been fully established. Jon Stallworthy and George Harper (who is transcribing the script for publication) seem to accept it as designated. Bradford does not. He says flatly that "George Yeats tried to divert him from his preoccupied gloom by faking automatic writing; the faked sentences were intended to ease his mind regarding Iseult" ("George Yeats," p. 393). Bradford says that the bent of her mind was decidedly "factual and practical," and that with this temperament the experience of "'mediumship'—whatever that is—may well have distressed her" (p. 394). He reports that she turned aside "all inquiries about her esoteric experiences, even tangential ones." Jeffares agrees that the writing began as a conscious attempt to distract Yeats but that the content of the "messages" surprised Mrs. Yeats herself (p. 191). Ellmann says that Mrs. Yeats had the ability to suspend her consciousness so as to give the unconscious play (p. 222). Bradford admits that Yeats's own personality produced psychic phenomena in others (p. 394). Whatever the truth of the authenticity of the writing and speaking, these activities consumed much time from George's housewifely duties and left her exhausted.

38. Marilyn Gaddis Rose, "A Visit with Anne Yeats," *Modern Drama*, 7 (December 1964), 301.

39. Bradford, "George Yeats," p. 397.

40. Jon Stallworthy, *Vision and Revision in Yeats's "Last Poems"* (Oxford: Clarendon Press, 1969), p. 34.

41. The roles of Solomon and Sheba were also in private use. Yeats scrawled these lines on a piece of blotting paper on one occasion when, in preparation for one of their frequent moves, George had packed books that he was using:

> When the Queen of Sheba's busy
> King Solomon is mute.
> 'Busy woman' ponders he
> 'Is a savage brute.'

George treasured that scrap of paper. She showed it to Bradford when he visited her in Dublin in 1954 (p. 396).

42. Hone, p. 311.

43. Jeffares, pp. 190 and 323n11.

44. The Maud Gonne Notebook.

45. Stewart, p. 61.

46. *Complete Works*, II, 389; quoted in Stewart, p. 86.

47. Stewart, p. 60.

48. *The Song of Songs: Commentary and Homilies*, trans. R. P. Lawson (London, 1957), pp. 108–09; in Stewart, p. 201n19.

49. MacBride, pp. 329–30. Maud seems to have submitted this account of the proposal to Yeats for approval when she asked his permission to quote his poems in her autobiography. In his reply he took issue only with the phrase "hopeless struggle" that she had originally quoted him as saying at the beginning of the passage. He declares, "I never felt the Irish struggle 'hopeless.' Let it be 'exhausting struggle' or 'tragic struggle' or some such phrase" (L910). She took his second suggestion.

Chapter 3

1. Oliver St. John Gogarty, *William Butler Yeats: A Memoir* (Dublin: Dolmen, 1963), p. 9.

2. Walter Starkie and Norman Jeffares, *Homage to Yeats* (Los Angeles: University of California Press, 1966), pp. 11, 13, 22.

3. MacBride, p. 332.

4. Ibid., p. 333.

5. Hone, p. 306.

6. *Yeats and Castiglione: Poet and Courtier* (Dublin: A. Figgis, 1965), p. 25.
   Yeats's weakened condition was not totally the result of unrequited love although that would fit the stereotype of the rejected courtly lover. It was rather the result of life-long neglect and some attempts to save money on food. As a child at school he often forgot to eat his lunch. His abstemiousness did, however, have an edge of romantic dedication, for in May 1887, he wrote to Katharine Tynan with a certain pride that he was practicing to be poor by eating the cheapest vegetarian dinners he could find as he would not "bow the knee to Baal" for meat (L36). While working at the British Museum he existed all day on a single roll and walked the miles between his home and the Museum. He reported many "collapses" to Katharine before he met Maud. One serious collapse followed his work on *The Wanderings of Oisin*.

7. George Moore, *Hail and Farewell: Ave* (London: William Heineman, 1937), p. 219.

8. Moore, p. 209.

9. Stephen J. Brown, S. J., *Ireland in Fiction* (New York: Barnes and Noble, 1969), I, 119.

10. *Cuchulain of Muirthemne* (1902) and *Gods and Fighting Men* (1906). Yeats wrote the preface for the first.

11. See Robertson, *A Preface to Chaucer*, p. 451.

12. Hone, pp. 221–22.

13. Castiglione, *The Book of the Courtier*, trans. Sir Thomas Hoby (London: Dent, 1956), p. 311; quoted in M157n3.

14. *Complete Writings*, ed. Geoffrey Keynes (New York: Oxford University Press, 1969), pp. 424–27.

15. CP gives the word as "reigns," but the *Variorum Edition* and *Collected Poems* (London: Macmillan, 1961) give the obviously correct "reins."

16. Harding describes the ancient beliefs that life rested at the full and dark of the moon and traces the origin of the sabbath day of rest to the Babylonian *Sa-bat* or "heart's rest," the day at the full of the moon when it neither increases nor decreases. That day is also the *Sabattu* or "evil day" of Ishtar, when she menstruates. Menstruating women could not travel and ate no cooked food, customs that became in Mosaic law the sabbath practices for both men and women (pp. 62–63). The mystery of menstruation also caused it to be associated with the dark of the moon. Harding, writing in 1935, says that the menses are often a period of conflict between the woman's "conscious attitude and the demands of her own nature," a point still much at issue in both medicine and law. The woman's judgment of life at this time is at the "dark of the moon," says Harding, and she advises women to "withdraw to arrive at unity of psychological aim" within themselves (pp. 74–75). Woman in her menstrual time was often portrayed in ancient images as fish, serpent, or half-fish— a mermaid—indicating her submersion in the unconscious, according to this Jungian writer (p. 81).

17. Harding, pp. 32ff.

18. Maud Gonne was in the habit of using drugs, particularly chloral, to calm herself for sleep. Millevoye strongly disapproved. When Maud once told him about finding a bottle of chloral that she had hidden and forgotten and calling the incident a mystical experience, he bluntly told her that she was like an alcoholic who could always get to the liquor when he wanted it. (Macbride, pp. 250–56)

19. Harding, pp. 101–03.

20. Ibid., p. 133.

21. Ibid., p. 146.

Chapter 4

1. Ellmann, p. 276.

2. W. B. Yeats and Margot Ruddock, *Ah, Sweet Dancer*, ed. Roger McHugh (London: Macmillan, 1970), p. 117.

3. Documented by McHugh in *Ah, Sweet Dancer*. McHugh says that Margot was born Ruddock and used her name from her first marriage, Collis, as her stage name. Hone agrees. Wade says that her stage name was Ruddock; she appears as Ruddock in the BBC broadcasts that he lists in his Bibliography of Yeats's writings. She is mentioned as Margot Collis in some of Yeats's letters. She was married to the actor Raymond Lovell when Yeats knew her.

4. Margot Ruddock, *The Lemon Tree* (London: Dent, 1937).

5. *Ah, Sweet Dancer*, pp. 19–20.

6. Ibid., p. 20.

7. Ibid., p. 30.

8. Ibid., p. 33.

9. Ibid., p. 31.

10. Monk Gibbon, *The Masterpiece and the Man* (London: Rupert Hart-David, 1959).

11. *Ah, Sweet Dancer*, p. 26.

12. Ibid., p. 35.

13. Ibid., p. 91.

14. Ibid., p. 118.

15. Bloom, p. 398.

16. Quoted in Hone, p. 429.

17. See G. G. Jung, *Analytical Psychology: Its Theory and Practice* (New York: Random House, 1968), pp. 190ff.

18. Barbara Hannah, *Jung, His Life and Work: A Biographical Memoir* (New York: G. P. Putnam's Sons, 1976), p. 125.

19. See C. G. Jung, *Aion: Researches into the Phenomenology of the Self. The Collected Works of C. G. Jung,* Vol. 9, Part II (New York: Pantheon, 1959), p. 6.

20. Robert Graves, *The White Goddess: A Historical Grammar of Poetic Myth* (New York: Farrar, Straus and Giroux, 1966), pp. 193–94; 253.

21. Phyllis Trible, professor of Old Testament at Union Theological Seminary, finds "male and female" to be the poetic parallel of "in the image of God" in the account of the Creation in Genesis I. She explains, "Detecting divine transcendence in human reality requires human clues. Unique among them, . . . is sexuality. God creates, in the image of God, male and female." In *God and the Rhetoric of Sexuality* (Philadelphia: Fortress Press, 1978), pp. 15–21.

22. See Journal entry No. 10 (M141–42).

23. Helen Vendler, *Yeats's Vision and the Later Plays* (Cambridge, Mass.: Harvard University Press, 1963).

24. F. A. C. Wilson, *W. B. Yeats and Tradition* (New York: Macmillan, 1958).

25. Ibid., p. 70.

26. O Rose, thou art sick!
    The invisible worm
    That flies in the night,
    In the howling storm,

    Has found out thy bed
    Of crimson joy:
    And his dark secret love
    Does thy life destroy.   (William Blake, *Complete Writings*, p. 213)

27. Bradford, "Yeats and Maud Gonne," p. 473.

28. Ellmann, *Eminent Domain*, p. 81.

29. *Ah, Sweet Dancer*, p. 65.

30. "Yeats and Maud Gonne," p. 473.

31. *Yeats*, pp. 422–24.

32. *Yeats's Vision and the Later Plays*, pp. 39 and *passim*.

33. *Ah, Sweet Dancer*, p. 112.

34. *The Dictionary of National Biography*, 1951–1960 (London: Oxford University Press, 1971), pp. 1041–42.

35. *Letters on Poetry from W. B. Yeats to Dorothy Wellesley* (1940; rpt. London: Oxford University Press, 1964), p. 174.

36. *Letters on Poetry*, p. 195.

37. Dorothy Wellesley, *Poems of Ten Years*, reprinted as *Selections from the Poems of Dorothy Wellesley* (London: Macmillan, 1936).

38. *Letters on Poetry*, p. 28.

39. Ibid., p. 70.

40. See remarks on courtly love by Susan Brownmiller in *Against Our Will: Men, Women, and Rape* (New York: Simon and Schuster, 1975), pp. 290ff.

41. Stallworthy, pp. 83–85.

42. Yeats and Maud had found the concept of spiritual marriage, or *mysterium coniunctio*, in their Rosicrucian studies as members of the occult Order of the Golden Dawn. For Jung it had been revealed through a series of dreams during his long illness of 1944. Of the *coniunctio* Jung wrote that it gave "the deepest bliss" but "darkness, too, and a strange cessation of human warmth."

43. Graves, p. 166.

44. Another private communication in the poem is the line "But no dogs barked," referring to the first midnight meeting of the Lover and the Chambermaid. Lady Wellesley had had trouble with strange dogs causing disturbance at Penns in the Rocks. Yeats refers to the dogs again in "To Dorothy Wellesley."

45. Sigmund Freud, *Standard Edition of the Complete Psychological Works* (London: Hogarth Press, 1957), XI, 185.

46. *Letters on Poetry*, p. 174.

Album of Illustrations

A romantic when romanticism was in its final extravagance ...

1. Yeats in youth

John B. Yeats, R. H. A.
National Gallery of Ireland, Dublin

Pallas Athene in that straight back and arrogant head

2. Maud Gonne in youth

unreasoning and habitual like the seasons ...

3. Mrs. John Butler Yeats

Portrait by John Butler Yeats, R. H. A.
The National Gallery of Ireland, Dublin

I overheard somebody say that she was the kind of woman who might make herself very unhappy about a man. I began to wonder . . . if it was my duty to marry her.

4. Katherine Tynan

Portrait by John B. Yeats, R. H. A.
The Municipal Gallery of Modern Art, Dublin

*... always in revolt against her own poetical gift ... and against
her own Demeter-like face in the mirror.*

5. Florence Farr

Routledge and Kegan Paul

. . . I could not give the love that was her beauty's right, but she was too near my soul, too salutary and wholesome to my inmost being.

6. Olivia Shakespear

Rupert Hart-Davis, St. Albans

Why should not old men be mad?
Some have known . . .
A girl that knew all Dante once
Live to bear children to a dunce.

7. Iseult Gonne

Portrait by AE (George Russell)
National Gallery of Ireland

. . . a perfect wife, kind, wise, and unselfish.

8. Mrs. W. B. Yeats
(Georgie Hyde-Lees)

Portrait by John B. Yeats, R. H. A.
Permission of Michael B. Yeats

That crazed girl improvising her music,
Her poetry . . .
. . . that girl I declare
A beautiful lofty thing.

9. Margot Ruddock

Permission of Mme. Simone Bertin

I long for your intellect and sanity. Hitherto I have never found these anywhere but at Coole.

10a. Dorothy Wellesley

b. Penns in the Rocks

Permission of the Duke of Wellington

Her present image floats into the mind—
Did Quattrocento finger fashion it
Hollow of cheek as though it drank the wind
And took a mess of shadows for its meat?

11. Maud Gonne in age

Photograph by Horvath
Permission of Sean MacBride, Esq.

. . . O that I were young again
And held her in my arms!

12. Yeats in age

Selected Bibliography

Andreas Capellanus, *The Art of Courtly Love*, trans. John Jay Parry. New York: W. W. Norton, 1969.

Appignanesi, Lisa. *Femininity and the Creative Imagination: A Study of Henry James, Robert Musil and Marcel Proust*. London: Vision, 1973.

Bachofen, J. J. *Myth, Religion, and Mother Right: Selected Writings of J. J. Bachofen*, trans. Ralph Manheim. Bollingen Series LXXXIV. Princeton: Princeton University Press, 1967.

Blake, William. *Complete Writings*, ed. Geoffrey Keynes. New York: Oxford University Press, 1969.

Bloom, Harold. *Yeats*. New York: Oxford University Press, 1970.

Boehme, Jacob. *Six Theosophic Points and Other Writings*, trans. Nicolas Berdyaev. Ann Arbor: University of Michigan Press, 1958.

Bornstein, George. *Yeats and Shelley*. Chicago: University of Chicago Press, 1970.

Bradford, Curtis B. "George Yeats: Poet's Wife," *Sewanee Review*, 57 (July–September 1969), 385–404.

––––––. "Yeats and Maud Gonne," *Texas Studies in Literature and Language*, 3:4 (Winter 1962), 452–74.

Brown, Stephen J., S.J. *Ireland in Fiction*, intro. Desmond J. Clarke. New York: Barnes and Noble, 1969.

Brownmiller, Susan. *Against Our Will: Men, Women, and Rape*. New York: Simon and Schuster, 1975.

Coxhead, Elizabeth. *Daughters of Erin*. London: Secker and Warburg, 1965.

Crain, Irving J. "The Origin of Love," *Diseases of the Nervous System*, 30 (1969), 774–76.

Daly, Mary. *Beyond God the Father: Toward a Philosophy of Women's Liberation*. Boston: Beacon, 1973.

De Lorris, Guillaume and Jean de Meun. *The Romance of the Rose*, trans. Harry W. Robbins. New York: E. P. Dutton, 1962.

De Rougemont, Denis. *Love in the Western World*, trans. Montgomery Belgion. New York: Pantheon, 1956.

Deutsch, Helene. *The Psychology of Women*. 2 vols. New York: Grune and Stratton, 1944.

Ellmann, Richard. *Eminent Domain*. New York: Oxford University Press, 1967.

––––––. *Yeats: The Man and the Masks*. New York: E. P. Dutton, 1948.

Florence Farr, Bernard Shaw and W. B. Yeats, ed. Clifford Bax. Dublin: Cuala, 1941.

Frank Pearce Strum: His Life, Letters, and Collected Works, ed. Richard Taylor. Urbana: University of Illinois Press, 1969.

Freud, Sigmund. *Standard Edition of the Complete Psychological Works*. London: Hogarth, 1957.

Gaster, Theodor H. *Myth, Legend, and Custom in the Old Testament: A Comparative Study with Chapters from Sir James G. Frazer's "Folklore in the Old Testament."* 2 vols. New York: Harper and Row, 1969.

Gibbon, Monk. *The Masterpiece and the Man.* London: Rupert Hart-Davis, 1959.

Gogarty, Oliver St. John. *William Butler Yeats: A Memoir.* Dublin: Dolmen, 1963.

Goldin, Frederick. *The Mirror of Narcissus in the Courtly Love Lyric.* Ithaca: Cornell University Press, 1967.

Graves, Robert. *The White Goddess: A Historical Grammar of Poetic Myth.* New York: Farrar, Straus and Giroux, 1966.

Gregory, Lady. *Coole,* comp. and ed. Colin Smythe. Dolmen Editions X. Dublin: Dolmen, 1971.

———. *Seventy Years, 1852–1922: Being the Autobiography of Lady Gregory.* Gerrards Cross, Bucks.: Colin Smythe, 1974.

Hannah, Barbara. *Jung, His Life and Work: A Biographical Memoir.* New York: G. P. Putnam's Sons, 1976.

Harding, M. Esther. *Woman's Mysteries, Ancient and Modern: A Psychological Interpretation of the Feminine Principle as Portrayed in Myth, Story and Dreams.* London: Longmans, Green, 1935.

Harper, George Mills. *Yeats's Golden Dawn.* New York: Macmillan, 1975.

Hone, Joseph. *W. B. Yeats, 1865–1939.* Harmondsworth, Middlesex: Penguin Books, 1971.

In Excited Reverie: A Centenary Tribute to William Butler Yeats, 1865–1939, ed. A. N. Jeffares and K. G. W. Cross. London: Macmillan, 1965.

Jeffares, A. Norman. *A Commentary on the Collected Poems of W. B. Yeats.* Stanford: Stanford University Press, 1968.

———. *W. B. Yeats: Man and Poet.* New York: Barnes and Noble, 1961.

Joyce, James. *A Portrait of the Artist as a Young Man.* New York: Viking, 1974.

Jung, Carl Gustav. *Aion: Researchers into the Phenomenology of the Self.* The Collected Works of C. G. Jung, Vol. 9, Part II. New York: Pantheon, 1959.

Analytical Psychology: Its Theory and Practice. New York: Random House, 1968.

Kingsford, Anna Bonus and Edward Maitland. *The Perfect Way: or, The Finding of Christ.* London: Field and Tuer, 1887.

Lakoff, Robin. *Language and Woman's Place.* New York: Harper and Row, 1975.

Lewis, C. S. *The Allegory of Love: A Study in Medieval Tradition.* New York: Oxford University Press, 1958.

MacBride, Maud Gonne. *A Servant of the Queen.* London: Victor Gollancz, 1938.

Mac Liammóir, Micheál and Eavan Boland. *W. B. Yeats and His World.* London: Thames and Hudson, 1971.

The Meaning of Courtly Love, Papers of the first annual conference of the Center for Medieval and Early Renaissance Studies, State University of New York at Binghamton, March 17–19, 1967, ed. F. X. Newman. Albany: State University of New York Press, 1968.

Moore, George. *Hail and Farewell: Ave.* London: William Heineman, 1937.

Neumann, Erich. *The Great Mother: An Analysis of the Archetype,* trans. Ralph Manheim. Bollingen Series XLVII. Princeton: Princeton University Press, 1963.

No More Masks! An Anthology of Poems by Women, ed. Florence Howe and Ellen Bass. Garden City: Anchor Press, 1973.

O'Casey, Sean. *Autobiographies,* II. London: Macmillan, 1963.

Pagels, Elaine. *The Gnostic Gospels.* New York: Random House, 1979.

Rees, Alwyn and Brinley Rees. *Celtic Heritage: Ancient Tradition in Ireland and Wales.* London: Thames and Hudson, 1961.

Robertson, D. W., Jr. "The Doctrine of Charity in Medieval Literary Gardens: A Topical Approach through Symbolism and Allegory," *Speculum,* 26 (1951), 24–49.

———. *A Preface to Chaucer: Studies in Medieval Perspectives.* Princeton: Princeton University Press, 1962.

———. "The Subject of De Amore of Andreas Capellanus," *Modern Philology,* 50 (1952–53), 145–61.

Rose, Marilyn Gaddis. "A Visit with Anne Yeats," *Modern Drama*, 7 (December 1964), pp. 299–307.

Salomon, Louis B. *The Devil Take Her: A Study of the Rebellious Lover in English Poetry.* Philadelphia: University of Pennsylvania Press, 1931.

Salvadori, Corinna. *Yeats and Castiglione: Poet and Courtier.* Dublin: A Figgis, 1965.

Seagrave, Barbara Garvey and Wesley Thomas. *The Songs of the Minnesingers.* Urbana: University of Illinois Press, 1966.

Shakespear, Olivia. "Beauty's Hour," *The Savoy*, August and September 1896.

Slochower, Harry. *Mythopoesis: Mythic Patterns in the Literary Classics.* Detroit: Wayne State University Press, 1970.

Stallworthy, Jon. *Vision and Revision in Yeats's "Last Poems."* London: Oxford University Press, 1969.

Starkie, Walter and A. Norman Jeffares. *Homage to Yeats.* William Andrews Clark Memorial Library. Los Angeles: University of California Press, 1966.

Stead, W. T. *Review of Reviews.* American edition, 5, No. 25 (February 1892), 6–7.

Stewart, Stanley. *The Enclosed Garden: The Tradition and the Image in Seventeenth-Century Poetry.* Madison: University of Wisconsin Press, 1966.

Taylor, Thomas. *The Eleusinian and Bacchic Mysteries: A Dissertation*, ed. Alexander Wilder. 4th ed. New York: J. W. Bouton, 1891.

Trible, Phyllis. *God and the Rhetoric of Sexuality.* Overtures to Biblical Theology. Philadelphia: Fortress Press, 1978..

Ulanov, Ann Belford. *The Feminine in Jungian Psychology and in Christian Theology.* Evanston: Northwestern University Press, 1971.

Vendler, Helen. *Yeats's Vision and the Later Plays.* Cambridge, Mass.: Harvard University Press, 1963.

Wade, Allan. *A Bibliography of the Writings of W. B. Yeats.* Soho Bibliographies. London: Rupert Hart-Davis, 1958.

Waite, Arthur Edward. *The Real History of the Rosicrucians.* London: George Redway, 1887.

William Butler Yeats: Essays in Tribute, ed. Stephen Gwynn. Port Washington, N.Y.: Kennikat, 1965.

Wilson, F. A. C. *W. B. Yeats and Tradition.* New York: Macmillan, 1958.

Woolf, Virginia. *A Room of One's Own.* New York: Harcourt, Brace, 1929.

Yeats, William Butler. *Autobiographies.* London: Macmillan, 1956.

――――. *The Collected Plays of W. B. Yeats.* London: Macmillan, 1952.

――――. *The Collected Poems of W. B. Yeats.* New York: Macmillan, 1956.

――――. *Dhoya and John Sherman*, ed. Richard Finneran. Detroit: Wayne State University Press, 1969.

――――. *Essays and Introductions.* New York: Macmillan, 1961.

――――. *A Full Moon in March.* London: Macmillan, 1935.

――――. *The Letters of W. B. Yeats*, ed. Allan Wade. New York: Macmillan, 1955.

――――. *Memoirs*, ed. Denis Donoghue. London: Macmillan, 1972.

――――. *Mythologies.* New York: Macmillan, 1959.

――――. *On the Boiler.* Dublin: Cuala, 1939.

――――. *The Secret Rose.* London: Lawrence and Bullen, 1897.

――――. *Uncollected Prose*, I, ed. John P. Frayne. New York: Columbia University Press, 1970.

――――. *The Variorum Edition of the Plays of W. B. Yeats*, ed. Russell K. Alspach. New York: Macmillan, 1966.

――――. *The Variorum Edition of the Poems of W. B. Yeats*, ed. Peter Allt and Russell K. Alspach. New York: Macmillan, 1957.

――――. *A Vision: A Reissue with the Author's Final Revisions.* New York: Macmillan, 1938.

――――. *The Wind Among the Reeds.* London: Elkin Mathews, 1899.

Yeats, William Butler and Margot Ruddock. *Ah, Sweet Dancer: A Correspondence*, ed. Roger McHugh. London: Macmillan, 1970.

Yeats, William Butler and Dorothy Wellesley. *Letters on Poetry from W. B. Yeats to Dorothy Wellesley*. London: Oxford University Press, 1964.

Zilboorg, Gregory. "Masculine and Feminine: Some Biological and Cultural Aspects," *Psychiatry*, 7(1944), 257-96.

Index